THE
RAGGED EDGE
OF
THE WORLD

Encounters at the Frontier

Where Modernity, Wildlands

and Indigenous Peoples Meet

EUGENE LINDEN

VIKING

VIKING
Published by the Penguin Group
Penguin Group (USA) Inc., 375 Hudson Street, New York, New York 10014, U.S.A.
Penguin Group (Canada), 90 Eglinton Avenue East, Suite 700, Toronto, Ontario, Canada M4P 2Y3
(a division of Pearson Penguin Canada Inc.)
Penguin Books Ltd, 80 Strand, London WC2R 0RL, England
Penguin Ireland, 25 St. Stephen's Green, Dublin 2, Ireland (a division of Penguin Books Ltd)
Penguin Books Australia Ltd, 250 Camberwell Road, Camberwell, Victoria 3124, Australia
(a division of Pearson Australia Group Pty Ltd)
Penguin Books India Pvt Ltd, 11 Community Centre, Panchsheel Park, New Delhi-110 017, India
Penguin Group (NZ), 67 Apollo Drive, Rosedale, North Shore 0632, New Zealand
(a division of Pearson New Zealand Ltd)
Penguin Books (South Africa) (Pty) Ltd, 24 Sturdee Avenue, Rosebank, Johannesburg 2196, South Africa

Penguin Books Ltd, Registered Offices: 80 Strand, London WC2R 0RL, England

First published in 2011 by Viking Penguin, a member of Penguin Group (USA) Inc.

1 3 5 7 9 10 8 6 4 2

LIBRARY OF CONGRESS CATALOGING-IN-PUBLICATION DATA
Linden, Eugene.
The ragged edge of the world : encounters at the frontier where modernity, wildlands
and indigenous peoples meet / Eugene Linden.
p. cm.
Includes index.
ISBN 978-0-670-02251-9
1. Indigenous peoples—Social conditions.   2. Indigenous peoples—Ecology.
3. Indigenous peoples—History.   4. First contact of aboriginal peoples with Westerners—History.
I. Title.
GN380.L555 2011
303.482—dc22
2010043578

Printed in the United States of America
Designed by Nancy Resnick

For my children,
their children yet to be born
and all those on whom it will fall
to restore this tattered planet

Contents

THE
RAGGED EDGE
OF
THE WORLD

Introduction

I never boarded an airplane before college, but just a year after graduation I began a series of forays to some of the most remote, wild and calamitous parts of the globe. First I went to Vietnam as a journalist, making a round-the-world trip out of the getting there and getting back. Then it was off to Africa and New Guinea during the writing of my early books, and then virtually everywhere else as a journalist reporting on global environmental issues for *Time,* and on assignment for *National Geographic* and other magazines.

These travels were prompted by diverse writing assignments, but all were informed by a hunger to see what I call the ragged edge of the world, the places where wildlands, indigenous cultures and modernity collide. Since my childhood, when I watched rustic neighborhoods give way to strip malls and tract homes, I've been acutely sensitive to change and loss. Those feelings intensified as I traveled to places such as Polynesia, Borneo, the Amazon and the Arctic. Time and again I saw traditional cultures encounter and succumb to the power of modern money, technology, ideas and images. Even places with no humans whatsoever feel the force of our presence. In the Ndoki, a remote and magical rainforest in the Congo where not even the Pygmies have ventured during the past thousand years, the impact of humanity intrudes in the dust that blows in from the desertified Sahel in the north, and in an ominous drying-out of the forest due to logging in the surrounding areas.

"Nostalgia" is the word we use to describe the bittersweet evocation of precious feelings that lie just beyond reach in the past. Often the emotion arises during rites of passage or out of the intricate matrix of personal history, memory and place, but what word or phrase adequately describes the feelings evoked by repeatedly observing the disappearance of an entire landscape, a people, a language, or a way of life? It is akin to forever showing up for the last scenes of a tragedy in which one can glimpse, but never fully experience, the past glory of the protagonist.

In the course of my career, I became a monitor of the march of modernity. Like some modern Josephus, in my forty years of travels I have witnessed the battles at the front lines of change, followed the retreat of the world where magic still lives and where animals and spirits dominate. And I have documented the human and animal detritus left behind in the aftermath of the advancing armies of the consumer society.

Today, many of the locales of my early travels bear little resemblance to the places I first visited. Even the most remote areas have become more accessible. Three years before I explored the Ndoki Forest, it took five days to negotiate the quicksand and swamps that guard the perimeter of this enchanted place. By 1991, when I traveled there, scientists had laid down some logs as a primitive path through part of the swamp, and it took us a day and a half to get from the tiny village of Bomassa to the edge of the river and swamps that isolate the Ndoki from the rest of the Congo. Now a car can take visitors to the banks of the Ndoki River in half an hour. Mike Fay, the explorer who brought me into the Ndoki, says that the first alarms about threats to the region were met with skepticism because a huge buffer of uncut forest surrounded it. Now every forest surrounding the Ndoki has been logged.

The Ndoki persists inviolate, however, while other places and peoples I visited haven't been so lucky. I traveled to the interior of Borneo in the early 1990s to write about the disappearing way of life of the Penans, a tribe of the last few hunter-gatherers remaining on that vast island. I witnessed firsthand a type of cultural Alzheimer's as Penans just a few years and a few miles from their ancestral forests were quickly shedding knowledge acquired over millennia. Schoolkids in Marudi could recall that their uncles would hunt boar after the appearance of a particular butterfly, but they could not recall which butterfly it was or when it appeared. Now only a handful of Penans preserve that culture in Borneo's fast-disappearing forests.

When I visited Chico Mendez's home in Acre, Brazil, in the late 1980s, Xapuri was a sleepy one-horse river town separated from the rest of the state by unbroken rainforest. Now the town has supermarkets and a highway connecting it to Rio Branco, the state capital. Some rubber tappers remain, but Xapuri now also has factories, and kids with bookbags walk along its suburban roads.

Some cultures have shown remarkable resilience in maintaining their identity while trying to reap some of the benefits of material advances. In Polynesia many of the outward trappings of the old ways have disappeared, but some islands retain a distinctly Polynesian spirit in their way of life.

Moreover, if that ragged frontier is retreating in much of the world, it is advancing in others. In some parts of Central Africa, modernity and its attendant infrastructure are disappearing, and traditional ways are re-colonizing peoples just as a strangler fig will gradually displace its host tree. Sometimes when the modern economy flounders, a toxic brew of banditry, superstition and cultural anarchy takes its place. In other regions, indigenous cultures reclaim modern myths and stories. At a Christian mission on an island in New Guinea, the presiding native priest (the European missionaries had long since departed) narrated to me a history of the island that seamlessly melded Christian and animist myths.

Even on our crowded planet there remain "lost worlds," places that seem to have escaped the intrusions of the consumer economy and persist in a time warp. From an animal's point of view, the Ndoki in the Congo is one such place, as are parts of Antarctica, and Vu Quang in the cordillera that separates Vietnam and Laos.

When writing about these and many other places, I almost always had some journalistic purpose that relegated the enchanting encounters and revelatory vignettes of my travels to the background. If I went to the Ndoki, it was because humans were encroaching and I wanted to raise the alarm. If I went to the Antarctic, it was to try to understand what role this vast and frigid continent might play in the world's rapidly changing climate. If I went to Borneo, it was to talk with Penan chiefs about the disappearance of their culture, or to report on the plight of the forest and its creatures.

To be sure, I'd take pains to try to evoke the flavor and wonder of these locales. It is hard, however, when writing for *National Geographic* about pygmy chimps, to venture into a digression about an encounter with a brutal, thieving commandante in the heart of Equateur. When reporting on cargo cults in the highlands of New Guinea and what they might suggest about the nature of consumer societies, it would be disruptive to veer off into an account of a trip with the police to arrest a grass-skirted rapist that included a pleasant stop on the way back to town during which the cop, the rapist and I toured a bird of paradise sanctuary.

Yet, when I think back on these travels, it is these vignettes that are freshest—my memory has inverted the priorities of my career. Perhaps I should pay heed to these persistent messages from my unconscious.

This book will offer some of my encounters at this slippery and fast-changing frontier. These are my stories not written. Psychologists have long pondered the syndrome in which facts, stories and jokes remain in memory until told or written and then disappear. I've noticed this at work in my own memory, but the halo around these stories comes from something else. Each is associated with a significant event in my life, but each also involves an encounter with some portion of the rapidly retreating ragged edge of the world. In the details of the stories that live most vividly in memory lie truths beyond statistics and theory.

Those living memories are testament to the quixotic priorities of the unconscious. Though it proceeds in unknowable ways, the unconscious is no fool. Perhaps these powerful memories of past travels are also its missives, delivering a message about what we have lost and are losing.

————

Before diving into the ragged edge, perhaps I should say a few words about the events that launched me on my travels. My first trip to Vietnam was a turning point in my life. I left for Southeast Asia only a few weeks after receiving an honorable discharge from the Navy. I should have been elated, but I was twenty-four and a walking monument to self-doubt.

To this day I remember those months before my departure as a low-water mark for my self-confidence. This is saying something given my subsequent career choice of journalism and writing, an occupation that delivers grievous injury to one's self-esteem with tidal regularity. (Happily, nothing that has happened to me since then has come close to that nadir.) I felt that I had wasted my college education, an opinion that I'm sure would have been endorsed enthusiastically by a wide range of Yale professors. I'd gone AWOL on a once-promising athletic career as a wrestler; I had uncertainties about my own position on the war; and I had serious qualms about whether I could deliver on my promise to do an investigation of fragging, which was the reason I was heading to Vietnam.

Fragging (as I later wrote) was a macabre ritual of the Vietnam War in which soldiers tried to blow up or otherwise kill their superior officers. It occurs in all wars, but fragging became pandemic in Vietnam, increasing dramatically even in the relatively safe rear echelons as American involvement in the fighting wound down. When I'd first heard about it from friends who'd returned from the war, I couldn't stop thinking about the notion of troops turning on their own officers. What did it mean? I was highly motivated to find out, as the phenomenon had received scant attention in the press. More important, a couple of years earlier I'd been well on my way to becoming one of those officers myself.

Perhaps fragging was the agon I'd been looking for, an event that would help me understand and integrate the various tensions of the war. I needed to know whether the misgivings that led me to leave the military and oppose the war were justifiable or merely convenient. An extraordinary encounter in Vietnam provided a spectacularly direct answer to this last question, and the journey itself changed my life.

I had an odd military history, to say the least. I had competed for and had been offered congressional appointments to all of the academies. My congressman urged me to choose West Point, because that year was another constituent's last shot at Annapolis. I agreed, but then ended up going to Yale on an NROTC scholarship.

Vietnam was only beginning to bubble to the surface as an issue when I entered college in the fall of 1965. Even when I was a sophomore, the biggest demonstrations were in favor of the war. The conflict escalated very quickly, however, and by the end of 1967, the antiwar movement was in full swing. Many fellow Elis began to develop a previously unnoticed interest in teaching, or started limping from long-forgotten injuries, or, in the case of George W. Bush (who was a class ahead of me), looked ahead to the possibility of war with Mexico and joined the Texas Air National Guard.

At that point, my own problems with the military were more personal. While I felt—and still do—that fighting for the defense of the country or one's family was the obligation of every able citizen, I had not really thought through the implications of the idea of unquestioning obedience. If a legitimate superior ordered you to kill someone in an authorized military action, it was your duty to carry out that order, regardless of your private opinion about whether the action was legitimate or the enemy posed a genuine threat.

But what if the war in question was undeclared, and what if U.S. involvement was based on a cascade of hypothetical events deriving from an unproven theory? Vietnam vividly framed this problem. No one had ever argued that Viet Cong were going to attack the United States, and some of us wanted something more convincing than the domino theory if we were going to accept orders to kill people.

I began trying to get out of the NROTC beginning in my sophomore year—not an easy task, given that I was on scholarship and officially in the Navy reserves. After I did very well in Marine training, however, the Navy officers in the unit apparently decided I wasn't a goldbrick and supported my efforts. I gave up my scholarship and was released from the unit. I was not, however, released from the Navy reserves. A few weeks later I got a letter from the Navy calling me up to active duty.

I immediately filed for discharge as a conscientious objector.

I insisted on doing this straightforwardly, without citing pacifism or other standard arguments used by conscientious objectors. In my statement I did not invoke religious prohibitions or even a repudiation of all wars. I wrote that, while I believed in the use of force to defend country and family, I also believed that life was sacred, and that I could not kill someone I did not know because of some abstract policy objective.

For reasons never explained, the Navy decided to grant me an honorable discharge (though it did not come about until after I graduated from college). Almost immediately thereafter I began thinking about going to Vietnam, wanting to see for myself whether my reservations about the war were justified. And so, with a document that allowed me to go to Vietnam unarmed, I set about putting myself in harm's way.

This was not easy. I was twenty-four, unpublished and completely broke. A friend told me about an organization called the Fund for Investigative Journalism, which had provided the money for Seymour Hersh's reporting on the My Lai massacre. I sent a letter to the fund and got a reply offering support if I had a commission. I managed to talk Norman Cousins of the *Saturday Review* into assigning me an article. I was going.

———

I arrived in Saigon with the remnants of giardia and other tropical bugs I'd picked up in Tahiti—more about that later—and I was continually drenched in sweat. I found a room at a modest hotel, which at that point was little more than a cathouse (the maids would come in to clean the room in the morning, then casually linger at the end of the bed and bat their eyes), but it was cheap.

Armed with a letter from the *Saturday Review* and another assignment I'd picked up from the *Overseas Weekly* (you needed two commissions to get accredited as a freelancer), I donned a lightweight suit and set off to get credentials from the Vietnamese and the American Military Activities Command Vietnam (MAVC). Still racked with fever, I looked within seconds of leaving the hotel as though I'd been thrown into a swimming pool. Although I got curious stares, I did get my credentials.

One piece of good fortune was an introduction to Kevin Buckley, then the *Newsweek* bureau chief. Kevin is one of the great raconteurs, and in 1971 his house was the wartime version of a salon. He generously included me in a lot of his gatherings, where drunken correspondents would challenge me with bewildering statements like, "You can't seriously believe that the U.S. can maintain its security commitments with less than five carrier groups, can you?" I regularly staggered back to my hotel well after curfew. The eye-batting maids became a de facto wake-up service, since they would come into the room whether I answered the door or not.

At that point Saigon was a wide-open city. Everybody knew the war was as good as lost, and that knowledge played out in different ways. Some were looking for a big score. I once hitched a ride in a rickshaw with two sergeants who were checking up on their investments in brothels and bars.

I was new to reporting and looked ridiculously young. I don't think that any of the great correspondents who trooped through Saigon paid me the slightest attention, but this turned out to be a tremendous asset. I was there to report a story that the military did not want to see reported, but they did not take me seriously enough to stop me. Moreover, since I was in Vietnam only for this assignment, once I got the story I did not care whether I was eventually thrown out of the country.

I discovered that my inexperience was usefully disarming. When I was given the name of a man jailed in Long Binh Stockade after being convicted of attempting to kill his superior officer, I simply showed up at the stockade (nicknamed LBJ) and asked to visit him. The Marine guard at the gate assumed I was a lawyer, took my credentials (which clearly identified me as a journalist), and had me brought to the man's cell. There, the young man told me the whole story of his attempt to kill his officer—in this case because the officer had volunteered the unit for patrol duty that deprived them of a hot shower! All the while I feared that the guard would actually read my identification more carefully and that I'd end up sharing a cell with my easily riled new buddy.

I did have enough sense to realize that once I started interviewing judge advocates general (JAG) prosecutors, shrinks and other officers, word would get out about what I was up to. When that happened, the MACV would soon tighten the leash. Consequently, I saved those interviews for the very end and spent most of my first few weeks talking to enlisted men.

If there was one overwhelming impression left by Vietnam, it was the randomness of the violence and the role of luck in one's survival. You might be the best-prepared soldier on earth, but if you were in the wrong place at the wrong time your number was up. Of the raft of Vietnam movies that followed the war, *The Deer Hunter,* whose central metaphor was Russian roulette, captured this best.

It was at Camp Eagle that I had the first of my spooky encounters. I had heard that a West Point–educated captain (whom I called Burke in the article) had survived a fragging attempt, and I asked to speak with him. The interview turned out to be one of the central stories of my article. The attack on the captain had grown out of racial tensions and his attempts to crack down on drug use in his unit. (One of the pithier quotes that came out of the investigation of this attack was a black soldier's comment to Burke before the fragging: "Why should I be here in Vietnam fighting a white man's war killing Vietnamese when I should be back in the States fighting a black man's war killing whites?") By all accounts the captain was a responsible officer who did not subject his men to needless risks at this late date in the war. For this reason, his story perfectly illustrated the bizarre factors that contributed to rear-echelon fraggings in Vietnam.

During the encounter I discovered things about Burke that made the interview even more compelling for me. Captain Burke had graduated with the class of 1969 at West Point. He had also wrestled varsity for the military academy, and had in fact wrestled against Yale. I felt as though I were meeting some version of my destiny had I not decided against West Point at the last minute.

In the bizarre, invisible world of quantum mechanics a particle has many equally valid destinies until some event channels it along a particular path. That's how I felt meeting Burke. Both of us were in Vietnam, but while he had felt the full brunt of the war, I had the luxury of examining it as a journalist.

Given my history, I suppose it makes sense that going to Vietnam would raise the probabilities of encounters charged with this quantum irony. The next one was even more pointed. It took place when I flew down to Quang Nai province to visit the 11th Brigade at firebase Colt 45, the last American fighting force still actively engaging the enemy.

The brigade, part of the Americal Division, lives in infamy as the perpetrator of the My Lai massacre. I caught a ride to the base with a Lieutenant Finnegan, who was piloting a two-man LOACH (a Hughes light observation helicopter). The lieutenant demonstrated some aerobatic tricks on the way out, which I might have enjoyed more were it not for the possibility that his showmanship might catch the attention of some bored North Vietnamese with antiaircraft capability.

The scene at the firebase was surreal. The Kit Carson scouts had found a "hot spot," meaning someone had shot at the GIs, and the officers were tremendously excited about the possibility of some real action. For the ambitious officer, combat experience was a prerequisite for rapid advancement. One major even effused, "Some boys are going to die tomorrow!"

The idea of an assault was less than wildly popular with the troops. Reactions ranged from fatalism to near rebellion. By this point no grunt wanted to be the last GI to die in Vietnam. Indeed, some soldiers told me outright that they had been planning to frag one particular officer because of his gung-ho attitude. (The same man had been pointed out to me earlier by the commanders as an exemplar of a good officer.)

I spent the afternoon getting opinions from both the officers and the troops, and what I discovered was one of the key factors in Vietnam's epidemic of fragging: The officers and the grunts lived in entirely different worlds, while the lifer sergeants who traditionally mediated between the two were as alienated from the troops as the officers were. If there was a lesson in this and, indeed, in my investigation of the demoralization of the Army as a whole, it was that troop morale is crucial for success in war. If political leaders can't credibly explain to soldiers why they are fighting, they will fight unwillingly and, ultimately, turn against their own.

Late that afternoon one of the officers asked me if I'd like to go along on the assault the next morning. I thought about the offer for a second. Though it wasn't technically relevant to my story, I'd also come to Vietnam to see what the war was really like—so I said, "Why not?" Then he asked whether I wanted a rifle.

My reaction must have mystified the group. Involuntarily, I burst out laughing. Once again I was being confronted with the quantum irony of my long journey to this spot at this time in Vietnam. Of all the possibilities of killing Vietnamese—as an infantry officer, as a pilot in the Navy, or as an enlisted man shelling them from a ship or gunboat—the one I hadn't considered was the possibility that I might have the chance to shoot one as a noncombatant reporter who had just gotten an honorable discharge as a conscientious objector.

I thanked the officer for his thoughtfulness but politely declined. Apart from my own history, I was concerned that if reporters started carrying guns, it would only reinforce the suspicion that we were all spies, and it would make every reporter fair game in the conflict. I never got the chance to regret that decision because in the end, the higher-ups decided to send the ARVN (South Vietnamese) troops on this mission and hold back the American soldiers.

By the time I got back to Saigon, the Army had figured out that I was onto a story that might prove embarrassing (by then I had spoken with psychologists and prosecutors as well as victims and perpetrators), and I was greeted with a welter of messages from press information representatives who wanted to "help" me with my reporting. I decided it might be best to gather my thoughts elsewhere, and so I made plans to head to Cambodia.

The night before I left, I had a drunken dinner with Kevin Buckley and a few others. Nick Profit (who died in 2006) was then just beginning his distinguished career as a war correspondent and urged me to "write the truth." If such advice now sounds trite, it was profoundly moving in the circumstances, and it's counsel I've never forgotten. Wobbling back to the hotel, again after curfew, I ran into the editor of the *Overseas Weekly,* who immediately asked about the piece I'd promised him. I was astonished that he actually expected something, but said I'd give him an article before I left.

Back at the hotel I made the unfortunate discovery that I could write while drunk. I worked all night and was stone sober by the time I finished. I delivered the article early the following morning and gratefully took my $300 payment in Vietnamese currency as well as the editor's helpful advice about which black-market moneychanger to use to convert it to dollars before leaving the country.

I left Vietnam with my confidence restored and at least the beginnings of a career. The *Saturday Review* published the fragging article as a cover story, and it received a great deal of attention. I felt ambivalent about profiting from the war, however (I still retained some of my killjoy moral inflexibility), and made sure that I was out of the country and incommunicado the week the story ran. With the perspective of hindsight and the knowledge of how difficult it is to make a career out of writing, I regret that decision to avoid publicity. I've learned since how rarely the brass ring is offered. But these regrets are mild. Much more important was the certainty that my misgivings about the war were more than an artifact of convenience.

And then there were the ontological issues the war raised. A need to know whether I was right about the conflict got me to Vietnam, but once I was there, coincidence or some law of quantum destiny gave me the opportunity to observe my life as it might have been lived had I taken another path. As a journalist I could meet my West Point doppelganger; as a journalist I found myself in the field confronting the very situation that as a thought experiment had impelled me toward leaving the military. What is a career compared with that?

Vietnam put me on the road, but I had no interest in becoming a war correspondent. Rather than cover wars between nations or the war on terror, I devoted the next thirty-odd years to another conflict: the war on nature. The reporting I did in 1971 enabled me to pursue the questions that underlie most of my subsequent travels and writings: What drives the consumer society and where is it going? How are we different from animals and how is the consumer society different from other cultures? What is the price of material progress? In what manner does the way we think impact the natural world? What are we losing, and what can be saved?

I stopped in Cambodia, Thailand, Iran and Ireland on my way home. I did not get back to Vietnam for twenty-three years. When I did return, the threat to the land was not war, but peace.

PART I

WAR AND PEACE

CHAPTER 1

Vietnam 1994

From the minute I arrived in Vietnam in 1971, I wanted to leave. During wartime any country will reveal its ugly side, and the conflict in Vietnam was one of the ugliest in which the United States had ever been involved. By that point we and the corrupt and incompetent regime we were propping up were well on the way to losing the war.

But the first thing that struck me about Saigon then was the heat: It was just impossibly hot and humid. Since that first trip I've been to many of the hottest and most humid places on the planet, and, until I returned to Vietnam in 1994, I had always wondered whether that initial experience reflected (a) a true measure of the heat or (b) the fact that in 1971 I really did not have much to compare it with. The answer, which became obvious as soon as I alighted in Hanoi in May, was (a): Vietnam has a combination of heat and humidity matched by few if any regions on earth.

If its climate was consistent, the Vietnam I encountered twenty-three years later was an entirely different landscape. Most of the surface scars of war had long since faded, and I was able to travel to parts of the country that would have been impassable three decades earlier.

I came back to Vietnam on assignment, in response to a series of reports that had come out of the country about discoveries of three new species of large animals in a lost world, a remote region high up in the cordillera that divides Vietnam from Laos.

The news of these findings was nothing less than astonishing, since only five new species of animals larger than 100 pounds had been discovered since the beginning of the twentieth century. One of the animals (variously called the Vu Quang ox, the pseudoryx or the saola) represented an entirely new genus, and only three other new genera had been documented in the century.

Since my visit in the early 1990s, other new species have been found in the region, and new species have surfaced in Borneo and the highlands of New Guinea as well. While welcome for science, this boom has an ominous side, as it is in part the product of disquieting forces at work around the world. The world's great wilderness areas have been so reduced that more and more animals are being forced into contact with humans. Similarly, with forests growing ever smaller and becoming more easily perforated by roads, humans, including scientists, are having a much easier time penetrating formerly impenetrable places.

To a degree this was the case in Vietnam, whose forest cover had been reduced from 50 percent to 10 percent during the previous half century. War played a complicated role in the discovery of these new species. One of the ironies of war is that while actual fighting takes a gruesome toll on both humans and wildlife—think about defoliation in Vietnam or guerrillas machine-gunning wildlife in the Congo—to the degree that animals can retreat beyond the reach of the troops, roaming armies do keep poachers away. Civil war in Nicaragua likewise stopped deforestation in its tracks for a number of years; in Suriname the presence of insurgent Maroons in the forests kept intruders out for decades, and whatever depredations the guerrillas themselves caused were more than compensated for by the recovery of its fauna and flora. The most intact ecosystem on the Korean Peninsula is in the demilitarized zone (DMZ), which is a perennial contender for the title of the place with the most land mines on the planet. (During the past fifty-five years the DMZ's big animals seem to have figured out ways of sidestepping the explosives.) The mention of such findings is intended not as an endorsement of war as a conservation strategy, but rather as an observation that nature takes her opportunities anywhere she can find them.

On the one hand, it could be argued that, but for the war, the new species in Vietnam might have been discovered years earlier, as the country's cadre of well-trained zoologists systematically explored its forests. In fact, biologists sometimes accompanied soldiers along the Ho Chi Minh Trail, and some of the boxes of bones lying around in the Institute for Ecology and Biological Resources had been collected on these forays. There is no question, though, that the war interrupted the cataloguing of these bones as more pressing matters (e.g., survival) demanded the attention of the scientists. Casually stored, the bones gathered dust for decades before reports began coming in that Vietnam might host a wondrous collection of large animals previously unknown to science.

One of the earliest indicators that Vietnam might play a special role as a refuge of ancient and archaic species came in 1990 when the skeleton of a poached Javan rhino was found in the south. The most endangered of all the rhinos, the Javan subspecies had been thought to be extinct in Vietnam. (Only a few dozen remain in Java itself.) The Vietnamese rhino population, which separated from the Javan group between 20,000 and 30,000 years ago, somehow held on, and now, with protection, a handful survive in the Cat Loc Reserve in a patch of southern lowland tropical forest.

That discovery whetted the appetite of field biologists to see what else existed in Vietnam's remaining forests. A particularly tempting target, revealed by a survey of satellite imagery, was the area surrounding Vu Quang, which constituted one of the last pristine patches of lowland evergreen forest in Asia. In May 1992, biologist John MacKinnon and a team of Vietnamese researchers set out on an expedition sponsored by the World Wildlife Fund to survey the animals of these moist, dense forests.

The area was especially active during the war, since its forests offered cover for the Ho Chi Minh Trail, by which the North Vietnamese moved men and matériel to the south during struggles with both the French and the Americans. It is hellishly hot, very steep, and, I was to discover, one of the most slippery places on the planet. Add leeches, malaria and the omnipresent threat of downpour, and it is easy to understand why the region was uninhabited until the 1950s, and not even the Vietnamese ventured there after the war wound down. Hmong and other tribes sometimes wandered in to hunt, but they had little interaction with the ethnic Vietnamese.

MacKinnon, a British expatriate, had worked as a field biologist in tropical Asia for twenty-five years, along the way doing pioneering studies of wild orangutans and authoring the celebrated *In Search of the Red Ape* (1974). While most of his early breakthroughs followed from painstaking research conducted over the course of many months, on this expedition he and the team found their first new species on the very first hike.

Returning from the forest, MacKinnon met up with Vietnamese zoologist Do Tuoc, who had spent the day talking with hunters from the nearby village of Kim Quang. The villagers had told him about hunting wild goats in the region, but when Do Tuoc asked to see one, they led him to a skull with long, curved, swept-back horns mounted over the front door of a local home. "You'd better show me," said MacKinnon, who had never heard of a Southeast Asian goat fitting that description.

When he saw the skull for himself, MacKinnon experienced the thrill of witnessing hard evidence of an animal heretofore unknown to science. Later, a Danish geneticist named Peter Arctander analyzed a specimen of its DNA, which revealed that the 220-pound animal was not only a new species but also a new genus, and had split from cattle-like relatives sometime between 5 million and 10 million years earlier. According to Colin Groves, a noted paleoanthropologist and taxonomist at Australia's National Museum, tropical forests tend to house more primitive forms of mammals, but this strange new creature was not just primitive, it was archaic. Its ilk, with small brain cases, primitive horns and long canines, had shuffled off the evolutionary stage millions of years ago. The discovery of what MacKinnon deemed "a whole new type of animal" suggested there might be something special about the dense, mysterious forests surrounding Vu Quang.

MacKinnon and other scientists soon uncovered two other deerlike species: one dubbed the giant muntjac, and the other identified by hunters as "slow-running deer," a name that immediately made MacKinnon fear for its future. Even more exciting, all of these creatures seemed to have primitive features, which suggested that they had remained unchanged for eons, and that the region had been both safe from outside influences and remarkably stable. Once I heard about it, I knew I had to get there.

In 1994, Hanoi still retained a good deal of the colonial charm and tropical clamor described by Graham Greene and Somerset Maugham. Mature trees shaded broad, bicycle-choked boulevards, and on many streets I encountered more carts than cars. Eschewing sightseeing, however, I made contact with David Hulse, the local representative of the World Wildlife Fund, and made plans to drive down to Vu Quang to meet up with the research team.

Before heading south, I met with MacKinnon, and we stopped by Hanoi's Institute of Ecology and Biological Resources. He showed me the boxes where skulls of the slow-running deer had been gathering dust since the late 1960s, when they were picked up during a Vietnamese collecting expedition. While we were there he took a quick look through some containers that had not yet been thoroughly examined. As he came upon a strange set of antlers—quite distinct from those of slow-running deer or the other new finds—he was pulled up short and remarked to himself, "Hello, what's this?" A fourth species? It defied the odds, but he set the bones aside for further investigation.

The trip to Vu Quang took several hours, at first along Vietnam's equivalent of I-95, and then on ever smaller, twistier and less-trafficked roads, as we headed west toward the foothills of the Annamite Mountains. At first glance the research station looked like paradise. Set in a clearing, the facility consisted of a group of simple thatch-roofed buildings. While sweltering, the air was clean, and a nearby stream offered relief from the heat. The stream and the vegetation, however, were festooned with leeches. Moreover, the supersaturated climate provided ideal conditions for slick algae that added a treacherous coating to virtually every surface. In this very steep terrain this provided the opportunity for continual slips, slides and misery with the constant threat of exsanguinations by leeches and mosquitoes.

The challenges of the terrain were one reason that all these wondrous creatures had survived in one of the most densely populated nations on earth despite forty years of civil war, and even local tribal hunters did not pursue game into the steep forests. The pseudoryx itself had developed sharp, narrow hooves, which were the best footing for the terrain, and they sported a short-haired, fast-drying coat.

We humans had none of those things.

Having been warned about the slickness, I'd brought along some reef walkers that turned out to be pretty good for getting a purchase on the ground. MacKinnon, who for years had found nothing that worked on the surface, was impressed. I left the reef walkers with him—with some trepidation: While it was fine to help MacKinnon do his research, I didn't want to come back in ten years and find that reef walkers had become the footwear of choice for local poachers.

MacKinnon was ensconced in Vu Quang with his new Chinese wife, Hefen Lu (also known as Monica). At that point the two of them were stuck in Vietnam, since she did not have a passport that would allow her to leave. An attractive and sophisticated woman with a wry sense of humor, Monica took her predicament with equanimity. Also in the camp was Shanthini Dawson, a vivacious biologist from India and the object of affection for one of the Vietnamese guides.

With some glee, MacKinnon told me about an earlier incident in which the guide, unable to write, asked a visiting journalist to help him compose a love letter to Shanthini. As MacKinnon told it, the crucial paragraph went something like this: "Clearly you are a woman of high station since you are fat, while MacKinnon's companion is clearly of low station since she is thin." It was not the kind of letter to endear the guide to many women in the twentieth century. MacKinnon's wife seemed to enjoy the retelling and her consignment to the lowest rungs of humanity.

MacKinnon himself was delightful company. To some degree he fit the stereotype of the eccentric British naturalist who had rejected a comfortable existence as a member of England's privileged class (he is a grandson of Ramsay MacDonald, the first British prime minister from the Labour Party, and is also a descendant of the sixteenth-century mathematician John Napier), but there was nothing eccentric about the distinguished body of work he had amassed during his years in Asia. After decades of dealing with physical discomfort and bureaucratic roadblocks, he remained affable and enthusiastic.

From the research station we set out on a few hikes—not with any expectation that I might see one of Vu Quang's rare creatures, but more to get a sense of how they might have managed to remain hidden for so many years. On one of our trips we stopped by an army facility that had been a hidden North Vietnamese base during the war. The post was neat as a pin and still manned. With undimmed memories of the violence of the war in my head, it was eerie to visit this absolutely peaceful encampment, which had more the flavor of a Boy Scout camp than a key mountain base for one of the most brutal and disciplined armies in the world.

We also visited the simple home of a hunter, which had the horns of a Vu Quang ox mounted over its door. MacKinnon told me that in other homes, the antlers were often used as hat racks or ceremonial altars. This particular hunter, named Bui Giap, explained that the pseudoryx was very difficult to find and that he only caught the animal at all by setting snares. Still, he talked about it as though it were just another creature of the forest, not a new discovery that had sent shock waves through zoology.

Hearing this for myself, I was astonished that it took so long for science to discover these animals, evidence of which sat in plain sight over doors and in boxes in museums for decades. Vietnam has a world-class cadre of scientists, and there are thousands of field biologists around the world whose careers would be made by the discovery of a new genus of large mammal. One of the lessons of this find is that the most dramatic new discoveries may come not from secret maps or an awed description delivered by a terrified native, but from the things we take for granted. The Vu Quang ox, the giant muntjac and the slow-running deer may be heady tonic for science, but for the local hunters these animals were just a meal.

The larger mystery lies in the clustering of all these archaic creatures in this one area of Southeast Asia. Geography and topography offer part of the answer. The mountains trap moisture evaporated from the South China Sea. During the rainy season, this moisture falls as incessant rain, while during the dry season dripping fogs maintain the moisture levels. The result is an unusually stable climate that may have persisted for millions of years. As Peter Arctander explained it, "With no fluctuations in climate, relic species can survive for a very long time." Before the discoveries of these animals, descriptions of new large mammals were few and far between. The forest giraffe called the okapi was discovered in 1901, and over the next century a giant hog, a peccary, and several species of monkeys had come to light, but Vu Quang, as MacKinnon put it, "is a zoologists' gold mine!"

It's possible that the Vu Quang ox never encountered the environmental pressures that led to the development of elaborate antlers, and that the giant muntjac never needed to develop antlers at all. This relic creature has large canine teeth that deerlike animals used in fights before they developed antlers. Colin Groves later told me that the Vu Quang ox resembles the himbos, a now-extinct species that lived in India some 5 million years ago.

It's probable that all these animals, and the ones since discovered in the region (like the northern buff-cheeked gibbon and the cricket-chirping frog), all roamed far more widely in the past. Climate change, ecological change and human pressures gradually reduced their range to the area where they now endure. As this region shrinks, it is likely that more new species will come into contact with scientists. But for how long can Vu Quang continue as a refugium?

Remoteness, topography, algae and geophysics may have protected Vu Quang for millions of years, and war might have bought it some additional time more recently, but hunters and loggers can enter the area, and given the extreme population pressures on the Vietnamese side of the border, settlers encroach, too. Both Vietnam and Laos have taken steps, however, to protect about 1.75 million acres of the region. Moreover, one of the most revered military figures from North Vietnam, General Vo Nguyen Giap, put his prestige behind efforts to halt the unchecked exploitation of natural resources.

Hearing that Giap had lent his support to the conservation effort brought the war back into my thoughts. While the human toll of the war is well known, the bombing, the defoliation and the dropping of millions of tons of poisons inflicted incalculable damage on Vietnam's ecosystems. In no sense does the fact that conflict slowed the commercial destruction of Vietnamese nature balance the scale. One clear beneficiary of the war, however, was Vu Quang. We will see whether it can survive the peace.

PART II

CULTURE WARS

CHAPTER 2

An Elusive Butterfly in Borneo

Borneo—three syllables of indeterminate origin that powerfully evoke the exotic. As is the case with a number of foreign place names, the word "Borneo" can most likely be traced back to a mispronunciation. In this case the garbled word was probably "Brunei," which, in turn, may be a corruption of a Malaysian expression, *Barunah,* which early settlers exclaimed when they saw what is now the Brunei River. The word has Sanskrit origins, and perhaps the best modern equivalent would be "Cool!" Borneo is not the name of the island locally in any event, as the largest native tribe calls it Kalimantan. Naturally, there is dispute about what that word means, too, but the theory I like best is that it comes from the Sanskrit word *kalaman-thana,* which means "an island so hot that it feels like the air is burning." So the island is both cool and hot—very apt.

Whatever its origins, the name "Borneo" has stuck. The island is enormous: Three times the size of the British Isles, it is larger than Spain and Portugal put together. When I first flew over Borneo in 1971, it was almost entirely forested, with a central massif whose rugged peaks rise over 13,000 feet. Hidden under its canopy—or what remains of it today—are flying snakes and flying squirrels, pygmy elephants and pygmy rhinos, orangutans and several species of gibbons, the most graceful aerialists on the planet. The Borneo rainforest is one of the oldest on earth, and nature has had the time to dabble in variation at leisure. One ecologist found 600 different species of trees in a single hectare, making the rainforest one of the most diverse of all ecosystems. Large, previously unidentified animals are still being discovered. In December 2006 a camera trap set up by World Wildlife Fund scientists snapped a picture of a mammal with a very long tail and red fur that looked something like a civet, but scientists really didn't have a clue what it was, and still don't.

I've been to Borneo several times, reporting on the plight of both its indigenous animals and its indigenous people. In even a moderately just world, Borneo's forests, orangutans and inhabitants would have been left alone in perpetuity. The place has a good deal of oil offshore, and an enlightened government might have used that resource to lift the lives of those who desired modernization without destroying Borneo's unique ecosystems and cultures.

But it is not a just world, and Borneo has had nothing even close to an enlightened government. In the states of Sarawak and Sabah, members of a Chinese clan that controlled logging also managed to get themselves installed in key agencies that regulated the logging industry and protected the environment. Indeed the minister of environment in the early 1990s, Datuk James Wong, was also part owner of the Limbang Trading Company, one of the country's largest logging companies. His environmental sensitivity was revealed in a remark he reportedly made when told that cutting the forests could lead to a drying-out in Borneo: "We get too much rain in Sarawak. It stops me from playing golf." The obnoxiousness of this remark was underscored during the droughts of 1997–98, when vast fires torched the island, sickened tens of millions, and brought commerce to a virtual halt in much of Southeast Asia.

Wong and his ilk were enriched thanks to a peculiarity of Malaysian politics. The national government, then headed by Prime Minister Mahathir Mohamad, needed the support of the governments of the states of Sarawak and Sabah to maintain its hold on power, and essentially offered the kleptocrats who ran the two regions an implicit deal: We'll take the oil; you get the trees.

Malaysia and Indonesia largely divide Borneo (the small, immensely rich nation of Brunei takes a chunk out of Malaysia's portion of the northern coast). While Malaysia and Indonesia have very different governments, they have been equal-opportunity exploiters of the giant island. On the Indonesian side of the island the federal government (with the encouragement of the World Bank) used the state of Kalimantan as a dumping ground for people forced off their land on other islands. While the poor cut the forest to survive, the rich razed it to grow richer. In recent years more than half the wood exported from Indonesia has come from illegal logging, and throughout Borneo, even where lands were designated for cutting, timber operations have proceeded with scant regard for ecological consequences.

The predictable result has been ecological and cultural tragedy. In the late 1990s the combination of an El Niño with uncontrolled land conversion resulted in the aforementioned calamitous fires. Ordinarily the peat that lies in Kalimantan's many swamps would be under water, but the combination of forest clearing and agricultural planting has reduced the water table to the degree that the peat is periodically exposed to the sun, which dries it out. When farmers burn cleared brush nearby, it easily catches fire.

Though they might seem merely a faraway curiosity for those living in the United States, these fires make remote Borneo a significant contributor to global warming. Indonesian estimates are that El Niño peat fires alone contributed 2 billion tons of CO_2 annually to the atmosphere through smoke and accelerated decomposition of unburned peat that is exposed to air. That figure represents more CO_2 emissions than are produced by all of Japan and more than 25 percent of total U.S. emissions.

I went to Borneo in April 1989 not to investigate its surprising contribution to climate change, but rather to look into a largely invisible conflagration. Indeed, my most memorable trip to the huge island was prompted by a casual remark.

In Djakarta, Indonesia, I had run into an anthropologist named Tim Jessup whom I'd met years earlier through family connections. We got together for a drink with some conservation-minded Indonesians and expatriates, and the conversation turned to the loss of indigenous knowledge around the world. Tim mentioned a story he'd heard about the Penans, the last hunting and gathering tribe that still pursued a nomadic lifestyle in the highlands of Borneo. He explained that while those in the highlands would hunt wild boar timed to the appearance of a particular butterfly, their children away at school in the towns were already forgetting this tidbit of local knowledge. They might vaguely remember that their uncle would pay attention to this butterfly, but they couldn't say why he cared about it, or which kind of butterfly it was. While such knowledge might seem trivial, Tim noted that the relationship between the butterfly and the boar might be linked to the fruiting pattern of a rainforest tree, and such ecological connections could be invaluable to scientists trying to understand the dynamics and vulnerabilities of the local ecosystem.

That story offered the perfect metaphor for a worldwide phenomenon

I was then studying—the loss of indigenous knowledge—and suggested that learning it could be as elusive, fragile and evanescent as a butterfly itself. Even though traditional lore might have been passed on for generations—perhaps for hundreds, or perhaps for just a few—it might vanish silently without any sense of loss in those who were losing it. And so I set about trying to get to Sarawak to hear more about the elusive butterfly and to meet the Penans.

—————

I got in touch with a remarkable young man named Harrison Ngau. A Sarawak-born lawyer and environmental activist, Harrison had taken up the cause of the Penans, who, having failed to get a fair hearing in any Malaysian or international forums, had taken to blockading logging roads to stop the remorseless cutting of their forests. This gesture, in which diminutive hunter-gatherers stood up against the police and powerful logging companies, did draw the world's attention, though it only marginally slowed the logging.

When I showed up in Borneo, these blockades were still going on, while Harrison was fully occupied trying to deal with the cases of the many Penans who had been arrested (for trying to get the government to enforce laws already on the books). He invited me to meet him in the principal town in the highlands, then a sleepy backwater called Marudi, situated on a bend in the Baram River. Many of the Penans who had been arrested at the blockades had assembled there for their court cases, and that offered me an opportunity to chat with chiefs from many remote longhouses.

Harrison had told me that the best way to get to Marudi from Miri (my port of entry) was by motorized longboat up the river. The two-hour trip was anything but the peaceful tropical river sojourn I had envisioned. The captain kept the tachometer redlined the entire trip, while a television blaring Asian martial arts B movies competed with the roar of the engine. I arrived in Marudi shaken, if not stirred, and since I wasn't scheduled to meet up with Harrison until the next day, I settled in at a local hotel and set about finding dinner. The only restaurant seemed to be an open-sided, thatch-roofed structure set on a lovely promontory overlooking a bend in the river. Through gestures I found a seat, and with elaborate formality the waiter handed me an English-language menu. There were pages upon pages of fish, chicken and pork dishes, and using sign language I pointed to some intriguing Malaysian concoction. The waiter shook his head. I pointed to another—this one? Again, the disappointed no.

This went on for some minutes until I shrugged in capitulation. The waiter took the menu and turned to the very last page, where a piece of paper had been pasted to the laminated menu. It offered two selections: "fish meat" and "pig meat." I pointed to the latter and enjoyed what turned out to be a delicious four-course meal.

The next day I found Harrison at an office where various Penans had gathered to prepare their cases. Sitting in the antechamber was a Penan happily reading a newspaper that he was holding upside down. I was brought into a small conference room and there, in various forms of dress ranging from shorts and T-shirts to loincloths, was a who's who of the Penans of Sarawak: Juing Lihan, the head of the South Penan Association; Peng Hulu Wan Malong, the major chief of Sungai Layun, which comprised twenty longhouses; Debaran Siden, a chief from Long Balau; Kurau Kusin, the chief of a group of Penans who were settled but who still pursued nomadic hunting; and so on. I don't know what Harrison had told the group about why I had come, but everybody was eager to talk, and Harrison graciously offered to translate.

From an anthropologist's point of view it was an extraordinary gathering, consisting of chiefs from settled tribes, seminomadic tribes, and nomadic tribes, as well as Harrison himself, who, while completely Westernized, had not forgotten his roots. The Penans may be among the oldest peoples on earth. One line of thinking places the tribes of Borneo near the roots of a radiation that eventually populated points north and ultimately the Americas. Indeed, my first impression was that I could see all races in the faces arrayed before me.

While the Penans assumed I wanted to talk about the blockade, they agreeably shifted topics when I brought up the question of traditional knowledge and the difficulties of maintaining that knowledge as tribes abandoned nomadic ways. One of the first to speak up was Kurau Kusin, the chief of a settled village, who was a bit defensive about his tribe's decision to settle. Demonstrating a distinctly Western gift for proactive argument, he noted that they still ventured far into the forest to hunt and gather, and that such activities kept the knowledge alive.

As he spoke, it became apparent that his tribe had developed something of a generation gap. From his comments I inferred that he and the other older members often waxed eloquent about the joys of a nomadic life. Like any exasperated elder dealing with a sassy younger generation, he noted that the young would ask him why they had settled if life had been so damned good back when they were nomadic. He said that his answer was that it was useful to have a permanent base from which to hunt. Well, yes, but one of the ecological benefits of nomadism is that moving around allows the forest and its game to recover. Kurau explained that while they did have to go deeper and deeper into the forest to find game, he blamed destruction by the logging companies and not the effects of settlement for the change.

The chief also said that although students regularly left the longhouse to go to secondary school, they usually came back. "If the land is there, the school is not a problem," he told me. "They will always come back. Their heart is still with us. Maybe they dress different, but their heart is still with us."

To some degree, poverty kept the tribe's traditions vital. I asked the chief whether they used guns to hunt. His somewhat ambiguous response was that it was traditional to use a blowpipe, which helped maintain knowledge about where to look for wood for the pipe and poison for the darts. But then he explained that if they used guns instead, they would have to buy both the gun and bullets, an answer that left the door open on whether the group might actually switch weapons should that financial problem be solved.

Kusan also said that the tribe transmitted its knowledge to its children by sending them into the forest to find bark and other plants. As an example he told of an accident that had occurred when a child playing with a blowgun accidentally shot another child with a dart. What could have been a tragedy had a happy ending, because the shooter knew where to find the antidote for the poison involved—a plant called *tebaran siden*.

The gun/blowpipe question frames how profoundly difficult it is to maintain traditions once a tribe becomes aware of the power of labor-saving technologies. Those like me who feel that something precious will be lost when the last Penan puts down his blowpipe always risk being accused of paternalism and hypocrisy, as well as inflicting needless hardship. What right do we have to insist that anyone hold on to traditions that we ourselves abandoned centuries ago?

Those tribal peoples who have tried to negotiate an entente with modernity have discovered that it's a slippery path. I witnessed the reductio ad absurdum of such compromises when I visited a tribe on Hudson Bay in Canada that used helicopters to commute to its traditional hunting grounds (at least until its money ran out). While the people may still feel a kinship with their forebears, the intimate bonds that tied this tribe to the landscape and its ecology were long ago broken.

While the dilemma of wrestling with how a tribe can accept the life-prolonging/labor-saving technologies of the West without losing its soul is a moral problem for outsiders like me, it is an ontological struggle for the proud elders of the Penans, who realize that maintaining their identity carries with it the price tag of living at a material disadvantage to those in the towns. The elders can only offer largely intangible rewards and philosophical arguments when the government or the younger generation urges them to abandon their backward ways.

The chiefs do try to muster a line of reasoning that the traditional life is better than life in the towns. Penans rarely get high-paying jobs, and they do not receive the quality of medical care typical of Western medicine. One of the chiefs observed that, in the case of the boy who had been wounded by a dart, a Western doctor would have cut the affected area to drain the poison, unaware of or unconcerned with the fact that the toxin could be neutralized by rubbing the puncture with herbs. Other chiefs cited various trees they used for common ailments like diarrhea, and named three—*getimang, nyekup* and *buhow*—whose bark could be chewed or boiled as a treatment for stomach disorders. Turning the conversation again to the blockade, they pointedly said that these trees were getting harder to find, and that if the trees disappeared, the knowledge of their medicinal benefits would vanish with them.

After further discussion of traditional medicine, the Penans addressed the role of ritual and taboo in their lifestyle and traditions. Yahya Sipai from Long Kidah said that an evangelical mission had been established in his area ten years earlier and had had a profound impact on their lives. In the old belief, women were not supposed to eat monkey, leopard, bear and python, but now that they had converted to Christianity, all dietary restrictions had been lifted. Korau Kusin from Long Kidah added that while they maintained some medicines that "attest to the natural," they had done away with those that attested to the old belief. I interpreted this to mean that they had kept those medicines that cure because of natural properties but had done away with those that involve spells and magic of the old beliefs.

For instance, the wood bark and roots from a five-foot-tall plant called *kenyatong* used to be employed as a balm to cure internal pain, but because it carried with it a taboo (it had to be handled according to a strict procedure—if put in a fire the wrong way, it would be harmful), it was now considered unchristian, and Korau Kusin would no longer use it, even though it provided effective treatment. He added that he and other elders would still tell children about the wood, but they would also warn them that it was now prohibited.

When I asked whether you could be a Christian and still be a Penan, one chief shrugged and remarked that the old way of life was still the same, irrespective of beliefs. He didn't mind giving up the use of potions to kill people. Others in the group, however, argued that switching beliefs came with a price. One Penan said that in the past, if you had good dreams you would have a good hunt; if you dreamed that you would catch a wild boar, for example, the next day it would come true. That didn't happen anymore, he said—while you might have the dream, the boar wouldn't appear.

This precipitated an animated discussion about the pros and cons of Christianity. I got the sense that Christianity was winning not because the Penans had embraced Jesus Christ as their savior, but because life was on the whole simpler under one god. As one chief put it, "Before we had all these taboos. If we had to walk from here to there, we had to think, *What was my dream last night, what route should I take?* Now we just go there."

Between the government, missionaries, loggers, competing hunters, liquor, Western movies and the lure of the towns, these chiefs and their still loyal longhouse members were being assailed from all sides. I had come to Borneo thinking how sad it was that out of the hundreds of millions of people who lived in the archipelago that extends from the Philippines through Malaysia and Indonesia, perhaps only a few thousand maintain the arduously acquired knowledge of the flora and the fauna. Listening to the accounts of these chiefs and hunters, however, I came away thinking it somewhat miraculous that anyone had been able to hang on to it at all.

At least, for that moment, that knowledge *was* still alive. The Penan group grew most animated when the conversation turned to hunting techniques and the various auguries they used to track boar. One bird, which they called *matui* and which looked a little like a hornbill, signaled the presence of certain kinds of fruit and correlated with the migration of the boar. So did a black, chickenlike ground bird with red and white feathers on its head. Another, whose Penan name was *be'ui* and which was described as a blue ground bird, signaled that not only boar but also barking deer were nearby.

The obsession with fruiting seasons may seem strange to those of us from temperate climes—after all, in one weekend any American schoolkid can learn when trees and berries fruit in New England—but the Borneo rainforest doesn't work like that. By far the dominant trees are dipterocarps, and, given all the seed predators waiting to pounce on fruit once it appears, the trees have evolved a strategy called masting to ensure their reproduction. What this means is that they produce an overwhelming amount of fruit at unpredictable intervals. This strategy, along with the great diversity of trees in the rainforest, reduces the odds that predators will adapt to a fruiting cycle and enhances the probability that seeds will survive. Thus, flying scouts like birds or insects provide invaluable intelligence to Penans and possibly animals as well about where the fruit and those animals who eat it can be found.

And yes, all the forest Penans gathered in Marudi knew about the butterfly. They called it *yap lempuhan,* a fast-flying insect that appears rarely but serves as a sign of fruiting season for many types of trees. Later, in Miri, I was introduced to a Penan secondary school student away from the highlands for his studies. When I asked him about the butterfly he looked at me as if I had three heads.

To put in perspective what I had heard from the Penans in Marudi, and during subsequent trips to longhouses in the highlands, I sought out Dr. Jayl Lanjub, an anthropologist trained at McGill University, then working with the state planning unit. He was fully aware of the problem of the loss of indigenous knowledge, noting that there were glimmerings of awareness in the government that something noble was vanishing. The maddening thing for Lanjub was that efforts to help the Penans were doing just as much damage as the destruction of the forests. "When a kid goes to secondary school," he remarked, "he's only home for three weeks a year. That's not much time to go out into the forest and learn." One of his proposals was to arrange for schooling in service centers that were a lot closer to the longhouses. From what I can gather, this policy has been implemented, though not to the degree the Penans would like.

He also said that he took the Penans' own protestations about their devotion to traditional knowledge with a grain of salt. "They talk a good line," he told me, "but like anybody, given the opportunity they are going to take the path of least resistance." For instance, he noted that whenever the planning unit visited the rural villages, its inhabitants requested guns. "Hunting with a blowpipe is very difficult," he explained.

When I left Borneo in 1990 there were eight nomadic groups. Now there may not be any that are truly nomadic, though a number of settled Penans still hunt and gather in the dwindling forests. The decline of nomadic groups has been matched by an increase in settlements, from about 78 in 1990 to 121 today. Some sense of deep identification with fellow tribe members might maintain Penan identity long after the last Penan forgets the significance of *yap lempuhan,* but that is only partial solace for what will be lost.

The march of so-called progress has been accompanied by a cultural entropy in the metaphorical sense, as distinct, well-ordered societies disperse into an undifferentiated mass after encounters with modernity. We can only hope that cultural dynamics are not as rigid as the laws of physics.

CHAPTER 3

New Guinea: The Godsend of Cargo

I f the ragged edge of the world is that moveable frontier where modernity, wildlands and indigenous peoples collide, then New Guinea has been on the front line of that silent struggle almost continuously since first contact between Europeans and the island's hundreds of tribes in the nineteenth century. (Contact with outsiders dates back much further, perhaps as early as the twelfth or thirteenth century, when traders from China and the Malay Peninsula would visit to collect bird of paradise feathers.) New Guinea's forbidding ecology and fierce tribes discouraged casual visits, and until World War II, many tribes remained uncontacted, meaning that they had not encountered Europeans face-to-face. That changed quickly after the war. New Guinea is rich in resources that the West covets and that in recent decades have brought many Europeans and Asians to the island, accompanied by the familiar pathologies of the active frontier—alcoholism, alienation, the breakdown of families, and the loss of indigenous knowledge. In this case, however, Western contact has also produced some surprises. Papuans (Papua was the name originally given to the entire island), for instance, have demonstrated more resilience in responding to modernity than many other indigenous peoples around the world.

I first went to New Guinea in December 1976, as part of the research for my book *Affluence and Discontent*. My purpose was to look into cargo cults, a bizarre phenomenon that took hold in New Guinea in earnest during World War II, when Stone Age tribes encountered airplanes and their cargo, and set about trying to integrate these seeming miracles into a view of the cosmos that held ancestors, not human endeavor, to be the transforming force in life. I was intrigued by cargo cults because I believed (and still believe) that they offer a crucial insight into the nature of consumer societies.

New Guinea is one of the strangest, most dramatic, and—for a nation not at war—most dangerous places on earth. Its strangeness is due in part to geography, as it lies on the Australian side of the Wallace Line, that invisible biogeographical barrier that separates the flora and fauna of Indonesia from the remnant relics and oddities of what was once the supercontinent Gondwanaland (now Australia, New Zealand and New Guinea). There are no primates in New Guinea other than humans, few poisonous snakes, and no large predators; the biggest native fauna are birds, not mammals. The meager assortment of terrestrial animals includes the kus kus, a golden-haired relative of the opossum; some small kangaroos; and pigs, which were brought there by humans in the distant past. Fruits abound, but there's not a lot of protein to be had, which may explain why different tribes made a habit of snacking on one another.

A number of cultural aspects of New Guinea are to some degree a reflection of its unusual ecology. For instance, the absence of primates or any other large mammals meant that as much as New Guinea's hunter-gatherers were a part of nature, they did not encounter any monkeys or apes to remind them that they themselves came from nature. By contrast, Africans are born Darwinians because the continent's primates serve as a daily reminder of our roots. In the absence of such reminders, ancient Papuans were free to speculate on human origins—a prerogative they seized on with great creativity. A number of New Guinean creation myths (not surprisingly, an island with several hundred languages has produced a great many such myths), for example, held that people originated in the sky.

Like many contemporary consumers, New Guineans are also highly materialistic; but delve deeper into this materialism, and Western consumers and Papuans rapidly begin to part company. Even today, good numbers of New Guinean natives believe that consumer goods (like people) come from the sky. It is this persistent conviction, which they cling to in some cases despite being physically shown how factories produce goods, that is key to the resilience of the Papuan worldview.

The belief that consumer goods have magical origins is at the core of each cargo cult. Cargo cults offered an explanation for European goods that fit within a native's traditional perspective. New Guineans would see great ships arrive and disgorge unimaginable wealth with no visible connection to the endeavors of the Europeans who brought them. (Papuans rarely saw Europeans working under any circumstances.) Local Europeans would also celebrate the arrival of ships, reinforcing the suspicion that the goods had magical origins. But the ultimate proof for many natives was the fact that the bumbling, sweaty whites who couldn't speak any native dialects just seemed too dimwitted to have produced such wonders. (This marked a decided downgrading of the original reputation of whites, many of whom were first viewed as deities, before the natives concluded that these strange newcomers did not live up to the behavior expected of a divinity.)

So, as the natives watched in awe, some local prophet would tell his one-talks (pidgin for people from the same clan) that the arrival of the rich whites was a signal that release from toil and strife was at hand. Often the prophet would announce that he knew the rituals that the Europeans used to produce the cargo, and equally often he would insist that the cargo rightfully belonged to the natives and that the whites had stolen it through treachery. Such claims often marked the point at which these cults moved from being quaint to being dangerous.

For me the persistence of cargo cults helped illustrate a simple but often overlooked idea: The mere desire for consumer goods does not a consumer make. In *Affluence and Discontent,* I tried to show that the genius of a consumer society is that it taps an endless source of power by translating religious needs into material appetites. The key to the power of a consumer society is that people are willing to organize themselves to earn the money to try to satisfy needs that can ultimately never be requited by material purchases. There's a lot more to the argument than that—a whole book's worth, in fact—but my basic point was and is that a consumer society is a system that integrates the production of goods and services and the consumption of goods and services. More specifically, a consumer society harnesses the very discontents it creates—in the form of disenfranchised and unrequited religious needs—to mobilize resources and extend its ambit. (For those interested, I developed this concept further in my more recent book, *The Future in Plain Sight.*)

Papuans loved the consumer goods, but they were not consumers. One of the most poignant illustrations of this involved a Papuan native named Yali who rose to the rank of sergeant major in the Australian army in recognition of his invaluable assistance to the Australian administrators of New Guinea during World War II. In most respects Yali was a model soldier, and he seemed to adapt well to modernity. During a training trip to Australia, he was taken to a factory where armaments were produced. When he returned to New Guinea he told his one-talks that, yes, he had in fact seen the place where goods were made, but the sneaky Europeans never showed him the secret room from which the ancestors directed the operations.

Talk to almost any anthropologist who has worked in New Guinea, and you will hear similar anecdotes about backfired attempts to contradict cargo beliefs. One researcher became alarmed at a nascent cargo cult near Garoka, the gateway to the highlands, and took one of the village elders to see a hydroelectric dam, hoping to enlist his help in defusing the cult. Instead, the sight of the immense structure instantly converted the elder into a full-blown believer in cargo, as he was convinced that no humans could build something that big.

Other such attempts produced unintended and amusing results. This was the case when, as the story goes, an expatriate took two village big-men up in a small plane to prove to them that it was nothing more than a machine. The pair were riveted by the experience and looked down with great interest as they flew over neighboring villages. After they landed they asked the pilot if the windows opened. When the pilot said yes, they asked whether they could go up again and fly the same route. Delighted that he was making progress, the pilot agreed. Once they were aloft, however, and flying over the neighboring village with the window open and the air blowing by, the men took out rocks they had brought with them and began throwing them down. The two natives might have reserved judgment on whether humans or ancestors produced airplanes, but they immediately grasped their military potential.

At first blush Yali and other cargo believers looked like consumers, but they lacked (or were blessed not to have) the critical parts. Traditional tribal culture had no concept of growth; the people saw no connection between expending effort and improving their material well-being. Indeed, in most tribes families didn't have to work any harder than the lazy Europeans, since an hour and a half's work a day was sufficient to secure a living (which makes one wonder about the putative lure of cargo cults being the release from toil).

Cargo ingeniously offered the Stone Age mentality a type of immunity to the most disorienting aspects of encounters with modernity. To a small degree, it allowed tribal peoples to eat their cake and have it also, since they didn't have to sacrifice their worldview to get access to some portion of Western goods. Indeed, the widespread notion that whites had tricked natives out of cargo that was rightfully theirs offered a perfect justification for stealing (not that most tribes needed any justification for stealing from someone who was not a one-talk). Consequently, crime was and is rampant in New Guinea. Port Moresby's murder rate is twenty-three times that of London, and in 2004 the *Economist*'s Intelligence Unit rated Port Moresby the most dangerous city on the planet—quite a feat when you consider that it was up against places like Baghdad.

The special flavor of Port Moresby became obvious when I first arrived in 1976. I found lodging with an Australian/Canadian expatriate couple. Over dinner they told me horror stories of the hazards of the city, including the experience of their previous guests, two travel-hardened women backpackers. The pair had declined an offer of a guest room and gone to camp instead on the beach. Both were raped within three hours of pitching their tent. Then and now, only the intrepid venture out at night, and the expatriate community was rife with cautionary tales of rapes, robberies and assaults.

The perpetrators of most of these acts were abandoned children and adolescents who had migrated to the cities. Many of them adroitly adapted to a life of crime, redirecting hunting and stalking skills they had learned in the mountains. (One expatriate told me of waking up one night to discover a young Papuan crouched silently on the nightstand next to his bed.) Dubbed "rascals," a deceptively endearing tag, gangs of these marauding outcasts and rebels-without-a-cause spread terror through Port Moresby. As one Papuan put it to me, "The influx of young into the cities is a sure indication that the elders are losing control over their sons and daughters."

Since World War II modernity has been coming at Papuans from all angles. Mining companies spread money around and hire the educated young, unintentionally creating a rift between young managers who have cash and their elders who control the land. In the 1960s colonial governors tended to be appointed from previous postings in Africa, where the conventional wisdom was to discourage tribalism in order to encourage national identity. Missionaries have a mixed record. Some of the fundamentalist Protestant sects have been the most assiduous demonizers of traditional practices and beliefs, but others, notably Catholics from the Divine Word order, have recognized the importance of cultural traditions to individual and village identity and have worked to link traditional culture with national pride.

There is a comic side to these collisions at the ragged edge of the world. On that first trip I flew up to Enga in the highlands. Enga, home to the Mount Hagen festival, was the last province to be contacted by Europeans. (Although he never talked much about it, my father was one of those first Europeans to enter the province, having served as a medical corpsman in World War II.) One evening I went to the local theater, which was showing Stanley Kubrick's *Barry Lyndon,* starring Ryan O'Neal as an eighteenth-century Irish adventurer and swordsman. Scattered among the audience were a number of Papuans in grass skirts, all of whom understood the plot perfectly, as it dealt with honor, betrayal and fighting skills. Later I learned that the theater had adopted a policy requiring natives to check their own weapons before entering, because some would become so caught up in the films that they would take sides and hurl spears at the screen.

Thanks to some friends who had worked in New Guinea in various UN programs, I had some contacts in the country. Thomas Unwin, the resident representative of the United Nations Development Program (UNDP) station in New Guinea, gave me an introduction to John Haugie, the minister of cultural affairs, who in turn wrote a letter to the provincial commissioner, noting that my journalistic visit had his official approval and support. This introduction magically opened doors, the most important of which was that of Chief Inspector Leo Debessa, the provincial police commander of Western Highlands province. Debessa was typical of the professionals I encountered in New Guinea: strong, well trained, and sensitive to the complexities of dealing with clans and tribes—perhaps because he professed himself only one step removed from the Stone Age ways of his family.

At the time of my visit, 4,000 Europeans were living in Mount Hagen, the provincial capital of Western Highlands. Debessa told me that in the previous year there had been 1,000 reported breaking and enterings. Since the majority of Europeans were there with their families, it was safe to assume that virtually every European had suffered a burglary or worse.

Chief Debessa was somewhat resigned to the persistence of such crimes. Since the theme of most cargo cults was that Europeans had come to possess their riches through trickery, theft was in effect a form of repossession, and that meme was far more widespread than the details of any particular cargo cult. Debessa was more worried about a rise in actual assaults, particularly that the unsophisticated tribesmen would get ideas from the violent films that were often shown in the theater, and that showcased the firepower of modern weapons.

Tribal warfare posed another headache for the chief. He was sensitive to the fact that the village bigmen achieved their rank through skills in war, and he needed their cooperation and the respect for traditional law to maintain order. At the same time he wanted to quell these wars, which could flare up over an issue as minor as an intemperate remark and disrupt regions intermittently for years. (As one weary expatriate remarked to me with considerable understatement, "People here are incredibly short-tempered.")

Once Debessa became comfortable with the idea that I was not in New Guinea to ridicule his country's backward ways, he began to offer me opportunities to accompany his men and associates on missions. Toward the end of my stay, he invited me to join a force from the elite Police Mobile Unit to try to stop a tribal war in Gumine between clans of the Yuri and Koksam tribes on one side and the Golin on the other. The battle had been raging on and off since 1973. I jumped at the chance. For one thing I was interested to see firsthand whether the natives still forswore modern weapons in their tribal conflicts. If that proscription was ever abandoned, the death toll in these conflicts would quickly rise to Congolese proportions.

I shouldn't have been so quick to accept the invitation, however, as the trip gave new meaning to the saying "It's not the destination, but the journey." Thirty-odd years later, that particular journey still stands as the most terrifying I've ever taken.

My driver was Group Commander Loki, a rail-thin but extremely rugged-looking leader of the elite force. As we headed out, he brought me up to date on both the conflict and the wearisome trials of being the first responders to violence in a country where men must prove themselves through fighting. In Bougainville he had had to deal with petrol bombs; in the coastal areas, slingshots; and in the highlands, bows and arrows. He said that the clans had guns and axes, but still hewed to traditional arms (except for using axes to chop up bodies of their victims—more about that later).

The most recent flare-up in the ongoing war to which we were heading had begun in June as the result of an argument over a woman. Loki resignedly noted that all wars trace back to disputes over land, women (either an insulting bride price or a rape), accidents, or pigs, or to some perceived insult. The regional police had been able to stop the June fighting, which had since been resumed. I tried to take notes as Loki talked, but my concentration was constantly interrupted by moments of sheer terror.

No road has clung to any mountain with less certainty than the narrow dirt track I drove with the Police Mobile Unit. While New Guinea lacks dangerous animals, it more than makes up for this omission through geography. With its huge, craggy mountains, unnavigable crashing rivers, and vertigo-inspiring ravines, the interior is treacherous in the extreme. In the 1970s many of the airports were "one-approach," meaning that if you blew the landing, there was no room to turn around, and you didn't get a second chance. Evidence of wrecks suggested that the stakes were similar on the backcountry roads.

This particular road consisted of an almost imperceptible indentation into a massive, supersteep mountain slope. Every few miles the track was partially cut by erosion or landslides, and peering out, I'd look thousands of feet down into bottomless canyons. One wants to put one's trust in the competence of the authorities, but my faith was sorely tested as the commander hurtled along these slick and treacherous passages at about 55 miles an hour, slowing down to about 30 at obstacles. After a couple of near-spinouts, I opted to hold my door of the Land Cruiser open, reasoning that when we went over the side, I would jump out and take my chances.

After safely arriving in Gumine, we went to the local counselor's house, where the magistrate (Loki's brother-in-law) brought us up to date. The fighters had gotten word that the Police Mobile Unit was coming and had melted into the bush. The patrol officer told us that he had settled the argument that had caused the latest incident, and while the counselor went outside to call (futilely) for the warriors to give themselves up, the troops entertained themselves by playing volleyball.

Given the gruesome toll of local conflicts around the world in recent years, a village skirmish in New Guinea might seem relatively harmless and innocent in retrospect, yet the details were anything but. The magistrate told us that six people had been killed in this go-round: One was beheaded, another was cut in half (postmortem), while a third was cut into so many pieces that Loki had to reassemble the body as if it were a jigsaw puzzle.

Such physical violence amounts to an extreme form of trash talk. The warriors disfigure the bodies of their victims and flaunt the parts in order to incite the other side to fight—in this case, taking the head they had cut off and driving a stick through the neck and out the eye, and then displaying the macabre tableau prominently.

Despite such gory specifics, the actual body count in these wars tends to be very low. For instance, a total of twenty-three people had been killed in this conflict, which had been going on for three years at the time of my visit in 1976. The mortality rate is even more remarkable when we consider the natives' extraordinary skill with bows and arrows—a typical hunter can shoot a bird out of the air. The difference might be that warfare is a hot-blooded affair, while hunting is done with calm and patience. It's possible, even likely, that natives get so fired up during warfare that it literally spoils their aim.

This, in fact, was the implication of an anthropologist's report to the administrator of Enga Province that I saw during that trip. The scientist, who was trying to explain why one native had murdered another from a neighboring village on a runway, noted that when a native encounters someone from a rival clan with whom he has an unresolved grudge, he will want to kill his enemy on the spot. She used the word "salivate" to describe the urgency of this desire to kill.

Whenever I have come upon a situation in which people are constantly fighting but few are getting killed, I tend to suspect that there is more than coincidence at work. The Columbia University anthropologist Marvin Harris once described the customs and taboos of Papuan belief systems as "tricks" that encourage natives to act in ecologically sustainable ways, regardless of their instincts. Thus *maselai* forests—tracts containing trees that house the spirits of the ancestors—remain standing even if a village has sold off every other tree, because the villagers believe that if you cut a *maselai* your wife will become barren and your crops will shrivel. Similarly, clan bloodlust might act to mute the effectiveness of individual homicidal urges, which likely enough serve their own purposes in clan relationships in the highlands. This was certainly the case in the war I visited. Both sides had worked themselves up to a frenzy and then filled the sky with arrows, but no one was killed during the official battle. All the casualties resulted from the odd warrior being in the wrong place at the wrong time.

I was to take one other excursion with the police during this trip, when Debessa asked whether I would like to accompany one of his sergeants to a village to pick up an alleged rapist and bring him back to Mount Hagen for arraignment. Debessa explained that this was one of those awkward situations in that the victim had been to a mission school and knew enough to bring a charge of rape, while the perpetrator was from a traditional village and probably had no concept of the crime.

The sergeant, the deputy and I hopped in a Land Cruiser and headed out. As we drove, I noticed a sign for the Baiyer River Bird of Paradise Sanctuary. I had never seen a bird of paradise, and I asked the officer if we might stop on the way back. He shrugged agreeably, why not?

The tiny, quiet village where the rapist lived seemed an unlikely spot for a violent crime, but just as a clan member might not consider it to be murder to kill a member of a rival clan, the same held true for rape if the victim was from a rival village. After some good-natured back and forth in pidgin between the sergeant and a village elder, the rapist was summoned from a grass hut. The smiling man appeared dressed in a grass skirt (*assgrass* in pidgin) and cassowary feathers, and the policeman gestured that he should jump into the back of the truck, which he promptly did. No handcuffs or guard seemed to be necessary.

I figured my side trip to the bird of paradise sanctuary was now moot, but as we approached its gates, the constable slowed and turned into the parking lot. I asked my new friend what he intended to do with the prisoner. "Hmm, right," he remarked. "I guess we should bring him along." Adopting a "when in Rome . . ." attitude, I bought four tickets (total cost, $4), and all of us set off for a tour. The deputy carried a butter knife, not the most serious weapon imaginable, but, I assume, sufficient to suppress any ideas of escaping that might come into the rapist's head.

No creature better captures the exotic flavor of New Guinea than the bird of paradise. Of the world's thirty-eight known species, thirty-four live only in New Guinea. Like most creatures on the island, the birds have been shaped by the relative paucity of ground-dwelling predators. Without the fear of surprise attacks on the ground from cats or other bird-eaters, they have developed elaborate courtship rituals, in which the males perform intricate dances to prove their worthiness as mates, displaying gaudy tail feathers that might be three times their body length. Their finery is as colorful and varied as ladies' hats at Ascot on race day, although there is much more drag-queen abandon to the presentations of the New Guinea males. For all the variety of design, ranging from elegantly curved feathers as tight as threads to long, long ribbon tails, most birds of paradise encounter only the designs native to the isolated forest niches in which they evolved.

The (accused) rapist seemed as engaged and interested as I was as we slowly toured the aviaries. He did not seem to be curious about why he was being shown the birds, only delighted to have a chance to admire a precious collection of creatures that he would gladly have hunted in the forest.

Then it was back on the road. One of the curiosities of New Guinea back then was that one passed an inordinate number of wrecks, even on roads not winding precariously up and down mountainsides. Many of the demolished cars and trucks looked brand-new. When I inquired about them, I was told that the wrecks were the result of money outpacing driving skills. As clans sold off timber and other resource rights, one of the first things they would do with their windfall would be to buy a Land Cruiser, a vehicle that would secure a bigman's status as a player. The Land Cruiser is a great car, but driving New Guinea's rutted, mired or rain-slicked roads of the 1970s would have presented a challenge to any driver, and was often fatal for the proud new owners.

The proliferation of these destroyed but otherwise spanking-new cars gave one enterprising Australian entrepreneur the idea of buying the wrecks and setting up an auto parts business. Alas, when he went to negotiate with various villages, he invariably came back disappointed. From the village elders' point of view, the value of the car was not in its utility but in its status, and their asking price was typically what they had paid for the truck before it bounced down to the bottom of a ravine. Indeed, one clan had its ruined Land Cruiser hauled up and installed as a monument at the entrance to the village.

My first trip to New Guinea gave me a feel for this special place, but it was motivated by a desire to understand how its tribal worldview differed from that of a consumer society. When I returned fourteen years later, it was to see how its tribes were coping with the continued onslaught of modernity.

CHAPTER 4

New Guinea Redux

In 1990 I returned to New Guinea, this time as part of the research for "Lost Tribes, Lost Knowledge," an article I wrote for *Time* on the loss of indigenous knowledge around the world. I flew in from Borneo, and my destination was the north coast, where I'd arranged to interview a number of remarkable men. One was Saem Majnep, a native of the Kalem clan from the Kaironk Valley in the highlands, who grew up to become a champion of preserving native knowledge. As a boy he discovered that his knowledge of local birds and ecology, learned on hunting trips, proved invaluable to Ralph Bulmer, who in the 1950s and 1960s was one of the world's leading ornithologists. Given the widespread disdain for native culture that Majnep had encountered in the expatriate and missionary communities, this was an eye-opening experience for him. It ultimately inspired him to become a motivational speaker who traveled the country assuring villagers that their hard-earned knowledge of the local flora and fauna had value and that it could disappear in the blink of an eye.

My other quarry was Father Frank Mihalic, a missionary from the Catholic order Divine Word, who as much as anyone had helped unify New Guinea by first codifying a grammar for pidgin, the common language that allows speakers of New Guinea's 800 languages to communicate. Mihalic, who died in 2001, had been in New Guinea since 1948, and with wit and sensitivity witnessed its bumpy encounters with the modern world.

Not entirely through coincidence, I also met up with my then-girlfriend, Tundi Agardy, a marine biologist, who was coming to New Guinea as part of her work in coral reef conservation issues. Even in 1990, New Guinea was still well off the tourist path, and many of its north coast reefs were completely unexplored. Indeed, Tundi had heard tales of marine biologists who discovered new species of clownfish on virtually every dive.

We met up in Madang, a pleasant enough coastal town where one still had the luxury of an evening stroll without the risk of being robbed by rascals. Tundi has impeccable scientific credentials, but she also has a strong adventurous streak. In short order we had lined up a dive trip with some other marine scientists, as well as an expedition up the Sepik River.

There are not many cities in the world where you would choose to go diving in the main harbor, but that's where we went. With virtually no sewage systems on the island, it stood to reason that the harbor was collecting a good deal of what scientists euphemistically call "nutrients." The waters in the outer part of the harbor were spectacularly clear, however, and it's possible that the reef waters were so starved for nutrients—the seas off New Guinea have perhaps the clearest waters in the world—that whatever was being delivered into the harbor was gobbled up before it even reached the outer harbor. Or, perhaps, we just missed the pollution. In any event, we got our dose of clownfish darting in and out of sea anemones as well as the usual cast of reef dwellers sporting colors with all the subtlety of a Greenwich Village Halloween Parade. The colors on such "poster fish," as they are called, serve as a type of semaphore system, reminding individuals whom they school with, mate with, and avoid in the crowded quarters of a reef.

We got to the Sepik courtesy of Peter Barter, then arguably the most successful tourism entrepreneur in New Guinea's history. Barter bears a passing resemblance to former NBC anchor David Brinkley, and went on to several high positions in the New Guinea government, ultimately earning a knighthood from Queen Elizabeth. When I met him, he remarked, "Three types of people come to Papua New Guinea: mercenaries, misfits and missionaries. I was all three." Barter was a bit of a showman, and I'm sure that I wasn't the first to hear that line. He first arrived as a Qantas pilot, then returned as a missionary pilot. As he got to know the country he saw an opportunity to bring affluent tourists in to see aboriginal life—and, he argues, benefit the locals as well. For every trip on the river, his foundation would donate about 5,000 kina, money that would go for boats, immunizations, school headmasters' salaries and the like. Tourists also created a lively market for scarification masks, shields and other artifacts, keeping skills alive.

I could argue in turn, and did, that there is a world of difference between creating artifacts for tourist souvenirs and carving sacred objects as homage to the spirits that animate a culture, but, given the array of threats faced by Papuan natives—which include fundamentalist missionaries who demonize their beliefs and burn *haus tambarans* (spirit houses used primarily by males for initiations and rituals), expatriates and teachers who ridicule their backwardness, and mining and timber companies that scorch the earth and poison the streams—Peter Barter's trips look veritably saintly. Moreover, the culture itself endured strongly in people's lives despite all these threats.

We joined a trip on the *Sepik Explorer,* one of Barter's boats. Our first stop was Manam Island. Most of my prior knowledge of the Papuan genius for interpreting modernity through a Stone Age mind-set came from readings and from conversations with anthropologists, missionaries and expatriates. On Manam Island, I encountered it firsthand.

The volcanic island sits 40 miles off the north coast of New Guinea. Since our visit, the volcano has erupted at least twice, most recently in 2004, an event that forced the evacuation of the entire population of about 9,500 people. Our destination was the village of Zogari. While the tourists bargained for artifacts with the villagers on the beach, Tundi and I set off, accompanied by an interpreter, to meet with the local parish priest, Teddy Boaroa. The last expatriate missionary had turned the parish over to local control some decades earlier, and with the white priests gone, the local spirits had been busy.

When I asked Teddy about the history of the island, he launched into a long story that beautifully merged Christian imagery with the traditional cosmology. We went on to talk to other natives, but just before we reboarded the boat, Teddy came running up to me. In the interim, he had taken the trouble to write down the history of Manam Island as he saw it. On the facing page is the paper he gave me.

THE STORY ABOUT MANAM ISLAND

3/02/90

MANAM ISLAND TRANSFER FROM SANAI BOSMUN.

BIPO MANAM ISLAND INO STAP OLSEM NAU, NAMDEL LONG BIKSOLO-
WARA. TAIM GRAUN I STAT NUPELA MANAM IS. I STAP LONG
WANPELA PLES LONG MAINLAND OL I KOLIM NEM BILONG DISPELA
PLES SANAI KLOSTU LONG KATOLIK MISIN STESIN BOSMUN RBMU.
SAMPELA YEAR BIHAIN EM I LUSIM PLACE SANAE NA EM I KAM
SANAP LONG BIAG LONG PLES KAYAN LONG NAMBIS. LONG BIAG TU
EM I STAP SAMPELA TAIM TASOL NA EM I PAININ SAMTING I
RONG LONG EM. BINATANG (INCECT) I KAIKAIM BOL BILONG EM NA TU I
BIN I GAT PLENTI NATNAT OLSEM NA EM I LUSIM BIAG LONG
PLES KAYAN NA EM I GO SANAP GEN LONG BIKSOLOWARA.
OLSEM TODAY YUMI LUKIM MANAM ISLAND I SANAP LONG SOLO-
WARA. TASOL ASPLES TRU BILONG MANAM I NO LONG SOLOWARA NO-
GAT. EM LONG SANAE. LONG DISPELA TAIM MANAM I KAMAP
NUPELA I GAT TUPELA MASALAI MAN NA MERI I STAP LONG
EM. NEM BILONG MASALAI MAN/EM AUROKA NA MASALAI MERI
EM EM ZARIA. TUPELA I ASPLACE MAN NA MERI BILONG
MANAM STRET. BIPO I GAT PICTURE/PIKSA TRU BILONG IABU NA
ZARI I STAP ANTAP TRO LONG STONE BILONG PAIA LONG ET BILONG
MANAM. ZARIA LONG RIGHT SOET NA IABU LING LEFT SOET
OLSEM MAN NA MERI TRU. MI YET MI LUKIM TUPELA TU
TAIM MI STAP 21 YEARS. LONG SANAE MANAM I BIN LUSIM
PLACE LONG EM. TODAY I GAT BIKPELA TAIS WARA I STAP YET.
INSAET LONG TAIS WARA I GAT TU PLENTI PIS. OLSEM TU LONG
SAMPELA MAK SANAE PIPEL NA MANAM PIPEL KLOSTU LUK WANKAIN
PLENTI TOK PLES I WAN KAIN. LONG YEAR 1965 MI GO LUKIM PLES
SANAE NA TU PLES WE EM MANAM I LUSIM LONG EM. I GAT YET
TAIS WARA BIPO I KAM INAP TODAY I STAP YET.

So EMTASOL PINIS BILONG STORY.

NEM BILONG MAN I RAITIM STORI
EM LONG: TEDDY BOAROA
PARISH TABELE 20GARI VILLAGE MANAM ISL.
PO BOGIA MADANG PROVINCE
P.N.G.

And here is a rough translation and interpolation as graciously done by Bruce Beehler, the renowned ornithologist and explorer who has spent many years in New Guinea.

THE STORY ABOUT MANAM ISLAND
MANAM ISLAND MOVED FROM SANAE

Before, Manam Island was not like it is today, in the middle of the ocean. When the land was new, Manam Island was a part of the mainland. This place was called Sanae, near the Catholic Mission Station at the Ramu River mouth. Years ago, it [Manam] left the place called Sanae and came and shifted to the place called Biag at the place called Kayan on the coast. At Biag also it stayed some time, but the place had problems. Insects stung his balls and there were many gnats, so he left Biag and Kayan Place and went back out into the ocean. Just like today where you see Manam in the salt water (ocean). But Manam's true home is not the ocean but at Sanae. At this time when Manam originated, it had two spirits, a man spirit named Auroka and the woman spirit named Zaria. These two were the original man and woman of the original Manam (as in Adam and Eve). There used to be an image of these two on top of a volcano on Manam. Zaria was on the right and Iabu on the left just as man and woman. I myself saw these images twice when I was twenty-one. The place in Sanae that used to be where Manam stood is today a big swamp. In this swamp there are now Sanae people, not Manam people. Much of their two languages and the people themselves are the same. In the year 1965 I visited Sanae—and the swamp was there as it is today. That's the end of the story.

Teddy Boaroa

The history as told by Teddy weaves elements of the Christian creation story with local tribal creation myths, with some plate tectonics thrown in for good measure. Keep in mind that Teddy was the resident Catholic presence on the island. Both Christian and aboriginal elements are background to the story. For instance, his account seamlessly shifts from the description of the island as a physical place to a personification of the island and has that unidentified "he" reacting to having his balls stung by insects by moving back to the ocean. What struck me about the whole episode was how unselfconsciously he wove these Christian and animistic elements together. It seemed as though Teddy felt no contradiction or conflict in integrating these two wildly different belief systems. I'm not sure which belief system will win out on Manam Island in the end, but at least in 1990 the spirits seemed to be holding their own.

From Manam we headed toward the Sepik River. As we made our stately way toward its mouth, I discussed further with Barter the uneasy bargain that tourism represents. Barter makes no apologies, pointing out that the number one priority of almost every village in New Guinea is to attract more tourism. At that point he was bringing about 7,000 tourists a year up the Sepik, and in a typical twelve-day itinerary, they would spend about 40,000 kina on artifacts.

As we entered the mouth of the river, I noticed that we had slowed to a crawl—and also that arrayed along either side of the boats were natives in dugout canoes. What I was witnessing was a variant of a scam I also encountered in Africa.

As Barter explained it, natives would position the boats so that they would be swamped if the *Sepik Explorer* came through at any speed. The grift was to then claim compensation, something that was all the rage then in New Guinea. Indeed, trumped-up claims against expatriates and the government for compensation probably ranked as a major source of income for those villages in contact with outsiders. Barter slowed his boats way down, but even so, natives who had spent their entire lives handling dugouts suddenly became all thumbs and would tip over, setting the stage for ludicrously large claims for compensation. If someone actually died, potential claims reached Lotto-like proportions. Barter told me of one enterprising headman who had precariously positioned his aged grandmother in a canoe, apparently with the hope he might make the mother of all compensation claims and rid himself of an expensive liability at the same time.

Barter had had it with this scam, and met with headmen from the surrounding villages and threatened to take his boats off the river unless they got this extortion racket under control. He also said that Michael Somare, then the prime minister, had backed him on this, suggesting that pulling Barter's boats was probably the only way to make the villagers desist.

While Barter gets irritated with nuisance compensation suits, he has built his life in New Guinea and asserts that he is sensitive to the vulnerabilities of native cultures. For instance, he notes that he won't visit certain villages unless his tourists are willing to spend an entire day there, because to do otherwise would be taken as an insult by their hosts.

He is also a bemused student of the deep resilience of New Guinean culture. He notes that the same natives who carve shields and masks for tourists will also produce works for sacred houses that they would never sell, or even show to tourists. Moreover, they adapt. Carvers noticed that tourists prefer flat to rounded storyboards, so they started making them flat. Others reduced the size of carvings so that they could fit in luggage. Christian imagery may be included on shields ostensibly decorated for ancestor worship. During World War II, Trobriand Islanders started incorporating pornographic images in response to the taste of GIs, a practice that has continued in different parts of Papua New Guinea to this day.

Conversations with Peter Barter turned out to be the most interesting part of the trip up the Sepik. While his boats are quite comfortable, traveling on a tourist boat, no matter how sensitive its operators are to the local indigenous people, invariably sets up a wall between you and the culture you've come to see. Encounters with the natives in such circumstances feel like staged affairs, and it's naïve to expect that the locals you meet in these circumstances will look past your wallet. I greatly enjoyed meeting Peter Barter, but I did not feel I was encountering New Guinea.

———

Back in Madang I immediately set about tracking down Saem Majnep. Diminutive in stature, Majnep is a member of the Kalem clan of the Kaironk Valley in the highlands, but he embodies the hope that New Guinea might come to terms with the modern world without abandoning the knowledge and culture that held its clans together for thousands of years. He was a student at a missionary school in the late 1950s when he was hired as a translator by the distinguished ornithologist Ralph Bulmer. Though he was studying evangelism in school, he spent his free time out in the forest with his relatives and friends learning about the habits of birds, the uses of plants and all the incunabula of a hunter-gatherer life.

"Unprepossessing" doesn't begin to describe how Majnep appeared at first glance, but he grew in stature almost from the first word. He was serious, but he had a ready smile and he radiated quiet dignity.

His story underscores a simple but profoundly important aspect of the worldwide loss of indigenous knowledge: that the toxin of cultural amnesia is often introduced as normally and benignly as sending children away to school. "If you stay in your village," he said, "it is easy to pick up this learning [about plants and animals] because it is all around you, but when people go to Madang, they lose it very quickly."

Bulmer picked up on Majnep's local knowledge and realized that he had found something more than a translator in the young man. He began interviewing him about the feeding and breeding habits of the birds he had come to study. Bulmer appreciated that the practical ecological knowledge of Majnep and other villagers could save him an enormous amount of time. Majnep said that at first other villagers resisted telling Bulmer their stories, but soon came to regard him as honest. Ultimately Bulmer gave Majnep credit in many of his monographs on the birds of New Guinea, and Majnep published a few in his own name.

As beneficial as this collaboration was for Bulmer, it was ultimately far more important to Majnep and the other villagers. Missionaries had tended to dismiss the traditional knowledge of the Kalem people as mere superstition, but here was a distinguished scientist from New Zealand who sought out their learning. This was an eye-opening experience for the whole village, and it had a profound effect on young Majnep.

For the first time he felt that his traditional culture had value. He began noticing the ways in which people used that practical knowledge in their daily lives, where the knowledge was being used, and where it was being lost. For instance, he noted that even though many of the young were ashamed of what they regarded as the backwardness of their parents, almost everyone still relied on traditional medicines and felt some ambivalence about going to a clinic if they were sick.

He also noted that a lot of critical knowledge was simply slipping away. Culturally illiterate young people no longer knew which trees made the best house posts or firewood, and would make themselves sick by burning what he called poison oak or by burning mango wood.

Majnep grew up as an eyewitness to the ways in which a traditional society can gradually become unglued. He saw the delicate equilibrium of slash-and-burn agriculture fall out of balance as populations grew, and people forgot proper procedures for rotations, converting forests to grassland and reducing the casuarinas, whose wood was used as firewood and whose sap was converted to gum.

He was also sophisticated enough to recognize that traditional beliefs can make people unwitting conservationists. One of the most powerful tools protecting the forest is the aforementioned *maselai*—the belief that the spirits of the ancestors inhabits certain trees, and if those trees are cut down, all manner of woes will be visited on the perpetrator. Majnep said that *maselai* still exerted a strong hold on the people of Kaironk. Even some of the more enlightened missionaries—Anglican, Catholic and Lutheran—recognized that *maselai* helped preserve the forest.

By the time I met him, Majnep had become something of an evangelist himself, and was spending a lot of time on the radio, broadcasting his message in pidgin to whoever among New Guinea's hundreds of cultures cared to listen. His message: "All I can do is try to help save the knowledge of my own culture. If you want to save yours, record it. If you want to lose it, it's your choice."

Saem Majnep could reach out to other cultures in part because of the works of another very good man, an American named Frank Mihalic. During his more than fifty years in New Guinea, Mihalic served as a living antidote to the narrow-minded fundamentalist missionaries who demonized traditional beliefs. Trained in the Catholic order Verbi Divini (Divine Word), Mihalic saw his role as a helper of the people, and if that meant recognizing that traditional beliefs were the glue that held their cultures together, he was ready to make that compromise. I caught up with him at the Communication Arts Department of the Divine Word University in Madang. With its louvered windows and simple concrete structures, the university had a sleepy, tropical feel. Mihalic was dressed casually in a short-sleeved, lightweight cotton shirt. He began our conversation by stressing the importance of establishing a grammar for pidgin.

"Pidgin was the first unifying factor of this country," he asserted flatly. "It's now spoken by 1.5 million people—half the population. Once you had pidgin, then through the radio, you could jump barriers and get this country to a state where someone could fly anywhere and be understood."

Linguistically, a pidgin is a trade language—one that stands as a bridge between two languages. There are about 170 pidgins in the world. Tok Pisin, the New Guinean pidgin, draws about 80 percent of its words from English; Swahili, the best-known African pidgin, draws most of its words from Arabic.

Mihalic first codified the New Guinea grammar in 1957, setting it on a path to becoming a language. He also started a pidgin newspaper called *Wantok* (One-talk), a pidgin word referring to individuals who speak the same language. For a priest, he showed unexpected flair as a newspaper entrepreneur. Knowing, for instance, that many villagers used newspaper to roll their smokes, he took pains to choose newsprint that had the best properties as cigarette paper, burning slowly and producing a white ash. In a communication with the Society of the Divine Word, he even joked about printing an exhortation on the front page: "Please read this newspaper before you smoke it."

Once a pidgin comes to be spoken as a first language, it achieves creole status. When I interviewed Mihalic, pidgin was the first language for about 40,000 New Guinean children. The process of gravitating to a single tongue is organic and probably inevitable in the evolution of Papua New Guinea as a nation, but each child who begins speaking with either pidgin or English means one less child learning one of New Guinea's 800 indigenous languages.

Languages die as silently as traditional knowledge. As kids go off to the city, schooling and business are conducted in English or pidgin, until one day the last native speaker of a given tongue passes away, and while he or she may leave dozens of descendants, a critical part of their culture has died. In many cases, traditional knowledge *is* the language—think of the many Inuit words for snow, or the subtle differences in Polynesian words for ocean water. Worldwide it's inevitable that at least half the languages now spoken will soon die out, primarily because they do not exist in written form, and the young have turned to English or Spanish or other dominant tongues.

Mihalic, who was well aware of the double-edged sword of spreading pidgin, saw his role in part as one of trying to mitigate the pain and suffering that inevitably accompany encounters at the ragged edge of the world. "The problem," as he explained it, "is that these people were forced to jump from the Stone Age to the atomic age with nothing in between. Many people in the highlands saw their first wheel in their lives in a plane. The director of aviation told me that he rode in a plane before he rode in a car."

He saw this as one reason why cargo cults flourished here but not in Polynesia. Father Mihalic recalled that when he posed that question to Margaret
Mead, she pointed out that the first Europeans the Polynesians encountered
arrived in ships. If something went wrong with a ship, ordinary men could
fix it, and the Polynesians could see that the ship was something built by
people, that it was a larger version of what they built themselves. By the end
of the nineteenth century, European machines—for example, the steam
engine—had become so complicated that they required specialists to attend
to them.

From his earliest years in the order Mihalic had been a different type
of missionary. Before he came to New Guinea he, like most members of
Divine Word, went through training in anthropology, linguistics and eth-
nology. His order believed not in supplanting cultures, but in learning about
them and then attempting to build upon them. He was proud that on occasion his order had stopped the government from burning *haus tambarans*.

Mihalic witnessed the alienation from traditional cultures growing from
generation to generation. "Students would wince when I talked about how
their dad or mom lived. They don't like history, because history is embarrassing. You won't find anyone in the library reading about Papuan history—for
students it's the least interesting subject on campus."

He then went on to describe how this delegitimization of traditional
knowledge led to larger problems in the society. "You leave your family and
go to school, which takes you away from the village for many years. You live
in a school atmosphere where everything is given to you. You're told that
education is the key to a job, but then you graduate and can't get a job. You
can't go back to the village, because that would be uncomfortable. Besides,
you'd miss the glamour. To make it even worse, in many cases your parents
don't want you to come back. They'll say, 'We spent all our money on you,
and you're still sponging off us—go out and get a job.'"

———

After leaving Mihalic I wanted to get the perspective of a Papuan who *had*
successfully dealt with those pressures. In Port Moresby I met up with John
Maru, who then worked in New Guinea's Ministry for Home Affairs and
Youth (and who later became chief superintendent of the Royal Papua New
Guinea Constabulary). He had grown up in the Sepik region in a village
about 20 kilometers from the coastal city of Wewak. One of eight children,

Maru acknowledged that he had no idea how his father managed to pay the school fees for all of them.

At first, after graduating, he said that he viewed the bonds of the traditional culture as useless, and the endless gift exchanges (elaborate ceremonies in which pigs and other items are exchanged to seal bonds between different families and clans) as a waste of time and money. He also freely admitted that the price of his schooling was ignorance of the local knowledge of his village. "If you asked me what plant to use if you were hurt or sick, I just wouldn't know," he remarked a bit ruefully.

But through his job in youth services, he also saw firsthand the costs of alienation from a supporting culture. "If you get rid of these gift exchanges," he noted, "you also lose your relationship to your family." He added, "An extended family ensures that there is no poverty. Everybody feels obliged to care for the handicapped."

A major problem for the modern Papuan is that an extended family also virtually ensures that there is no material advancement. Maru admitted that one reason he didn't take a plum job as a provincial planner in Wewak was that "every Tom, Dick and Harry would drain me on payday." If it had been only immediate family, it would have been fine, but he worried that if he refused a maternal uncle or aunt or, God forbid, one of his many nephews, "I couldn't face up to my sisters again."

So Maru tried to walk a fine line. He didn't pay a bride price. When he broke that news to his parents he said, "You can do this with my sisters because you're alive, but in my time it's over."

His position was entirely sensible, and many in John Maru's shoes would do the same. But, the ingenious resiliency of the aboriginal Papuan worldview notwithstanding, it is hard to see how New Guinea's hundreds of diverse cultures can survive as their most intelligent and dedicated youths are compelled to make this same choice.

CHAPTER 5

Polynesia Lost and Found

The time when Tahiti represented the ragged edge of the world probably ended over 200 years ago, but like an aging femme fatale, the place still casts quite a spell and remains many people's idea of the epitome of a tropical paradise. One of the first reactions of those charmed by Tahiti (which often meant European men who couldn't believe their good luck with easygoing Tahitian women) was an immediate sense that the special feeling of the place couldn't last. One enduring and probably apocryphal story has the British explorer Captain James Cook running into Captain Samuel Wallis back in England some years after they had separately explored the South Seas. After listening to Cook go on and on about the charms of Tahiti and Polynesians, Wallis supposedly responded that Cook should have visited the islands two years earlier, in 1767, when Wallis discovered them and before the natives were spoiled by contact with outsiders. Visitors have been repeating variants of this theme ever since, and continue to do so even today when Papeete has suburbs, slums, traffic jams and satellite TV.

Today one would be more likely to find the Polynesian equivalent of the ragged edge in some of the more northern and remote islands of the Cook chain, or perhaps the less accessible Austral Islands. Indeed the aphrodisiac overtones of the spell Tahiti continues to cast over the Western imagination are something of an affront to the actual tragedies unfolding at the real ragged edge of the world. Polynesia has not escaped the cultural holocaust affecting so many once serenely isolated areas of the world, and, as I will explore later, its bitter encounters with the outside world in centuries past resonate today. But the aftermath of contact also offers valuable insights into the nature of this moveable frontier, insights that are accessible once you look past the gaudy facade of sex and indulgence. What you find is that if a people remain in place, and the ecology retains some continuity with its past, then a type of deep culture lingers even after the natives abandon most of their traditional ways. It's a bad bargain, and its price is most of the knowledge that is a culture's patrimony, but to the degree that some form of deep culture can endure, there is hope for the world's indigenous peoples.

If you manage to get away from Papeete and Bora Bora (now blanketed with hotels), embers of the old Polynesian magic still burn here and there. While many of the places I've visited succumbed to modernity in the blink of an eye, Tahiti has held on to some degree of its essential Tahitianness for hundreds of years. The common refrain is "It's changed, but it hasn't changed." Polynesians were once very warlike (and even today, they are disproportionately represented on the front lines of America's most bellicose sport—NFL football), but in Tahiti the locals long ago abandoned fighting foreigners in favor of seducing them. Most Tahitians gladly embrace modern conveniences, but far fewer are willing to make the sacrifices we make to climb the slippery pole of upward mobility.

I initially went to Tahiti in 1971, on my way to Vietnam on assignment as a journalist. I financed the trip through a Rube Goldberg contrivance of loans and grants, but since I intended to go around the world on my first real trip outside the United States, I decided to make the best of it, and one thing I wasn't going to miss was a stop in Tahiti. I'd fantasized about the place (in line with the standard-template fantasies for males of European ancestry) since high school days, reading Michener and Maugham, Jack London and Conrad, and getting lost in the paintings of Gauguin. Its appeal wasn't based just on sex, though. As I got caught up in the baby boom rat race to get into a decent college, nothing had more appeal than Tahiti's reputation as a place where nothing mattered, where a living could be plucked from the sea or a nearby mango tree. It may sound preposterous for a seventeen-year-old suburban American to be dreaming of a place famous for the acceptance and restoration of human wreckage, but then, when have teenagers ever displayed a sense of proportion?

Looking back today, I find it easy to perceive the narcissism at the core of the fantasy of the South Seas. Nathanael West skewered the tawdry French postcard image of Tahiti beautifully in *Miss Lonelyhearts,* when he had the demonic editor Shrike sarcastically and systematically torment his miserable reporter:

"You live in a thatch hut with the daughter of the king, a slim young maiden in whose eyes is an ancient wisdom. Her breasts are golden speckled pears, her belly a melon, and her odor is like nothing so much as a jungle fern. In the evening, on the blue lagoon, under the silvery moon, to your love you croon in the soft sylabelew and vocabelew of her langorour tongorour. Your body is golden brown like hers, and tourists have need of the indignant finger of the missionary to point you out. They envy you your breech clout and carefree laugh and little brown bride and fingers instead of forks. But you don't return their envy, and when a beautiful society girl comes to your hut in the night, seeking to learn the secret of your happiness, you send her back to her yacht that hangs on the horizon like a nervous racehorse. And so you dream away the days, fishing, hunting, dancing, swimming, kissing, and picking flowers to twine in your hair."

Take away the context and the sarcasm, and Shrike has captured the essence of the dream. The image is powerful enough to make visitors overlook all the changes that centuries of contact have wrought.

What put me over the top, however, were stories recounted by a friend from Yale named Jeff Stookey. Jeff graduated a couple of years before me, and after getting a glorious 4-F from his draft board, he miraculously recovered from his disabling knee injury and went off to explore the world. He got to the South Seas intending to stop for a few weeks and remained for two years.

Jeff spent most of his time in Tahiti working at a tiny English-language newspaper in Papeete, but he also spent time on Western Samoa. Indeed, Jeff pretty much lived out Shrike's taunting vision: In Samoa he fell into a relationship with the chief's daughter on an out-island, lived by spear fishing, and, as he told me with pride, went close to a year without wearing shoes. For me the message was that the Tahiti that enthralled Europeans for two centuries still existed—you just had to dig a little to find it.

Jeff might have stayed forever, but he was eventually gnawed by the feeling that he hadn't given real life a fair shake. He had been around Tahiti long enough to know that after a few years it would be difficult for him to live "in a place where nothing matters." In fact, he observed that it was difficult for almost any American to live where no one cares what you've accomplished. After ten years or so, expatriates typically went into a decline often described as "Pacific paralysis." Or, as Jeff put it, "The tragedy of the *popaa* who comes to live in Tahiti is that he left civilization to free himself of what is not important, and while he succeeds in this, he almost invariably loses the energy or the desire to seek what *is* important."

Ten years seemed a long time off to me when I was an undergraduate, and listening to his reasons for leaving after hearing the descriptions of his idyllic life in the South Seas, I thought he was crazy to have left and wrote it off to his Puritan ethic. He was no slacker, and the longer he stayed the harder it would have been not to succumb to his sense of guilt that he was indulging himself. My attitude was, "If that's the way you feel, well then, that's your problem." It's fair to say that the idea that grace might be achieved through humility, diligence and self-denial had somewhat less of a hold on me at that age. As I set off for Vietnam, I budgeted just a few weeks for stops on the way there, but in the back of my mind I kept my options open.

Jeff had given me the names of a few contacts in Tahiti, and I quickly found a welcome presence when I arrived in August 1971. The first person I looked up was Jim Boyack, who over the years edited some of the island's tiny English-language papers. If Stookey's analysis of Pacific paralysis was considered, Boyack's was succinct: "Tahiti is a giant, green, sweet-tasting stupid pill!"

A tall man with a genial stoop, Boyack then lived not far outside Papeete with his wife, Vera, and two children. Through him I met a number of Tahitians and other expatriates, many of whom had come to the island drawn by the paradisal dreams its name had conjured. Some of them had had actually succeeded in living those dreams.

Homer Morgan, owner of the Bel Air Hotel, told me that he had initially come to Tahiti on vacation in 1952. One of the first things he did was find a bicycle, planning to spend a few days cycling around the island. After his first few hours pedaling, he stopped to ask an old man where he could find an inn. Because he spoke neither French nor Tahitian, he used a slate and chalk to illustrate his needs. The old man turned out to be the chief of the district and insisted that he stay with him. That night everybody feasted and drank in Morgan's honor. The next day he awoke and groggily started to pack his bike, only to discover that his clothes were missing. He angrily confronted his host, who merely smiled and pointed to the freshly laundered clothes drying in the sun. Clearly their guest could not leave until they had properly dried. Three days later Morgan prepared to be on his way, only to be gently trapped into another round of feasts. By the time he returned to Papeete, more than a week behind schedule, he was making plans to stay permanently.

The magic that entrapped Morgan and others like him was something other than the sheer physical beauty of the place. The landscape is dramatic, with mountains, grottoes and waterfalls, but the islands of French Polynesia are not nearly as lush and diverse as the Hawaiian chain, 1,500 miles to the north. What ensnares expatriates is the *feel* of Tahiti. For most American visitors, though, the Tahitian way of life most often hovers like an entrancing sprite, just out of reach.

Some of those I met achieved only the surface trappings of the dream. They built airy houses on beautiful promontories, met and married enchanting Tahitian wives, but they had a difficult if not impossible time entering into what might be called the Tahitian state of mind, a worldview in which the simple satisfactions of life on a small island—family, fishing, feasts and music—are sufficient.

The cruel twist of Tahiti is that a constrained worldview is not just sufficient for life on a tropical island; it is also necessary for long-term contentment. And, as I was to discover many years later, the consequences of a Westerner's inability to accept the boundaries of island life could be far more ugly than Pacific paralysis.

During that first trip I did meet one man who managed to pull off the trick of living in a place where nothing matters. Ed Ehrich, a potbellied gray-haired American expatriate, was in his late sixties in 1971. When I met him, he lived with his Tahitian *vahine* in a self-designed meld of airy Polynesian and Cape Cod styles on a point in the Papara district, then quite a ways removed from the bustle of Papeete. After dropping out of the Yale class of 1927, Ehrich had lived in Greenwich Village for a year (where he roomed with a young vaudevillian named Archie Leach, later to gain fame as Cary Grant) before taking up a short career in broadcasting. He eventually realized that he didn't have any particular ambitions and did not want to work that hard, so in 1950 he set off for the one place that he imagined would suit him.

"All that's necessary for an American to be happy in Tahiti," he told me in 1971, "is that he be preternaturally lazy." Apparently Ehrich had strolled that walk for two decades, professing to have done nothing other than build a place to live, tend his garden, and read. The reading helped maintain his wry pedantry. Ehrich told me that a few years before my visit a Yale undergraduate had dug his name out of an alumni register and had contacted him in the hopes of securing an invitation to come visit. (Apparently Jeff Stookey and I were part of a long line of Yalies who had a thing for the South Seas.) In his letter the young man wrote, "I've always had a certain amount of fascination for the South Pacific," to which Ehrich promptly replied that his grammar suggested that the South Pacific had always been fascinated with him, and Ehrich doubted that this was the case. What a comedown Ehrich's reply must have been for the hapless undergrads whose dreams of escape were probably fired by the hope of escaping precisely this kind of nitpicking.

Among the American expatriates, Ehrich was famously hermetic. One very social hostess remarked to me with unintended irony, "I just don't understand why Ed doesn't come into town. Some people come to Tahiti and just cut themselves off." But what worked for Ehrich didn't work for most Americans, who couldn't suppress their characteristic restless knee syndrome. They started businesses, built hotels, took on hobbies, or became drunks—sometimes all of the above.

One American I ran into, Jean Jacques Laurent, had his own solution to dealing with the confines of the island. To break what he called "the monotony of the climate," he would go off on expeditions each year to collect artifacts from Polynesia and Melanesia. His Tahitian-style thatch-roofed *fare* was festooned with totems, charms, masks, shields and skulls. The gods must have found it a very confusing place. When I joined him for dinner one night, he recalled a bartering trip in New Guinea during which he had pointed to a weathered old mask in the corner of a tent and asked in pidgin, "How much?" The mask turned out to be the chief's very much living grandmother, and the chief promptly offered to sell her to Laurent for $20.

When Ed Ehrich first arrived in Tahiti, horses and buggies plied the streets of Papeete. By 1971 that Tahiti no longer existed, though after I got over the shock of traffic jams in Papeete, it was possible to see if not partake in the naïve ebullience of the place. I spent the first few days in the Hotel Stuart, a dump back then, but a famous dump where many of Tahiti's most celebrated expatriates stayed when they first arrived. I then spent a few days camping out in the offices of the *Tahiti Journal*. Finally, Jim Boyack offered me a place in the guest bedroom at the top of the stairs, just under the thatch roof of the house where he and Vera were staying.

My first night there, the Boyacks had to go out to dinner, and I stayed behind with their two young children and the babysitter, an achingly beautiful young Tahitian who later won a Tahitian beauty pageant. Having flown many time zones west, I was still suffering from jet lag and went to bed early. I'd never slept under thatch before, and one of the tricks it plays is that the leaves amplify the wind, and until you get used to it, your body reacts to the sound they make by generating heat to compensate for the cooling suggested by their rustling. Consequently, I was shortly soaked with sweat under the sheets, but cold when I threw them off. After tossing and turning, I got up and groggily wandered to the landing at the top of the stairs. I looked down, and there was the future Miss Tahiti, looking up at me with a bold frankness that I'd never before encountered in any girl. I didn't need Homer Morgan's chalk and slate to figure out that there for the taking was the image that had lured me to Tahiti in the first place.

So what did I do? Nothing. For one thing, I didn't know how old she was, and didn't relish spending the rest of my youth in a Tahitian jail (if they had such things). I also felt that accepting that invitation would somehow violate the hospitality of the Boyacks, who, after all, had assumed that they were only offering me a place to stay, and not the consummation of a *rite de passage*. In another sense, to have the dream so close at hand, and so soon after my arrival in Tahiti, was simply overwhelming. Oh, and I did have a girlfriend back in the United States.

I'll never know what might have been. Had I accepted the unspoken invitation, I, too, might have succumbed to the succulent allure of the South Pacific, maybe even ending up like Ed Ehrich. (Although that was unlikely, since one undiscussed ingredient of his successful indolence was money—something I didn't have, not even a little bit.)

While my subsequent encounters with Tahitians were never so heavy with promise, I did get a firsthand look at some of the ways Tahitians incorporated the constant assault of modernity into their lives. For instance, one evening a group of us went to a show, ostensibly put on for the benefit of some French sailors. The promoters had unaccountably imported a stripper, and the most enthusiastic members of the audience were not the sailors but the Tahitian girls who came by out of curiosity and who with gusto and hilarity cheered on the somewhat startled performer. On another occasion I attended a dance where modern pop alternated with traditional Tahitian dance music. The Tahitians, both men and women, were amazing dancers, and the song that got everyone on the floor and engendered the most excitement was José Feliciano's "Feliz Navidad," with its refrain "I want to wish you a Merry Christmas." The dance took place in August.

———

Since 1971, I've been back to Polynesia twice. I returned in 1976 when I was researching my book *Affluence and Discontent* (in which I used Tahiti to illustrate the point that there is much more to a consumer society than a simple desire for consumer goods). Then, in 1995, I returned again on assignment for *Condé Nast Traveler*. During these subsequent trips I was able to move away from the somewhat self-referential perspective on the elusiveness of the South Pacific dream, and looked a little deeper into Polynesian culture and how it was adapting to modernity.

To that end, for instance, my then-wife, Madelaine, and I went in 1976 to Bora Bora on the cheap and found lodging with a Tahitian couple who had a small guesthouse called Chez Aimé. The accommodations would have met with approval from the most austere Amish. Our room (no bathroom, of course) was sparsely furnished and lit by a single bare lightbulb, which went off with the generator at 11 p.m. After a few days, though, we felt ourselves falling under a spell. A beguiling order slowly emerged from what initially looked like a mere haphazard tropical garden in the front yard. Aimé began showing up with fish that he would catch before he went off to work in a copra plantation. He grew and ground his own coffee. We were inundated with fresh fruit—papayas, mangos, bananas and pineapples. He took us snorkeling. He eschewed swim fins, claiming (in French) that his feet could propel him perfectly well.

He and his wife lived what could be called a mixed subsistence economy. But what a subsistence! Apart from the aforementioned fruits, he grew manioc, breadfruit, vanilla and coconut. He kept hens and a sow. His tools were old and outdated, but they all worked. I left thinking that if World War III broke out, Aimé might not notice.

Back in Tahiti, we had a comical encounter with one of those charming scoundrels who prowl the backwaters of the world. I met Emil Yost through Madelaine, who found herself the object of a Gallic full-court press (including several rum punches) while I was off on an errand. When I returned to the bar at the Tahiti Village, Emil turned his charm on me, treating me to a monologue in broken English. "Yes, I have vineyard in

California—Brookside, you have heard? . . . My house is next to Bob Hope. . . . We play golf, just off Hollywood Boulevard. . . . But I think I sell vineyard and move to Miami. . . . I try to buy this hotel [the Tahiti Village]. . . . I have four million in Swiss account, three millions in New York, yes! . . . and certificates of General Motors. . . . I say to my son, 'Why work when we have money?' But he want to travel. . . . Donald Nixon, a good friend, but bad businessman . . ."

We arranged to play tennis the following day, but he didn't show. Then I got a call from him. "I'll meet you at the bar at 9:30. . . . I will explain." Emil arrived with an official-looking man in uniform, and begged off. "I am sorry, I have appointment at 10:00, I forgot, yes?! But maybe I not go to Bora Bora and we meet later."

That was the last I saw of Emil. Later, talking with another expatriate, Nick Rutgers, I discovered that Nick had run into Emil at the gendarmerie later that morning, and that Emil had been carrying a briefcase. He told Nick that he had an appointment, but Nick knew that he had just been convicted for passing bad checks, and suspected that he was at the police station to begin his sentence.

I did live out one small fantasy. During the 1976 trip, Madelaine and I visited Western Samoa before I went on by myself to New Guinea. Traveling around the green, green island of Upolu, I remembered a story Jeff Stookey had told me about snorkeling through an underwater passage that linked two caves, each of which opened to the ocean. You could swim in the mouth of one cave, take a deep breath and swim underwater until you saw the light hitting the surface of the water at the back of the other cave. Although the caves were linked at the back, their mouths on the ocean were several hundred feet apart. On a whim I asked one of the locals if he had heard of these caves, and somewhat to my disappointment (because I knew that if I went to the cave, I was going to have to try to make the swim) he had. He gave me directions. Madelaine was very dubious about the whole idea.

After I donned my snorkel and fins, I swam into the entrance of the cave, where I saw a teenage Polynesian. I asked him where the passage was, and he pointed toward the back. I asked him how long you had to swim before you saw light, and he was pretty vague. He was more definitive when I asked whether you could turn back once you had entered the passageway. He shook his head vigorously; the answer was no. Swell!

I couldn't back out at this point. I made a couple of exploratory dives so that I could efficiently locate the entrance to the passageway. Each time I surfaced the Polynesian boy encouraged me with hand gestures. After a bit more procrastinating I hyperventilated to saturate my lungs with oxygen, took a deep breath, and headed into the passageway. Any claustrophobia I might have felt took second place to my desire to keep going until I saw the light. It took several strokes, but then I did see a bright spot ahead and set out toward it, surfacing exultantly after a few more strokes. Piece of cake, really, and I'm sure every boy and girl on the islands makes that swim often with nary a thought.

By 1995 the Tahiti that had greeted Ed Ehrich and Homer Morgan was long gone, and even the Tahiti that had greeted me in 1971 had succumbed to the remorseless tide of visitors and the contagion of modernity they brought with them. Foreigners still sought out the Tahitian dream, but if they wandered into a club frequented by locals they risked getting beaten up. Rates of family violence, incest and rape had risen, and the poorest neighborhoods had the flavor of slums everywhere.

Tahitian nature was also a far cry from the ferns and forests that greeted the early sea captains. Bougainville began a trend by introducing oranges and pineapples, and Harrison Smith soon followed with grapefruit, breadfruit and rambutan. Miconia, a weed brought in for the botanical garden, seemed to be taking over the island. Hibiscus, flamboyant and bougainvillea, everywhere associated with the beauty of the tropics, were all exotics—non-native—as well. Even global warming might have been having an impact. Powerful El Niños had produced superheated waters and attendant coral bleaching.

The atmosphere of the neighboring island of Raiatea (the old royal center of Polynesia) remained similar to that of the Tahiti that had greeted me in 1971. The pace was slower, and each house had well-tended tropical gardens. It so happened that we (I was joined by Mary, then and now my second wife) arrived on a day of feasting before an armada of replicas of the huge double-hulled canoes set sail to re-create one of the great Polynesian feats of navigation—the trip from the Society Islands to the Marquesas and then up to Hawaii. The crews were to navigate using methods developed by their forebears, who would read stars, ocean currents, clouds, the feel of different waves and the movements of birds to find their way around the otherwise undifferentiated vastness of open water.

The food at the feast was authentic, too. Served on thatched plates made of palm leaves, the cuisine was a loving monument to carbohydrates. The menu offered an assortment of sweet potatoes, taro root, breadfruit and papaya, along with pig, chicken and fish. Here, laid out before me, was the answer to why Polynesians are the heftiest people on the planet.

One of the guests of honor was Ben Finney, a University of Hawaii anthropologist and a prime mover in the resurrection of the art of Polynesian navigation. He was beaming at the success of the venture because, among other things, he hoped the voyage would help restore Polynesian pride, which, as he put it, had taken "a real beating" in the modern world. He noted that thirty years earlier, the average Tahitian could build his own house; supply himself with food by fishing, gathering fruits in the mountains and farming; and then cook his meals in a traditional earth oven. "Today," he said sadly, "most Tahitian young can't do those things."

Finney's simple remark starkly underscored what is really meant by the statement "Tahiti is being spoiled." What's being lost is not some playground created for the benefit of uptight, overworked Europeans (and now Asians and oil tycoons from the Middle East), but arduously acquired knowledge about the life and rhythms of the largest ocean on the planet and those few, widely scattered islands and atolls that dot its surface. What's being lost is the culture that bound the Polynesians to the sea and to one another, and that gave their lives meaning.

Consider, for instance, how Polynesian navigators voyaged from Tahiti to Hawaii before the advent of global positioning systems. They relied on the sun, the wind, the stars, the feeling of the sea, the color of the sky and the movements of birds. Here are the beginning of their directions, literally, as I wrote them down in my notebook: "Turn right towards the setting sun when blows the *Maraouu*. 2) Blue-green sea and the sky is the color of the sea. 3) When the star *Tetia Hoe* plunges in the night—that is his guide follow her. Wind push—the star pulls. When the sun rises . . ."

By 1995 Finney's observations were a familiar variant of comments I had been hearing all over the world: about the Penans in Borneo, the Cree on Hudson Bay, the Machiguenga in Peru, and dozens of other tribes from the Arctic to the equator. In some cases the loss was happening before my eyes, while in others it had taken place long ago. In almost all cases, however, the unifying theme was that the loss was voluntary, as tribes abandoned their knowledge and ways in favor of the conveniences and seductions of the consumer society.

But Ben Finney was not just rehearsing an old lament: He had hope. He retained the belief that traces of Tahitian identity remained alive in what he referred to as "deep culture, the knowledge and attitudes one learns at one's mother's knee." Finney was confident that the embers of Tahitian identity might one day flame again, particularly since most Tahitians still spoke their language and controlled their lands. And no matter how Westernized Tahitians appeared to be, he argued, at times of critical life decisions, their reactions were characteristically Tahitian.

If human culture is anywhere near as resilient as nature, there may indeed be cause for hope. The west coast of the Americas was repopulated with elephant seals from just a few dozen that remained on remote islands off Mexico after being given protection by the Mexican government in the early twentieth century. While human cultures are far more intangible, they might have some capacity to rebound similarly. Perhaps it's the remnant embers of Tahitian culture that perpetuate the lure of the South Pacific, and still give Tahiti a feeling different from that of Hawaii, however much Tahiti itself seems hell-bent on acquiring all the surface trappings of the Mall of America.

Tahiti retained its magic for me long after I outgrew any fantasies of exploring the lagoons with Povana's granddaughter, the iconic maiden of the South Pacific featured in Michener's *Return to Paradise*. I realized that it wasn't so much that I wanted to indulge in the idyllic lifestyle Tahiti offered, but rather that I wanted the reassurance that someone, somewhere on this hectic planet, still had the opportunity to live that way.

This dream should not be viewed as some romanticized, Rousseau-flavored misinterpretation of full-blown Polynesian culture, which, after all, involved warfare, human sacrifice, and other unsavory practices alongside its luaus and liberal attitude toward sex. Tahitians did not need to perform human sacrifice in order to navigate the Pacific, any more than Americans need to resort to torture to protect our borders. To say "Tahiti is a place where nothing matters" only underscores how important it is that certain things matter to the person saying the sentence. The real Tahiti is a place where the fundamentals matter—nature, life, intellect, hospitality, family, honor.

This special magic was very much on my mind when I left Tahiti for Vietnam in 1971. As I waited to leave for the airport, I watched two Tahitian women lounging under a palm tree by a lagoon in a tableau that might have been witnessed by Gauguin many decades earlier. I had little notion of what Vietnam might bring me, but the war was killing people by the many thousands each week, and while its reverberations echoed around the world, I felt certain that they wouldn't reach Tahiti. I wanted to stay, but I left. Tahiti was for Tahitians. Maybe someday it would be for me, but not yet. The deep culture I learned at my mother's knee was more akin to Jeff Stookey's than to a Polynesian's.

Twenty-four years later I stood on the atoll of Rangiroa, watching the sunset across the second largest lagoon in the world. As I described the scene in *Condé Nast Traveler,* the horizon turned pink and yellow; I followed the progress of showers marching across the waters. Such is the size of the sky that the dominant color remained blue for both sky and water despite the thunderheads scattered over the lagoon. Looming over the tiny village of Tiputa, illuminated by the fading sun, was a cloud that had assumed the perfect shape of a *moai,* one of those mysterious Polynesian idols erected in bygone times on the shores of Easter Island. For a brief moment, this diaphanous echo of ancient Polynesia floated over the atoll and its people like a shadow of the past. Its unreadable features gave no indication of whether they were baleful or benign, but its presence was somehow reassuring, a transient reminder of the deep culture that hovers over the present. Even as this thought entered my mind, the *moai* began to disassemble as it was buffeted by the complex air currents of the onrushing evening.

PART III

ROADS TO RUIN

CHAPTER 6

Rapa Nui: The Other Side of the Story

It was my long-standing desire to see real *moai,* not just an accidental evocation in the clouds, that prompted the last part of my trip to the South Seas in 1995. From Tahiti, I went on to Pitcairn and Easter islands, each of which, for very different reasons, offers evidence that not every Polynesian island made its peace with modernity. Some met fates every bit as sordid as war-torn Europe, and demonstrated that island living can be as brutal as life anywhere else on the planet. Polynesians weren't always as outwardly easygoing as cliché has it today. Indeed, in the fate of Easter Island, Polynesia's bequest to posterity is a cautionary tale of the horrors of ecocide.

I particularly wanted to visit Easter Island (the European name for Rapa Nui) because through the years its catastrophic decline has served as testimony to the dangers of overpopulation and ecological degradation. Its story has been variously told, but the basic elements are as follows: Polynesians arrived on Easter Island somewhere between AD 400 and AD 800, and by 1600, the population had soared to 7,000. In the ensuing years the natives stripped the island of its trees, ultimately depriving themselves of the very material from which to construct fishing boats. A brutal competition for resources started a descent into cannibalism and barbarity from which the Easter Islanders never recovered. By the time Europeans arrived in 1722, the population had been reduced to 3,000, living in primitive conditions. So complete was their cultural devolution that the survivors had supposedly forgotten the purpose of the great stone heads called *moai* that had been erected during the island's glory days.

It's an irresistible story, and variants of it appear with numbing regularity. The most notable recent iteration was offered by Jared Diamond, who in books and articles has spun a narrative in which the fatal mistake of the

Easter Islanders was the overharvesting of trees in order to transport the *moai* from the center of the island, where they were quarried, to the shores, where they were erected to face out toward the ocean. Easter Island still stands as an example of ecological folly, but its ruin likely took an even more circuitous path than Jared Diamond imagined.

I traveled to these remote islands in style. To reach the eastern Pacific I agreed to be a speaker aboard Cunard's five-star liner *Sagafjord* on the segment of its annual world tour that took it from Tahiti to Chile with stops at Pitcairn and Easter islands. My accommodations were comfortable, and the food and wine were spectacular. For a significant percentage of those on the cruise, the boat served as a type of ultraluxe assisted living. Many of the passengers were widows, a good percentage of whom made the trip every year. Some left a full wardrobe on the boat to save the trouble of shipping steamer trunks back and forth, and even though every night at sea was black-tie, I was reliably informed by one of my dinner companions (a woman who was a regular herself) that many of the guests brought enough clothes to go through the entire world cruise without wearing the same outfit twice.

Those of us speaking and entertaining were an odd lot. One of the other speakers was an expert on Captain Bligh's astonishing feats of navigation after he was set adrift from the *Bounty;* another, an astronaut who had piloted the space shuttle. Dino Anagnost's Little Orchestra Society from New York played during the evenings, and the musicians filled me in on some of the peculiarities of life at sea with septuagenarians. I learned, for instance, that there was a morgue on board with capacity for fifteen bodies. Although I did not try to verify the stories, I was also told that when a hubby conked out during the cruise, on more than one occasion the widow put his body into cold storage and continued the cruise.

As there were many widows on board, Cunard thoughtfully provided dance partners for these women. My orchestra friends said these jobs were highly sought after, and had a heavy representation of gay men from the Midlands of England. One attraction for the dance partners was that these women were quite affluent and quite old, and sometimes, if things worked out, they married the dance partners, ensuring their financial security.

Also on board was a young lawyer who was traveling to Pitcairn from New Zealand as part of a periodic visit to look after the island's affairs. He told me about some of the problems that came from managing a population of a few dozen people who lived almost completely removed from any contact with modern society. Their naïveté, he said, set them up for violent cultural collisions for which they were completely unprepared.

For instance, apart from the rare appearance of a cruise ship, the only visitors to Pitcairn were freighters that occasionally came near the island. Sometimes these ships would anchor for a couple of hours offshore so that the sailors could barter for the artifacts and stamps the islanders sold. The sailors were a rough lot, however, and among the items they would offer in barter were pornographic videos. The unsuspecting islanders would then convene the entire population, including children and the elderly, to watch these movies. They would come away from these viewings believing that they were normal fare for the outside world. (Years later, when I saw news reports of the uncovering of widespread sexual abuse among the Pitcairn Islanders, I thought back to the lawyer's account.)

Our own stop at Pitcairn was very brief. We anchored off the tiny town that clung to the leeward side of the island, but because the seas were frothy, the islanders rowed out to the boat rather than risk the wrath of elderly ladies getting soaked as they rode the surf to shore. (Pitcairn really doesn't have an easy entrance to a harbor, and in fact doesn't have much of a harbor at all.) I bought some stamps and a beautifully carved model of a longboat from one of the residents who rode out. Like many, he was a descendant of Fletcher Christian, the mutineer from HMS *Bounty* who settled on the island in 1790.

Pitcairn is about as far from the image of a Polynesian paradise as might be imagined: It's little more than a rock rising out of a frequently angry Pacific, with scraggly vegetation and no lagoon. Perhaps the most amazing thing about it is the fact that it still retains a cadre of residents.

Easter Island, however, was my principal goal on this latest Polynesian foray, and it did not disappoint. Once we were deposited in the port I hired a cab for a tour. If I hadn't known that it once supported 16 million palm trees I never would have guessed it. The island today has the appearance of a giant meadow, albeit one that is guarded by its *moai,* which look forlornly out to sea. It's a place where a hundred golf courses could be built without changing a feature in the landscape (exactly what some developers intend to do). Still, the setting is charged with all the questions it raises: What was once there? What's the story behind those giant statues? Most of all, what happened?

As noted, Jared Diamond's account, spelled out in his books *Guns, Germs, and Steel* and *Collapse,* is one of ecocide, a cautionary tale of overpopulation and overexploitation in which the population overtaxed the resource base and denuded the island. In this telling, an increasingly desperate population devolved into civil strife and ultimately cannibalism.

Almost from the moment Diamond advanced this narrative, his interpretation prompted vociferous rebuttals from a number of anthropologists, who have subsequently shown through painstaking examination of ancient pollens, charcoal, soils and other evidence that trees persisted on Easter Island long after Diamond and others assumed that it had been completely deforested. Questions were also raised regarding the dates when the island was settled, the rise and fall of its population, and when and how it became deforested. No one doubted that the story of Easter Island was one of ecological collapse; the debate was over whether it had been overpopulation that drove the ecocide.

I first began encountering these critiques in the mid-1990s, but they came to a head in early December 2005, when I was asked to be part of a presidential panel at the annual meeting of the American Association of Anthropologists. The subject was anthropology and the media, and the moderator was Lisa Lucero, a specialist on the fall of the Maya. When I arrived, she informed me that while the panel would proceed as planned, she'd been asked to give time to a group of anthropologists who wanted to respond to Diamond's interpretation of Easter Island's collapse, particularly as it had been unquestioningly echoed by the media.

The most detailed rebuttal came from Terry Hunt of the University of Hawaii. After summarizing the various scenarios of the rise and fall of Rapa Nui, Hunt reviewed the evidence and offered a picture strikingly different from Diamond's. Hunt argued that Easter Island was settled much later than most estimates, probably around AD 1200, and that deforestation began immediately. The culprits were not humans, according to Hunt's research, but rather one of their fellow travelers, the rat. By Hunt's calculations, just a few rats arriving with the natives could have populated the island with 20 million to 30 million descendants within a decade. The Polynesian rat is a seed predator, and Hunt argued that the rats already had demonstrated their capacity for forest destruction, having earlier killed the palms on the Ewa Plain on the island of Oahu in Hawaii. In support of his view about the sequence of events on Rapa Nui, Hunt argued that the carbon dating of charcoal fires and other evidence of settlement showed that the palm forest began declining before humans began exploiting it, although he admits that humans probably hastened the decline through their own fires and cutting.

So what actually did do in the Easter Islanders? Not overpopulation, according to Hunt, who asserts that Rapa Nui had probably reached a relatively stable population before contact with Europeans. Hunt looks past undeniable ecological collapse to diseases like smallpox that were introduced by contact and the repatriation of slaves and other returnees. As for the cannibalism that Diamond argues was symptomatic of the degradation of the culture, Hunt argues that there is no evidence of cannibalism before European arrival and that accounts of it were most likely overheated reimaginings of precontact society by disapproving European chroniclers.

Hunt does not let humans off the hook—he is careful to stipulate that the arrival of Polynesians was an ecological catastrophe for Easter Island (as it has been on virtually every island humans have colonized or visited)—but he avers that a good portion of their destructive and self-destructive impact was an unwitting side effect of their arrival, rather than the direct result of human activities. This is an intriguing argument that has been advanced for other extinctions and collapses coincident with the appearance of modern humans in virgin habitats. For instance, Ross McPhee, who is one of the world's more creative thinkers about prehistory and who is now at the Smithsonian, has argued that the pattern of extinctions of large animals that regularly followed soon after humans penetrated new areas was not (as Diamond argues in his so-called Blitzkrieg hypothesis) the result of their wholesale slaughter, but rather was the result of diseases introduced by the dogs and livestock that accompanied human migrants. With no immunity to these novel organisms, the large, slow-reproducing animals would have easily succumbed to disease. The smaller animals, with more offspring and faster reproductive cycles, would have been better equipped to adapt.

I suspect that Diamond's and McPhee's narratives of the mass extinctions that seem to follow soon after human arrival are not mutually exclusive. It's easy to see how diseases imported by pets and livestock could impact concentrations of large animals adapted to a high survival rate of their young. It's also easy to see how human hunting (as well as predation by pets and fellow travelers) of naïve animals could finish off the job.

It's tougher to find common ground between the very different scenarios offered by Diamond and Hunt. Hunt argues that the Polynesian population had reached a sustainable equilibrium before the Europeans made contact in 1722. It's hard to make the argument that ecological collapse proved fatal for the Polynesian culture if in fact it was smallpox and other European-introduced diseases that brought about a catastrophic drop in numbers.

Still, even if we accept that Diamond was wrong about the chronology of some crucial events, I'm left with questions: With no trees left to make boats or houses—even if some of the deforestation took place after the arrival of Europeans—how could the residents of Rapa Nui fish, and what could they use for shelter? How could they have avoided the fate that Diamond describes? I don't think we've heard the last word on this catastrophe, and I suspect that the mysteries of Easter Island will engage scholars for years to come.

CHAPTER 7

Bangui, Bayanga and Bouar

I made my first trip to Africa in 1974 while researching a book about the impact of voluntary aid on the continent (eventually published by Random House as *The Alms Race*), with an itinerary that took me to Liberia, Zaire, South Africa, Lesotho (the focus of the book), Kenya, Ethiopia and Egypt. I have returned to Africa many times since. In 1982, I went to Senegal and Gambia to report on an attempt by Janis Carter to return a female chimp named Lucy to the wild. Lucy had been raised in suburban Oklahoma and had been the subject of early attempts to teach chimpanzees language. Then, in the late 1980s and early 1990s, I made several more trips to Francophone Africa. In 2001 I traveled to Kenya and Uganda with the goal of reaching a chimpanzee research station in Kibale and seeing firsthand a group of chimps that had been observed using weapons.

In the course of this quarter century, I've watched as the continent—at least its sub-Saharan part—has suffered inexorably escalating misery and depredation. Its population has exploded, but standards of living have continued a remorseless and accelerating decline. Every time I visited, it was hard to imagine that things could get worse for ordinary people, and yet every time I returned, that was indeed the case. Civil wars, genocide, starvation, killing epidemics, and kleptocratic and/or sadistic rulers have been the order of the day. For the most part, aid projects only worsened the situation by lining the pockets of corrupt politicians or displacing the primitive but effective structures of village life, while offering no alternative.

For wildlife the decline has been even more precipitous. During the span of my travels, most of the continent's wild elephant populations were hunted down and killed—so, too, its rhinos. Chimps and gorillas that have managed to escape poaching and habitat destruction often fall prey to diseases such as Ebola that have been loosed by the wholesale disruption of the continent's ecosystems.

Why, then, do I recall my journeys there with such fondness? At various times I've been held hostage by greedy officials, chased by mobs, threatened by trigger-happy soldiers, robbed, and weakened by Africa's infinite supply of superambitious microbes. During one particularly bad stretch on my first trip, I slept with a pistol under my pillow after someone attempted to break into my hut. Still, when I look back on them, my first thought is how great each of those trips was, and my second is gratitude that I had the opportunity to get close to the mysterious, awesome power of the continent.

———

My visits to Africa in the early 1990s revolved around four different stories. Three of them were for *Time*—"Inside the World's Last Eden," which recounted my trek into the pristine Ndoki rainforest with the botanist and conservationist Michael Fay; "Megacities," which ran in 1993; and "Lost Tribes, Lost Knowledge," which ran in 1992. The fourth was "Apes and Humans," an article I wrote for *National Geographic* in 1992. Since "Apes and Humans" and "Lost Tribes" were both extremely expensive to research and involved many of the same locales, I did a lot of splitting of expenses to minimize the burden. My motivation was not concern for the bottom line (I knew tales of expense account extravagance that would bring a blush to the sultan of Brunei), but rather pure self-interest: I was hoping that my efforts to limit expenses would be recognized by the suits the next time I proposed one of my globe-trotting assignments. Thus, when I had to get from Bangui, the capital of the Central African Republic, situated on the shores of the Ubangi River, to Bayanga, a small river town on the Sangha, which forms part of the western border of the country, I decided to accept a ride in a truck rather than spend the $5,000 or so to charter a plane.

While driving in New Guinea was physically terrifying, getting around the country was otherwise a fairly straightforward process. Africa has its share of bad—make that impassable—roads and broken-down aircraft, but it's the cumulative impact of bureaucracy, mechanical problems, creative scheduling, roadblocks, and weather that makes traveling in Central Africa more arduous than in any other place I've yet encountered. Much of life is taken up with getting from one place to another. In this respect, the trip to Bayanga did not disappoint.

The origins of this trip dated to 1989, when Mike Fay came through New York and we talked about the region. By that time Mike had already spent several years in Africa, first as a Peace Corps volunteer and then as a graduate student/conservationist working on his PhD in botany. Although he had not yet achieved the conservation superstar status brought by his subsequent work in the Ndoki and his walks across Africa, he exuded a great sense of purpose and intensity. Because I was writing about both apes and conservation issues, my interests intersected with Mike's in several different areas. Mike was tremendously excited by the densities of lowland gorillas he was finding in the corner of Africa where the Central African Republic, the Democratic Republic of the Congo and Cameroon met. At the same time he was outraged by the corruption (he told me that the party chief in Bayanga had already been caught ten times for poaching with no penalties whatsoever) and the out-of-control poaching that was killing elephants as well as gorillas and every other large African mammal.

Even then, Mike was hard-core. Back when he was a Peace Corps volunteer, he had spent time up in the north part of the Central African Republic, hard by a large tract controlled by a French national named Michel LaBureur. Although he had come to help the people, rampant poaching had convinced Mike that direct action was necessary. He teamed up with LaBureur on daily poaching patrols during which they regularly got into armed confrontations with Sudanese hunters. In the bush Mike often travels with Pygmies from various groups, and after one particularly arduous trek with Ba'Aka Pygmies they gave him the nickname "Concrete."

When I arrived in Bangui on September 17, 1990, Mike was not yet back in the Central African Republic (CAR), but he had put me and *National Geographic* photographer Nick Nichols in touch with Andrea Turkalo, a biologist studying elephants who was also based in Bayanga, and who was then Mike's wife. Andrea was in Bangui on business, and it was she who offered us the truck ride out to Bayanga. We set off from Bangui on September 18 for what we hoped would be an uneventful 530-kilometer drive across the country. The route would take us along the border with the Democratic Republic of the Congo, and then south into the extreme southwest corner of the CAR—a toothlike projection bordered by Congo to the east and the Sangha River and Cameroon to the west.

We'd intended to leave at 6:30, but we didn't get off until 10:30, since Andrea was suffering from food poisoning, courtesy of a goat meat lunch she had consumed the day before. Not long out of Bangui, we drove by signs for Bimbo, one of the CAR's small towns. (Looking at a map, I see that there is also a city called Bazoum, causing me to imagine the headlines if the then-president of Gabon came for a visit—"Bongo Visits Bimbo; Raves about Bazoum!")

Not long thereafter we encounter the first of ten roadblocks we had to negotiate during the drive. The excuse for many of such barriers was that the roads were impassable because of rain, but in this case the rain had ended hours earlier. Guards would seize any excuse to keep the barriers up, and after cadging bribes would let us continue on the supposedly impassable roads, or would insist that we could not pass unless we gave a ride to X or Y (who had presumably paid them off). Sometimes we encountered roadblocks ostensibly set up to guide cars around potholes, and in these cases workers would be energetically using picks and shovels to repair the damaged road. They would drop their tools and flag us down to help pay for the worthy public works (leaving us to wonder how long before we arrived they had actually picked up the tools). Andrea muttered that it had been her experience that often the repairs were being done on potholes that had been diligently dug earlier by the very same crew. If the road had a pothole with water in it, another scam was to stand innocently beside it and, when splashed by a passing vehicle, demand payment for dry cleaning. I was amused by the idea of there being a dry-cleaning establishment in towns that lacked electricity. (I was familiar with such compensation scams from my trips to New Guinea, and if the ingenuity that went into these petty attempts at extortion could be directed more productively, both Africa and New Guinea would be economic superpowers.)

Wearying of the constant demands at roadblocks, we developed a good cop/bad cop routine. I assumed the role of the big boss from the United States, admittedly a bit of a stretch, but in his bush attire Nick looked more like an unstable soldier of fortune than a visiting fireman on a site visitation (the unintentionally hilarious word—conjuring the image of visits from the spirit world—often used for official visits). When we were accosted for a ride, Andrea would start to accede to a demand and then turn to me, whereupon I would sternly remind her of company policy against giving rides to non-employees because of liability problems in the past. It worked for a while—if exposure to the developed world has given Africans anything, it is experience with bureaucrats and their leaden rules.

Andrea knew of a shortcut—a relative term in the Central African Republic—that required us to head through a logging concession. The logging roads were an obstacle course of mires and deep ruts, and we inched along, often precariously balancing the wheels on the ridges between the ruts. After some hours of lurching and bucking travel, we arrived at a beautiful river in the middle of the concession. To get across we had to take a rudimentary ferry, which, attached by a rope and ring to a cable strung across the river, used the current against the attitude of the boat to go back and forth. For instance, if the prow was pointed slightly upriver, the current would push the ferry in that direction, since the cable to which it was attached by a ring would not permit the boat to go downriver. To get back, the ferry masters simply pointed the prow in the other direction.

We arrived at the river crossing at 5:10, knowing that if we didn't get across before dark we would be spending the night in the truck. Unfortunately the ferry sat abandoned on the other side of the river. On our side we saw a bunch of empty pirogues, and when we located the crew members at a palm wine stand, they all turned out to be drunk. Judging by their unsteady state, I could tell that our good cop/bad cop act, polished and rehearsed at a dozen roadblocks, was about to be tested to the limit.

When they saw us, however, the crew sobered up considerably at the prospect of easy money and hustled back to work. The chief demanded 5,000 Central African francs, payable in advance, to take us over. With the gravity of a hard-nosed executive accustomed to cutting budgets, I refused, and Andrea began protracted negotiations. Against my advice Andrea agreed to pay about half that sum once we were in the middle of the river, but at least that got the ferry over to our side of the river. Once we were aboard, the still-half-in-the-bag crew mishandled every conceivable maneuver, including the simple task of untying the ferry. Then, after we got the truck on the boat, they again demanded payment, and again we refused, anticipating they would simply demand more. When we finally reached the other side they refused to put up blocks for the truck without additional payment. By now it was growing dark, and Andrea finally lost her temper. In rapid French she scolded them: "I've been here ten years helping Africans, and these people have come from the U.S. Is this the impression you want them to have of your country?" Finally, they relented, and we were on our way.

Six hours later we arrived at Andrea's simple bungalow in Bayanga, passing only one car heading in the other direction during the entire trip. We entered to find that three Peace Corps volunteers had moved in during her absence. After a thirteen-hour drive, and weakened by food poisoning, Andrea was ready to cry.

The volunteers, however, affably agreed to find other digs, and even offered to cook dinner. Having written about the impact of voluntary aid on Africa over a decade earlier, I was interested to hear what the volunteers had to say about the results of their work. One of them, Rebecca Hardin, was nearing the end of her stint, and had no illusions about the failure of efforts to bolster local economies. She told me of a Peace Corps review of a fifteen-year effort to improve beekeeping; to its credit, the Corps wanted to know why this long-term project had failed. Rebecca pointed out that the Africans had done sufficiently well with their inefficient method of collecting honey by smoking the hives to chase away the bees (which often killed the queen in the process). Moreover, they made the rational decision that selling the honey in local markets for smaller amounts of money was better than the added work and risk of bandits that selling the honey in Cameroon for twice as much would entail. A similar study of fish farming produced similarly disheartening (from the Peace Corps' point of view) results, as the villagers proved unwilling to do even the minimal maintenance needed to keep the ponds viable.

Rebecca's story resonated with some ideas that Dan Phillips, the American ambassador to the Republic of the Congo, had offered earlier during a dinner in Brazzaville. He speculated that one reason why the social contract—the idea that individuals would cede some rights to the government in return for the security and opportunities that being part of a larger community offered—was so underdeveloped in sub-Saharan Africa might be that the penalties of going it alone were not so terrible for an African villager. Food—in the form of fruits and carbohydrates—was often readily available, and that knowledge skewed the risk/reward calculation when villagers were asked to put aside immediate self-gratification for the vague and unreliable prospect of larger gains that might accrue from investment in the community. When one examines them from this perspective, one reaches the disheartening conclusion that the petty extortion schemes we encountered on our trip might have been the result of an entirely rational risk/reward analysis.

One story Rebecca told, however, stayed with me. While my main purpose in Bayanga was to gather material for a *National Geographic* story on apes and humans, I was also doing some reporting for my *Time* article on the loss of indigenous knowledge. Rebecca had mentioned a Western-educated health administrator named Bernard N'donazi who had decided that the traditional healing techniques that he had been taught as a child were more effective, more available and cheaper than the Western medicines he had been trained to distribute. He was based in Bouar, a few hundred kilometers to the north, where Rebecca and her boyfriend were living. Before she left, I mentioned that I might want to talk to her again. At that time, I had no intention of going to Bouar, but the French Foreign Legion changed those plans a few days later.

I spent the next few days interviewing various people in connection with the apes story, and taking desultory hikes to different *bais* (a *bai* is a type of clearing) scattered through the forest, in fruitless search of gorillas. One of the reasons I was interested in the area was that it had populations of both gorillas and chimps. Mike Fay theorized that chimps tended to fare better where the forest was denser, while gorillas prospered where it was more open so that sunlight could penetrate to spur the growth of monocots and other so-called terrestrial herbaceous vegetation. According to Mike, the key to this seesaw was the elephant, which diligently opened the forest by tearing down trees. It was an interesting theory, in part because it offered the promise that humans, chimps and gorillas could find a way to live in harmony—if humans stopped short of clear-cutting. "Looked at this way," Mike told me, "humans are nothing more than mechanized elephants."

We found only teasing evidence of the presence of gorillas on this trip—severe hunting pressure had made them very wary of humans. Nick Nichols spent twelve days walking the forest and had a single distant contact. In the course of several days of hiking, I saw only one gorilla, and that was by the side of the road on the drive back from Bai Hokou. During these forays I began to think again about a wondrous forest that supposedly lay directly to the south, an area that had been characterized as perhaps the most perfectly intact rainforest haven on the planet—a place where gorillas, chimps and other animals never encountered humans—but I had no plans to go there.

Mike Fay had described this area to me when we had first talked about Africa. Then, in July 1990, I went to the International Primatological Society's congress in Nagoya, Japan, where Masazumi Mitani told me about his research in this forest, which he called the Ndoki. He said the conditions there were "very, very difficult," and well aware of the Japanese field researcher's legendary capacity for enduring hardship, I could only imagine that the Ndoki must be a very tough place indeed.

During my initial research forays for the apes and humans article, however, I also felt that such an unknown and unspoiled area should be left alone. With no protection in place, the last thing the Ndoki needed was publicity that might inspire an influx of adventurers, hunters and their camp followers. The situation changed in 1992, but during this first trip to Bayanga, I still felt that the Ndoki's best protections were its remoteness and obscurity.

If the Bayanga region proved to be a disappointment for seeing gorillas in the wild, it held many other charms. There was Dzanga Bai, for instance, a clearing in the Dzanga Sangha park, where tens of thousands of African grey parrots and scores of elephants would gather in the evening for a couple of hours of raucous socializing before settling down for the night. Before Dzanga Sangha received protection a few years earlier, the elephant population had been poached mercilessly, but now numbers were recovering, and elephants that had earlier moved away because of the poaching were starting to come back.

Access to the *bai* was through a relatively short trail. The only real hazard was the omnipresent danger of inadvertently surprising an elephant. Elephants are admirable in almost every respect, but they are also known as the most dangerous animal in the rainforest. Nick Nichols had photographed every conceivable African animal, but during one of our walks to the *bai* he remarked that he knew very little about elephants. After he was nearly trampled during one attempt to photograph them, I told him that I had prepared a motto to be inscribed on his tombstone: "He died as he lived, knowing very little about elephants."

Mike Fay believes that elephants play by different rules when they enter human-controlled areas than when they are in the forest. Typically they aren't aggressive when they encounter humans on human turf, and they expect humans to reciprocate when they enter the elephants' domain. In any event they don't react well to being surprised (a few years after this trip, Mike barely escaped being crushed after an unscheduled encounter with a female elephant in Gabon), and I was always alert for elephants on the walk to a mirador that had been constructed as a perch from which to watch the life of the *bai*.

On these hikes to *salines* and *bais,* I was accompanied by Andrea, a few Ba'Aka Pygmies, and, sometimes, Nick. To attract gorillas, one of Andrea's Pygmy assistants, Teti, made a scream like that of a female gorilla, but none appeared. Later he tried to call chimps by making the screams of a duiker (a tiny deerlike ungulate) giving birth; chimps will often come when they hear these screams, hoping to eat the placenta (or, some claim, the baby duiker). Again no luck, but two blue duikers did show up. The richness of the area was evident in the constant parade of wildlife we did encounter, including white-nosed monkeys, bongo, and on and on.

Later still we came upon an extreme rarity—a yellow-backed duiker. Andrea had seen only two of them in the previous five years. Somewhat larger than the diminutive ungulate that most people think of as duiker, the yellow-backed version has a golden patch on its back. There's speculation that it was a sighting of yellow-backed duikers that gave birth to the legend of the Golden Fleece.

<hr>

On another trip to a *bai* we encountered a group of paratroopers from the French Foreign Legion. At that time, the French maintained troops in a number of Francophone sub-Saharan countries. Ostensibly, they were there at the invitation of the government to help preserve stability, but they also served as a subtle reminder to corrupt leaders of their former colonies that there were limits to their sovereignty. While the French had high tolerance for these leaders' abusing their own people, French expatriates were off limits, and economic ties and commercial relationships, which gave French businesspeople a decided edge over other expatriates, were not to be tampered with. Great Game–like maneuverings aside, we were happy to encounter the Europeans. Their captain told us that they had flown out for some R and R, and they wanted to visit the *bai.*

In the course of the conversation we discovered that they planned to fly back to Bangui later that day. I was looking for a way to get back to Bangui, and, preposterous as it sounded, I asked if I could get a lift with the paratroopers in their military plane. The captain pondered for a moment and then said, *"Pourquoi pas?"* Only in Africa would a military commander agree to such a request, and before he could change his mind I dashed back to gather my gear, agreeing to meet up at the airstrip.

When I reached the strip, however, I learned that there had been a change of plans: The legionnaires had received orders to take part in a military exercise, and instead of flying to Bangui, they were heading north. My ears pricked up when the captain told me that they were stopping in Bouar. With an eye to trying to meet up with Bernard N'donazi, the healer Rebecca Hardin had mentioned, and knowing that it would be easier to find a lift to Bangui from Bouar (which is connected to Bangui by a decent road), I made an instant decision and asked whether I could at least accompany them to Bouar. Again, the captain agreed.

Compared to bouncing in the back of a lurching truck, the minimalist benches of the paratroop transport felt as comfortable as the seating on a private jet. The trip was an easy one, and though the Legion contains some of the toughest and most disciplined soldiers on earth, my companions were affable and easy to talk to. I fell into conversation with a paratrooper from Ireland and another from Turkey, both of whom were looking forward to French citizenship. The etiquette of the Legion prohibited any discussion of why they could not return to their native lands.

Though larger than Bayanga, Bouar is still a small town, and I quickly found Rebecca at home with her French boyfriend, Pascal. One of the charms of Africa is that you can drop in on someone you hardly know and be met with genuine warmth. They offered to put me up while I was in Bouar, and Rebecca began making inquiries so that I could meet N'donazi.

As noted earlier, many of the organizations and experts attempting to foster African economic development regard indigenous practices as impediments to progress and indigenous knowledge as worthless. (There's a practical, if wrongheaded, reason for this: The entrepreneurial spirit is anathema to many indigenous peoples whose cultures stress communal decisions and sharing of wealth.) Once exposed to the power of the West and its images, many young tribal people adopt these same prejudices, either physically abandoning their people or, as I saw in New Guinea and Borneo, simply checking out mentally from their tribe. The depressing result in Africa, as everywhere, has been a silent holocaust in the realm of knowledge, as wisdom—about the medicinal properties of plants, about the migration patterns of animals, about the interplay of different species—disappears, simply because nobody speaks the language of the wisdom keepers or wants to listen to the elders.

N'donazi proved to be a perfect subject for my story. As a boy he had been initiated into some of the healing knowledge of his Souma tribe while spending time in the male house. Part of his initiation rite involved enduring an incision that had been cut into his side and that briefly exposed his intestines. (Rites like this probably make it easy for the young to abandon tribal ways.) N'donazi was one of the last initiates to live in the male houses since his father, a village elder, fell under the influence of a Catholic abbot who considered the rituals pagan. His father ordered the destruction of the male house, and with its burning, the tribe lost a cultural and medical tradition that extended back to antiquity.

N'donazi, however, had not forgotten everything he had been taught. After receiving training as a health technician, he discovered that many Western medicines derived from plants. He began wondering why it made sense to sell poor villagers prohibitively expensive Western drugs when there were plants right at hand to treat many common ailments. He began documenting the knowledge he remembered from his youth as well as what he could collect by interviewing local healers.

N'donazi's vindication came some months before my visit, when he was contacted by nuns from a nearby Catholic mission hospital. One of their patients was suffering from a gruesome ailment in which subcutaneous amoebae were eating away the skin covering his chest cavity, leaving cysts to develop and eventually explode.

The nuns reached out to N'donazi because the man's infection had failed to respond to any treatments they had available. After examining the patient, N'donazi tried a treatment he had learned from his father, washing and crushing soldier termites and applying them to the open wounds. The patient, named Thomas Service, made a remarkable recovery, as attested to in photographs N'donazi showed me. Service himself showed up during one of my interviews, as since his recovery, he has made the 17-kilometer trek from Kpocte to N'donazi's clinic every Sunday, bearing a gift to express his gratitude.

As in every story in Africa, however, things are never as straightforward as they first seem. When William Coupon, the celebrated photographer contracted to shoot my story, arrived some months later to shoot a portrait of N'donazi, the healer's family essentially held Coupon hostage and demanded that he pay a fee of a few thousand dollars before they would let him depart. Since he had chartered a plane to fly in, they may have felt that he was rich, and photography arouses intense emotions in Africa. Whatever their motivations, Coupon's story left a sour taste about the healer.

My own exit from Bouar was smoother, though less elegant than departure by chartered plane. The saintly Rebecca found me a lift with Patrice, a local businessman who with his driver was making the 445-kilometer trip back to Bangui. For a reasonable sum (I paid for the gas), I could go along. The first part of the drive took us through savannah-like country, marked by tall grass and low trees. We passed through many Fulani villages, all traditional. About 100 kilometers out from Bouar a tire went flat. The competent driver managed to fix it, but now we had no spare.

After finishing the repair, he started the car with a screwdriver. This aroused slight feelings of concern, since we still had several hundred miles to go. Another 85 kilometers down the road, the car overheated. When Patrice lifted the hood we discovered that there was no radiator cap—only a rag stuffed into the hole where the cap should be. Patrice was irate, but we had no choice but to make do with the rag, given that we were in the middle of nowhere. (Once we left Bouar we didn't see another vehicle for 300 kilometers.)

As we entered more populated areas I was treated to the one-size-fits-all tendency of African drivers. Flying through villages and populated areas, they seem grimly determined not to touch the brakes. Consequently we left behind us a wake of vehicular mayhem whose victims included a chicken, a goat and at least one old dog. I understood why the driver didn't stop—we'd have been mobbed by angry villagers—but I couldn't get him to slow down.

Safely in Bangui, I cleaned up at the Sofitel (whose amenities shop featured hard-core French comic-book pornography in its bookstand). The next morning, the transportation comedy continued as I tried to make my way to the airport. Having failed to wave down a succession of fully loaded taxis, I hitched my way to the center of town, where I finally found a cab. No sooner did we start for the airport, however, than we ran out of fuel. The driver headed off with a quart bottle to a nearby gas station, but when he poured the gas into the tank the car simply died, my guess being that the fuel had actually been flavored water. I found another taxi and managed to get to the airport, where I headed for the relative civilization of Kinshasa.

CHAPTER 8

Equateur Devolving

I was standing in the dilapidated, sweltering office of a tinpot commandante of the gendarmerie in a two-bit town called Djolu in the heart of
Equateur, Zaire. With me were an affable missionary, Father Piet; Mike
Chambers, a capable Canadian fixer; and Frans Lanting, the wildlife photographer. While Mike negotiated with the swaggering commandante, I idly
glanced at the crude paintings that had been chosen to enliven the walls
of the jail. One showed soldiers flailing at half-naked women with clubs.
I suspected that the commandante himself was the artist, and that he was
drawing from memory. I knew then that I very much wanted Mike's negotiations to succeed.

We shouldn't have been there at all, of course. Father Piet, who was from
the local Mill Hill mission at Yamoseli, had agreed to have his driver take
us out to a pygmy chimp (or bonobo) research station near the neighboring
village of Wamba. Earlier, back in Kinshasa, the capital, we had arduously
gathered all the requisite permissions to report and take photographs as part
of an assignment from *National Geographic*. As was customary in Africa, we
had come with a letter of introduction that was so bedecked with seals and
stamps that it looked like an international treaty. But the commandante,
who'd desperately bicycled out to the dirt airstrip where we'd been dropped
off an hour earlier, had taken one look at Frans's many cases of expensive-
looking equipment and promptly declared in French, "You don't have *my*
permission."

He had a point, given that we were a long way from Kinshasa, not that official permission would have gotten in the way of a bribe-seeking opportunist
in the capital city, either. In any event, Mike persuaded him to expedite his

"permission" for something like 110,000 Zaires (at this point in 1991, about $30), and we hightailed it to Wamba before the extortionist could decide that he had lowballed us. Since we had the benefit of the only working car for miles around, we assumed that once we were at the research station we would be beyond the reach of his bicycle. This turned out not to be the case.

I've visited primate research stations all over Africa, Asia and Latin America, and Wamba was one of the more primitive facilities. It consisted of a series of mud-brick and thatch huts, and its outhouses were mere pits. On the other hand, it had a nice bamboo shower, and water carriers brought visitors one bucket of warm water in the evening.

Takayoshi Kano, who had founded the station seventeen years earlier, may have intentionally avoided making improvements. For one thing, Japanese field researchers are about as tough a group of scientists as there are, and they seem to take some satisfaction from enduring hardship. Kano also may have kept things as austere as possible so that he did not live noticeably better than the natives in the village a few kilometers down the road. That would minimize resentment, and also reduce incentives for thievery.

On arriving at the station we were greeted warmly by Kano and Ellen Ingmanson, an American then doing graduate work on bonobos. Over dinner we heard some of the gossip about other field researchers, including news of one eminent primatologist whose wife left him after getting word that he had slept with a local. "Absence makes the dark grow blonder," muttered Frans, quoting the apt but politically incorrect remark of an expat British wildlife cinematographer.

We spent the next couple of days observing the bonobos in the field. Every time I've been in Africa I have marveled at the logistics involved in getting to the field—sometimes a week of transits and travel is required to reach a spot for a three-day visit. Once I am out in the forest with the animals, however, memories of all the hassles fall away. The air is clean, there is a heady mixture of fragrances from various flowering plants and trees, and the only sounds are the creatures of the rainforest. Around ponds and clearings there is often a tympanic symphony of frogs and crickets. It's a magical restorative.

As we roamed the forests around Wamba, the first Gulf War unfolded a few thousand miles to the north. At dinner we speculated about what it must be like for Iraqi troops, surrounded by hostiles and cut off from food, fuel and water. "You've just described Wamba," observed Frans.

Indeed, the food was simply awful, and in such small portions. We began referring to dinner as rice and pets, since chickens and goats mysteriously disappeared from the yard only to appear on the dinner table a few hours later. On the other hand, a magic fruit grows in Wamba. It's red and larger than a berry with a nice-tasting but skimpy flesh surrounding the pit. Its virtue is that it can turn anything sweet. If you eat it and then eat a lemon five minutes later, the lemon will taste sweet, no matter how sour it is otherwise.

Three days into our reporting and photographing, an exhausted minion of the commandante showed up, having made the 70-kilometer trek on a bicycle. Shyly and politely he informed us that the commandante and also the commissionaire de zone needed us to return to Djolu immediately for further discussions. Clearly the commandante had figured out that there was more money to be had if he could only get his hands on us. Kano seconded this assessment, based on his own experience.

Once, when the researchers had caught a poacher, Kano had one of his native trackers take the man to Djolu to be charged. Realizing that the poacher had no money but that the tracker had Kano's supposedly deep pockets behind him, the commandante promptly released the poacher and arrested the tracker. Kano had to pay 40,000 Zaires in ransom to get his man released.

We decided to avoid any further encounters with the commandante. I knew that a Missionary Air Fellowship flight was due in about five days, so all I had to do was stall for a while. We gave the messenger a meal and sent him back with our regrets and the word that we would be out there for several more weeks. By the time the enraged commandante dispatched a stronger posse or message, we would be gone.

That's exactly how it worked out. We'd arranged for the car to pick up Mike and me in a week, while Frans decided to stay on to do more shooting. Since we had official permission, we could not ignore the invitation from the commissionaire de zone, so we engineered an exquisitely timed exit in which we would stay at the Mill Hill mission in Yamoseli, 30 kilometers out of Djolu, and then make a lightning stop with the commissionaire before heading for the airport. To implement the plan we had to promise to replace all gas used, so scarce was fuel in the interior.

The mission at Yamoseli was a lovely and tranquil place where Father Piet and a couple of lay nurses spent most of their days dealing with the public health tragedy that has been unfolding in Africa. Father Piet had been in Zaire since 1947, and when he retired or died, there would be no one to replace him—a scenario that was being played out at all the Mill Hill missions in Zaire. In 1991, the youngest Mill Hill missionary in Zaire was sixty, and their number was down to eighteen from the sixty-four who had been there in 1955.

Once settled in my little room at the mission, I got a chance to see myself in the mirror for the first time in several weeks. I was astonished at how much weight I'd lost, mostly due to lack of appetite for such research station entrées as crocodile and goat guts. I was revisiting weights that I hadn't seen in decades.

To minimize opportunities for extortion during our brief time in Djolu, we left all our gear at the mission. Father René came by and said that Ida, a longtime missionary, wanted to meet the new commissionaire. We welcomed Ida's company, since opportunities for shenanigans decrease as the number of witnesses increases.

As it turned out, everything went swimmingly. We'd sent the bicyclist back with a letter hinting that we'd report any further harassment once we returned to Kinshasa, and the last thing the new commissionaire wanted was a negative review submitted to the governor of Equateur. As we headed to the airport a bicycle-riding soldier flagged us down and demanded that we see the commandante. Mike suspected that he wanted to retrieve the illegal convocation he had sent us before it came to the attention of the commissionaire de zone, who, whatever his policy on extortion, was probably not in favor of freelancing by his subordinates. Tough luck. We had already given the commissionaire the letter.

We reached the airport and boarded the plane before anyone else could intercede and flew on to Basankuso, where presumably a boat was waiting to take me to another pygmy chimp research station in truly remote Lomako. Formalities in Basankuso passed without a hitch, and I foolishly allowed myself to begin to think that it might be possible to work in Zaire. I couldn't have been more wrong. I never made it to Lomako. In fact, the Wamba visit was the most successful part of this particular trip.

———

Why is it so difficult to do the most basic things in Africa? Tasks we take completely for granted in the United States—making a phone call, getting the mail, paying a bill—require strategy and cunning. Why is it that, despite decades of development projects, the roads, railroads and services on the continent are but a shadow of what they were at the end of the colonial era?

I kept thinking back to Ambassador Dan Phillips's speculation about the lack of a social contract—the deal between citizens and their government in which people cede some of their incomes and rights in return for the security and benefits of being part of a larger community. In Africa people did cede their income and rights, if often at the point of a machete or gun, but never received anything in return. In Kinshasa I was regaled with stories of American aid projects that languished even after the money had been approved because Zairois officials saw no reason to sign documents unless they got a piece of the action. I didn't have to hear such reports, however, since I encountered the corrupt face of Central Africa at almost every turn.

This was not for lack of preparation. After many previous trips to the continent and other remote areas, I was familiar with the drill of dealing with corrupt officials, mechanical breakdowns, logistical failures, simple incompetence, civil disorder and natural disasters. By no means do I seek out adventure—if I'm traveling somewhere, it's for a purpose, not for thrills—but I do have reasonably good improvisation skills when I encounter the unexpected. However, Zaire was in a class by itself.

The country was rotten to the core, and as eventually happens in the last stages of rot, things began to fall apart. Encounters with corruption began at the airport in Kinshasa, where weary arrivals had to run a gauntlet of state-sanctioned thievery. In a country where nothing works, officials become punctilious to the extreme as they pore over customs forms and visas looking for any irregularity that might provide an opening to extract a bribe. If they can find none, they still declare the forms improper. On the other hand, offered a generous bribe, they would turn a blind eye if someone arrived carrying vats marked "Ebola virus."

The airport gauntlet dated back to my very first trip to Zaire in 1974. I remember arriving and hiring a local for $20 to negotiate customs. The young man sitting next to me smugly said he was going to go it alone, since he spoke perfect French. As I whisked past customs, I saw him sweating heavily, his bravado long gone, while a pack of armed men picked through every piece of his luggage as though they were at a one-day sale at Filene's Basement.

For a time I would fly into Brazzaville in the Republic of the Congo rather than directly into Kinshasa. In Brazzaville you had to contend with the occasional uprising, but at least you could get through the airport in one piece. From the airport I would go straight to the port on the Congo River and take a short *vedette* ride across to Kinshasa, where the border guards were much easier to deal with. The kleptocracy quickly figured this stratagem out, however, and learned to take aside Westerners and others with baggage. Brazzaville benefited in many other ways from Zairian corruption. When diamond mines in eastern Zaire were looted during riots in the interior, the big diamond buyers happily set up shop in Brazzaville and bought the stolen diamonds for much less than they would have had to pay the government monopoly.

Sometimes the corruption verges on the comical. In the early '90s, rather than wait hours to get a dial tone and pay extortionate rates for international calls, many savvy expats would make private arrangements with those working for the government phone company. The phone worker would put through the call for an agreed-upon price and then assign the charges to some deep-pocketed foreigner. When officials at the U.S. embassy bought some new lines, they were surprised to find themselves billed for thousands of dollars before the phones were even installed.

I learned this last tidbit while watching a rugby match with the American ambassador, some staff from the embassy, and Harry Goodall, the son of missionaries and an American expatriate in Kinshasa. Frans Lanting and I had hired Harry to help expedite our trip to the interior. One of the rules of the road in Zaire is that the more expensive the equipment you travel with, the more opportunities for extortion, if not theft, and Frans traveled with cases and cases of expensive cameras and lenses. Harry's team greased our way through customs, found us a reliable charter plane to take us to the interior, and set us up with Mike Chambers, who would accompany us on the trip.

Just before we had left for Wamba, Harry obtained 30 million Zaires on the black market, so that we could settle accounts in cash. The scene in his office looked for all the world like a drug deal as we sorted out the stacks of cash. Frans set up a shot of him shaking hands with Harry while each was surrounded by a mountain of Zaires and had $100 bills sticking out of every pocket.

Nothing expressed the soul of Mobutu's banana republic better than his currency. In 1974 the Zaire was worth more than the dollar. As hyperinflation took hold in the '90s, the decline of the currency was vertigo inducing. During one of my visits the currency stabilized briefly, yet it turned out that this was not the result of some incongruous return to fiscal sanity, but because Zaire had failed to pay a bill to the German company that printed its money, and the Germans had simply stopped the presses. At the Bank of Zaire the government regularly had to redeploy the soldiers stationed to guard the building—after a week or so on duty they would start asking employees entering the building for money. "You have so much in the bank," they would say. "Give us some."

———

Needless to say, I couldn't wait to get out of Kinshasa, and Mike Chambers turned out to be the perfect guide through the interior. He traveled light, carrying only a small gym bag. His Lingala and French were good, and he knew how to *hondle*. One personality trait was both an asset and a liability—a stubborn streak that manifested itself in the most impractical ways.

His friends regaled me with tales of his adventures. Once, when he was cheated by a politically connected Zairois on a business deal, he pursued the matter so thoroughly that his former partner used his political connections to have Mike thrown in jail. Rather than simply buy his way out, as was local custom, Mike stayed in jail and loudly demanded justice until the dumbfounded and embarrassed officials relented. I was to witness this stubborn streak firsthand in Basankuso.

The plan on arrival from Wamba was to meet up with the head of a palm oil plantation partially owned by an American expatriate named Elwin Blattner, and then take Blattner's boat—described as a fast and comfortable cabin cruiser—up the Maranga River to the Lomako River to the research station, which was then run by Richard Malenky and Nancy Thompson-Handler. Lomako was actually not far as the crow flies from Wamba, but there was no passable road or navigable river that would get you there directly.

By this point there were few passable roads in all of Zaire. Harry had told us that within his memory one could drive from Kinshasa to Kisingani, a few hundred miles east of Basankuso, stopping at filling stations and well-maintained hotels along the way. Now only a few thousand kilometers of the 144,000 kilometers in gazetted roads were still passable. During the dry season many river towns were completely isolated when the water got too low for boats.

We'd made the deal for our boat in Kinshasa with Elwin, who had assured us that his staff in Basankuso would be alerted and ready and waiting for us when we arrived. Elwin, who had recently been profiled in the *New York Times* as a nice Jewish boy from New York who had decided to become an entrepreneur in Zaire, seemed every bit the competent MBA, and despite the certainty of the unexpected in Zaire, I figured that orders from the patron would be heeded.

Things start going awry upon our arrival at Basankuso's rudimentary airport. Mike had been bantering with the locals, and became alert when he heard a rumor that our boat was about to head down the Lulonga River to the Congo and toward Mbandaka, the opposite direction from Lomako. We cadged a lift from the local Mill Hill mission vehicle and raced to the port. There, waving Elwin's card, we confronted various Compagnie de Commerce et des Plantations (CCP) officials, and we gave them the news that the boss of all bosses had promised us that his boat would be available for this most important journalistic mission.

We could see the boat, or what appeared to be the boat, given that it was completely covered with Zairois. Elwin had made it sound like a sleek vessel, but what we encountered was a run-down wreck surrounded by befuddled people looking at the engine and scratching their heads. So the rumors were true: The chef de personnel had plans to take the boat to Mbandaka, and it looked as though he had paying customers. I doubt that Elwin knew about this little business venture. Mike exacted the chef's word that he would not leave until we cleared the matter up with the plantation's general manager.

We jumped into our commandeered mission vehicle and goaded the driver to hurry to the plantation, which was 16 kilometers away. There we were greeted warmly by the director general, who told us that he'd gotten a message from Elwin that we were coming. He reassured us that the chef would not leave without his say-so, and gave us a letter confirming that we had the use of the boat. Once again we hit warp speed on rutted roads getting back to the port.

There histrionically cringing officials told us that the chef and the boat had departed, despite their efforts to stop him. Apparently, he had decided that the amount he would net from this excursion would more than compensate for any loss of income that would follow from his being fired when he returned. I was furious, and when an official said, *"Il est parti,"* I responded, *"Il est fini!"* Mike went ballistic, scattering dark threats like cluster bombs to everyone in earshot, before we stormed back to the Mill Hill mission, hoping to find lodging. By now I'd been spending so much time at Catholic missions that I might as well have converted.

That evening we had a beer with Father Dick, another member of the Mill Hill gerontocracy in Zaire, and Father Otto, an affable Gyro Gearloose type who spent much of his time fiddling with half-assembled, obsolete electronic equipment. Father Dick brought us up to date with the inexorable decline of Basankuso. Equateur had the misfortune, shared with much of Africa, of producing goods that the rest of the world was either giving up or making more efficiently: coffee, palm oil (rich in saturated fats), and rubber (easily replaced with synthetics). Inefficiency and corruption added costs that made even these products uncompetitive. Asian palm oil, shipped in from halfway around the world, was offered at the port of Kinshasa at exactly half the price of locally produced oil from the CCP plantation in Basankuso.

The result was that money had dried up like a puddle in the sun. Father Dick said that in the early 1970s the priests would go down to the local cafés and share a beer with townspeople who had gotten off work. It was pleasant and helped seal the mission's bonds with the community. Now a beer cost a day's wages and was rarely to be seen. If they did go to the few remaining cafés, the only people who could afford to join them there would be state officials on the fiddle. The Mill Hill fathers avoided such encounters, because being seen with the roundly disliked officials would cost them the trust of the townsfolk. Father Dick said a bit wistfully that he missed the old days.

I ask Father Dick why the town seemed so devoid of goods. Earlier in the day, I couldn't find even a Coke, the world's most ubiquitous product. He explained that the lack of hard currency was one problem. (Indeed, during one of my visits just after Zaire switched to a new currency, preparatory to launching yet another round of hyperinflation, many in Equateur continued to use the ostensibly worthless old bills because people knew that at least no one would be printing any more of them.) The other problem was the disappearance of the *petits commerçants,* the traders who used to deliver goods to the interior. As the plantations fell into disrepair and closed down, the transportation system crumbled (I was to discover how much it had crumbled in the days to come), money vanished, and traders found it no longer worth their while to deal with the thousand hassles and payoffs required to get deliveries, particularly since no one had any money to buy anything.

The scarcity of money produced demographic oddities. Frans had told me about virtual towns springing up around potholes in eastern Zaire. Long lines of trucks would be backed up as they gingerly negotiated the deeper potholes, and locals would gather around the stopped trucks, setting up food stands. The settlers would give the villages names from the Mobutu family. Prostitutes would flock to these spots, too, until a little impromptu village had sprung up. Naturally, the locals would have little incentive to fix the pothole.

These villages and other truckstops brought AIDS to the interior as well as goods. Even in 1991 AIDS was everywhere (in fact, AIDS was so prevalent in Central Africa by the 1990s that I'm surprised there has not yet been a population collapse). When I asked him what the mission was doing about it, he said that they were handing out condoms and trying to educate the locals to use them. Thinking of the pope's position on condoms, I raised an eyebrow. "It's a long way to Rome," replied Father Dick.

After drinks we sent several messages by radio to the mission at Monpoko, 120 kilometers downriver, with the notion of intercepting the boat and ordering it to return. (In the end, it didn't limp back into Monpoko until late the following afternoon, too late to do us any good.) Mike struck up a conversation with the mission's sentinel, who stood guard with a spear. When he told us he was from the Lomako area, I could see the germ of an idea form in Mike's stubborn Canadian brain.

It turned out that Mike had long had dreams of setting up an ecotourist site in Lomako, and he was determined to get there whatever the cost. I, meanwhile, had to get to a gorilla sanctuary in eastern Zaire and then to Burundi to meet up with Jane Goodall. Without a fast boat, the trip to Lomako by motorized pirogue would take at least three days, assuming we could even get something organized. I would obviously have to skip Lomako. By radio I asked Elwin to see whether any planes might be coming through Basankuso in the coming days. In the meantime I helped Mike get provisioned for his trip.

After he hired various members of the sentinel's family to find a *baleinière* to take him to Lomako, we headed into the center of this ruined and crumbling colonial town to buy provisions. The streets were rutted and scattered with the useless hulks of abandoned and stripped automobiles.

Untended gardens sprouted weeds everywhere. At the local store what few goods were available lay strewn about, with piles of soap on the floor and, incongruously, an ancient stack of scratched 45 rpm records perched on a table. The look and feel were postapocalyptic.

Basankuso was becoming Africanized again. Within a few decades all traces of the colonial era may have vanished. I kept thinking about an article by William Pfaff, who argued that forty years of Russian domination could not erase Eastern Europe's millennium years of orientation toward the West. Why, then, should a century of colonialism have succeeded in erasing cultural attitudes that dated back thousands of years, and that were supported daily by climate and geography?

It is possible to meet rudimentary daily needs with very little effort in much of Africa, particularly if you are a man, since women do so much of the work. Mike took this idea even further, arguing that part of the nutritional problems in the interior were due to the typical village preference to grow manioc, which required relatively little work, instead of more varied and nutritious crops that might demand more attention.

Sunday morning we walked into town, where Mike haggled with fishermen over the rental price of a pirogue. One fellow we spoke to was a dignified older man who looked as though he had been working the river forever. I liked the cut of his jib, and we arranged to meet with him again that afternoon.

Back at the mission we were introduced to a newcomer, Father Kerwin, who was en route to another Mill Hill mission situated in Waka. He bemoaned the quality and paucity of young recruits for the mission, noting that many joined the priesthood with mixed motives. In this impoverished country, the priesthood was actually a step up for almost everyone. More to the point, in the interior, it was the fastest way to get a car. Missionaries, using French, referred to the priesthood as *"vocation Toyota."*

Efforts to find a plane proved fruitless, so I prepared to spend two more days at the mission while waiting for the next Missionary Air Fellowship flight. I helped Mike with his final preparations for his trip upriver. It was beginning to look like Stanley's expedition, and Mike seemed to be well on his way to becoming the biggest employer in town. He had hired the three sons of the sentinel, as well as two river men with a boat and a motor. Apart from money, Mike brought to the negotiations a drum of fuel, which was as scarce and expensive as caviar. The director general, a decent man who was mortified by the loss of face of having his subordinate disobey a direct order, sold him the fuel at cost as compensation for the disaster.

Mike's departure was delayed by some last-minute negotiations when the captain's unsavory cousin and an equally unsavory companion tried to insert themselves into the trip. The piratical-looking cousin insisted that Mike had agreed to a price 100,000 Zaires higher, and Mike ended up splitting the difference in order to devote his energy to keeping the unsavory cousin off the dugout. I watched the proceedings with joy in my heart that I would not be going along, and then waved bon voyage as Mike and his dubious crew pushed off and started putt-putting upstream.

———

With time on my hands I decided to follow a path into the fields to find the headwaters of the endless procession of women commuting by foot past the mission. Stanley wrote that women were the beasts of burden in Africa, and apparently nothing had changed in the 100-plus years since he offered that insight. Father Dick said that one reason that the women live longer than the men in Equateur might be the physical endurance they gained from their physical labor. Another might be that they don't have the leisure to drink and smoke as the men did. In Wamba the men often could not bear the loads regularly hauled by their wives.

The women carried their burdens strapped to their backs with cords looped around their foreheads and shoulders, which led to their building up huge calluses. Father Piet had earlier suggested that I conduct my own survey and see how many younger women were making the trek. I saw very few young women, leaving me to wonder what they were doing.

To be fair to the men, they did clear the fields in the countryside in the dry season, and they fished and hunted. But in the towns they did very little. Mike said that in Kinshasa the female employees were often more disciplined and honest. I wondered what kind of state Zaire might become if the women could take charge.

The next morning I went down to see Father Piet's woodworking shop. Using local labor, the shop produced an impressive variety of doors, chairs, and other furniture for all the missions, as well as for people who bought them on commission. At the shop a group of apprentices waited for instructions from Piet. He told me that until three months earlier he had had an experienced crew of woodworkers, some of whom had been there for ten years. Unfortunately he discovered that they were robbing him, and after giving warnings to several of them, he finally caught one of them red-handed. The man revealed that the entire crew of seven had organized a ring to steal wood, tools and furniture in cahoots with the watchman. Piet fired them all, and for several months he was so depressed that he worked alone.

Before coming to Africa, Piet had run a similar operation in India, between Hyderabad and Madras. That business had been a great success, and the neighborhood so honest that he never once locked his shop or quarters. What was the difference? The moral structure, he offered, but also the ecology. The Indians lived in a harsh, semidesert envrironment that forced them to work hard to eke out a living, while in Africa, according to Piet, the forests and rivers supplied game quite readily. Ambassador Phillips was not the only one in Africa who believed in ecological determinism.

We were interrupted in this conversation by the reappearance of Mike—something I'd expected, but not quite so soon. The trip had been a disaster. The piratical companion had rowed out in another boat and jumped aboard carrying a wicked-looking blade, which he always had at hand. Mike finally got rid of him by threatening to call the gendarmes. The motor on the boat broke down halfway to Waka, and they returned to Basankuso by floating with the current, arriving at 2:00 a.m.

There was no way, however, that Mike was going to give up. With yet another fine display of his legendary tenacity, the next morning he set off for the port, determined to recover his 100,000 Zs (as Zaires were called) and then rent another boat with his remaining fuel. It hadn't yet dawned on him that Lomako might not be the optimum choice for an ecotourist site. I wished him luck and fully expected to see him again soon.

My final night in Basankuso was enlivened by stories about the justice system, such as it was, in the interior. The fathers told me about the aftermath of a rape as an illustration. The family of the victim reported the crime to the police, who immediately asked how much it was worth to them to have the police arrest, jail and beat the perpetrators. Once they settled on a price, the police then went to the families of the perpetrators and asked them how much it was worth to them *not* to have the police jail and beat the malefactors. Apparently, the bidding was still going on.

Basankuso had reset my reference points for standards of luxury, and by now I couldn't wait to get back to Kinshasa, which had acquired the allure of Paris. Mercifully the MAF plane arrived the next day, and I headed back

to the very city I could not wait to leave a few weeks earlier. Before heading
off to Goma and then Burundi, however, I was to have one more memorable experience on this particular trip to Zaire.

———

On my return to Kinshasa I contacted Harry Goodall. I'd earlier expressed
an interest in watching his rugby team, the Kinshasa Barbarians, play the
Zairois paratroopers, and he said that there was a game scheduled for the
following day, and that he would pick me up in the morning. On the way
to the game, Harry handed me a uniform.

"What this?" I asked.

"What does it look like?" he replied.

As it turned out, they were a man short. I'd never played rugby (and in
fact had seen my first match only a few weeks earlier), and the idea of playing
against a team of paratroopers did not seem like fun. But I could hardly back
out, so as we drove to the match, Harry hastily told me some of the rules.

I can't say that I was much of an asset, and although I'd played a bit of
football, I was now utterly confused. This was not a good thing, given that
bodies were flying around like NASCAR vehicles hitting the wall. Everybody
on both teams was tough as nails. A couple of our guys were members of the
SAS contingent guarding the British ambassador, and, whatever their skills as
soldiers, the Zairois paratroopers were still mean and fit. I endured the entire
afternoon, however, and left with only minor injuries (one lost big toenail).
Mike Sheehan, an accident-prone lawyer and avid Barbarian, cracked a molar.

It was not until a subsequent trip to Kinshasa that I learned what happened to Mike Chambers after I left Basankuso. His second attempt to get
to Lomako proved no more successful than the first. In all it took him about
a month to reach his El Dorado, and when he did, he could stay for only
a couple of hours or he would have found himself marooned there indefinitely. Mike eventually came to the conclusion that Lomako might not
become the ecotourist magnet he'd envisioned.

Postscript

As the region descended into anarchy and civil war in the middle '90s, the
situation in Equateur grew ever worse. Takayoshi Kano was forced to pull

out of Wamba, leaving his beloved bonobos in the care of a dedicated but undermanned and underarmed local staff. Bonobo numbers suffered from poaching. Researchers were forced to abandon Lomako as well. With the miseries inflicted by civil war, economic collapse and the remorseless spread of AIDS, the corruption of the Mobutu era now looks like the good old days. One fading ray of light is the dwindling, aging, saintly Mill Hill missionaries, who've taken it as their charge to help those they can as long as they can.

PART IV

APES AT THE BRINK

CHAPTER 9

Travels with Jane

For indigenous peoples today, the risks of living at the ragged edge of the world are a matter more of identity than of survival. While the natives manage to live on, their culture withers and dies. For our closest animal relatives, the risks are more existential. A great ape living at the ragged edge of the world faces loss of habitat, loss of livelihood and loss of life.

I've been writing about our poor relations since the beginning of my career. After returning from Vietnam, I switched gears from war reportage to writing about the sign language experiments conducted with chimpanzees in *Apes, Men, and Language* (1974). Since then I've visited research stations studying chimps, gorillas and bonobos in Africa, and gibbons and orangutans on Borneo and Sumatra. But until *National Geographic* assigned me to write "Apes and Humans," I'd never traveled with Jane Goodall, though I had met her on several earlier occasions.

Jane had long been one of the great apes' most eloquent champions, but even as her fame and recognition soared, the wildlands around her beloved Gombe Stream Reserve in Tanzania disappeared, marooning a few dozen chimps amid a sea of humanity. The chimps' insurance policy was Jane's international status, but their lives—basically a simian version of *The Truman Show,* as they lived and died in the fishbowl of Gombe—offered a poignant metaphor for the plight of great apes in general. And so I resolved to meet up with Jane. As usual in Africa, this turned out to be an adventure in itself.

———

Back in Kinshasa after my involuntary, but mercifully brief, exile in Basankuso, I immediately began planning to go to eastern Zaire, Rwanda and Burundi. Apart from connecting with Jane Goodall, I hoped to meet up with Diane Doran, who was then running Karisoke (the famed refuge for mountain gorillas that had been established by Dian Fossey); visit a lowland gorilla site in Zaire called Kahuzi-Biega; and then travel to Gombe Stream Reserve in Tanzania. It was Jane's work in Gombe that launched her career as a primatologist and ambassador-at-large representing the interests of the great apes. My itinerary was ambitious, given that it involved numerous trips and border crossings, and always on my mind was the inviolate lesson of Central Africa: Traveling can never be taken for granted, no matter how meticulous the preparations.

On a late November Sunday I headed off to the airport to catch a plane to Goma in eastern Zaire, meeting up at the airport with a group of American embassy personnel who were going there as well. All went smoothly until, just as we were accelerating down the runway, the pilot aborted the takeoff and, with no explanation, returned to the terminal, where we were herded to various *salles d'attente*. Meanwhile we watched as the plane was towed off, a fact for which I suppose we should have been grateful.

Five hours later we finally did take off, and headed for the stunning high-country towns of Goma and Bukavu. Bukavu was built as a resort town for the Belgians, and, though run-down, it retained a decaying colonial charm. The Orchid Safari Club, where I arranged to stay, had spectacular gardens winding down to Lake Kivu. The hotel had been purchased by a former Belgian mercenary, who insured his investment by buying a neighboring house, which he promptly gave to the minister of justice. Now, I heard, trouble was afoot. The minister wanted to sell the house, and he was asking more than the Belgian could afford. No one seemed to question the morals of trying to gouge the man who had given him the gift in the first place. (Americans can't get too smug about this, of course, since fourteen years later a similar sordid drama unfolded in California, when Congressman "Duke" Cunningham bought his house below market and sold it above market thanks to the generosity of MZM Inc., a company whose government contracts were subject to the committee the congressman chaired.)

At that time Bukavu and Kivu were probably among the few places on earth where people basically had to leave the country to make a phone call or send or receive mail. Expatriates and Zairois officials alike routinely made a 45-kilometer trek to Rwanda for precisely those services. A popular theory in town held that Mobutu had fostered the collapse of the country's infrastructure because it made it more difficult for any rebellion to be organized.

Still, despite the brutality of Zairois soldiers and the corruption of the politicians, the Zairois remained a cheerful and charming people. Waking up Tuesday morning, I heard the fishermen singing, just as I heard them the night before as they paddled out in the evening.

My one brief mission in eastern Zaire was to visit Kahuzi-Biega, which was situated between two volcanoes of the same two names. At that time— before refugees and rebels overran the park when neighboring Rwanda descended into genocidal madness—it was probably the most accessible place for visitors to see habituated gorillas in the wild. Tourists could get very close to the gorillas as they calmly munched in their natural salad bowl. In fact the scene was quite comical. Given their diet, a good deal of fermentation seems to go on in the gorilla gut, and the reverential mood of the tourists watching these magnificent animals was persistently undermined by the sound of stentorian gorilla farts reverberating through the air.

After returning to Goma, I made plans to set off for Burundi. The drive to Bujumbura—which now took four to five hours rather than the standard two and a half, because rebel activity forced us to drive on Zairean roads— was a pleasant enough trip through mountain passes. Very little forest cover remained in this most densely populated part of sub-Saharan Africa. Coming down through the pass just before we entered Burundi, we drove onto an enormous plain, and then suddenly Lake Tanganyika came into view, vast and blue and guarded on every shore by tall mountain ranges.

At the frontier the Zairean guards were dressed in ragtag clothes and fatigues, while on the Burundi side they were smartly decked out in blue uniforms with blue berets. Unlike Zaire, which did not pay its soldiers (all but guaranteeing that they would steal to support themselves), Burundi had a well-compensated, highly professional army. Once in Burundi, we drove on paved roads with lots of other vehicles sharing them. I was astonished to see real stores selling real merchandise. Burundi had its share of serious problems, but compared to its neighbor, it felt like Switzerland.

After installing myself at the Novotel, I ran around town trying to locate Jane. Realizing that I wouldn't get far on foot, I hired a car and drove out to Geoff Creswell's house. A former zookeeper, Geoff then ran the Jane Goodall Institute in Bujumbura. When I arrived, he was playing nanny to three orphaned young chimpanzees while the institute looked for a permanent site where they might be rehabilitated. Within two minutes, Max, a two-year-old chimp, was climbing into my arms. Geoff told me that Jane would be arriving the following day and going down to Gombe on Saturday. I decided to make a quick road trip to Rwanda to check on Karisoke and then return in time to go to Gombe with Jane.

That night I bought Geoff dinner at the Lake Tanganyika restaurant, a spacious legacy of colonial days now run by a Belgian couple. Geoff began telling stories about encounters with chimps and orangutans during his zookeeper days. I just sat and listened.

He began by saying that he remained taken with the chimps' rampant intelligence. Whatever he was doing at the house, they would try to imitate. Once when Ali, the little female, was throwing a tantrum, Geoff decided to distract her by digging a hole in the sandbox in the backyard. Soon Ali came over and peered at what he was doing. Then she pulled his hand out and peered in the hole. She sniffed his fingers, but he just kept scooping sand. After a few more seconds, she started digging her own hole, right next to his. Then, said Geoff, a minute later, the dog came over. After looking at both of them, he started digging, too.

Geoff said that the difference between chimps and orangutans was that a chimp would try to grab your keys every time you walked past, while an orang would make an attempt only if it was certain that it would succeed. Usually, Geoff could get the keys back simply by asking. From Geoff's perspective, orangutans were also the best liars in the zoo world. At the Topeka Zoo an orangutan named Jonathan would steal something, keys or the like, and then when a keeper called for him to return the items, he would first act surprised that he was being addressed and then offer a stick or something else he had picked up, all the while concealing the keys with his foot or other hand.

The females sometimes used a different strategy for getting what they wanted. When one of the female orangutans at the Topeka Zoo got fat, it fell to Geoff to deliver her new, reduced rations. At first she decided that Geoff was trying to starve her and would greet him with threats and tantrums. When this had no effect, she suddenly started to present to Geoff sexually whenever he appeared.

One story Geoff told stayed in my mind. He said that every orangutan keeper had heard the zoo legend of a male orangutan at the Omaha Zoo that repeatedly escaped from his cage. In Geoff's version, the keepers notified the police only to discover that the orangutan had been picking the lock with a piece of wire he secreted in his cheek. The orangutan got caught only because he neglected to relock the door after escaping.

Geoff got a couple of the details of that account wrong, but its essence was spot on. While it did not fit into the article I was writing for *National Geographic,* some part of my unconscious must have recognized it as important because I never forgot it. As noted in the introduction, there is a phenomenon in psychology in which important events remain fresh in memory until you have written them down. Whatever the phenomenon, it wasn't until a few years later that the significance of the story finally fell into place.

Over the years I've written a great deal about animal intelligence, including a few books and many articles. When I was reporting on the experiments to teach chimps sign language, I doggedly kept up as experimenters and critics pursued a joyless trench warfare in which each assertion about evidence of a higher mental ability in an ape or dolphin would be dismissed as flawed, usually because there was a possibility that the experimenters were cueing the correct answer, or because the answer was ambiguous and subject to overinterpretation.

By the mid-'90s I had had enough of this debate. It had been easier to end the Cold War and defeat communism than it was to get scientists to agree on what a juvenile chimp named Washoe meant when she combined the signs for "water" and "bird" when she saw a swan on a pond. (In fact, that debate remained unresolved when Washoe died at the age of forty-two in 2007.) Then, in the late 1990s, I woke up one morning thinking about Geoff Creswell's story once again, it finally dawned on me: Here was an ape who was demonstrating a suite of higher mental abilities—reverse engineering, innovation, deception—regardless of the motivations of his keepers. Maybe animals did their best thinking when it served their purposes and not those of a scientist, whose audience was his or her peers and not the animals themselves.

Out of this "aha" moment came my book *The Parrot's Lament* (1999) and its sequel, *The Octopus and the Orangutan* (2002). I mention those books here only because they may be the most enduring results of that trip to Africa, and yet the conversation that eventually prompted me to pursue that line of thought had very little to do with the purpose that brought me to Bujumbura.

Before heading off to Kigali, I had breakfast with Mimi Brian, a sunny, competent woman attached to the American embassy who had taken it upon herself to facilitate Jane Goodall's efforts to help chimpanzees. After making arrangements to ensure that I connected with Jane when she arrived, I headed off to the airport to try to get on a flight for the short hop to Kigali.

Airline schedules in this part of Africa seemed to be closely guarded secrets, released to pilots but not to airline officials, ticket agents, or, God forbid, passengers. My first flight to Rwanda was canceled, but then rumors began circulating about a flight the next morning. That would give me a day to talk with Diane Doran and catch up on doings at Karisoke during the fighting. (Paul Kagame, now president of Rwanda, had launched his first invasion of the country the year before.) No one, however, would admit that this flight existed—not the ticket agents, airport personnel or anyone. At the airport Mimi and I managed to contact the control tower (only in Africa!), and the guy who answered assured us that the flight was coming in and returning to Kigali.

When I arrived in Rwanda, Kigali was a ghost town. There were no taxis, only a few vehicles of any kind on the streets, and an eight o'clock curfew, after which you were likely to get shot. This was probably why, when I finally did reach Diane Doran, she instantly proposed that we drive back down to Bujumbura. I agreed, somewhat reluctantly, since I was not looking forward to six hours in a vehicle. On the other hand, there was no chance of getting to Karisoke, which had been evacuated. I realized that three hours in Kigali was enough for me, since there was no way to get around and, to all appearances, no one to see.

Ordinarily, the evacuation of a research station like Karisoke would have been fatal for the unprotected animals, but I had reason to be hopeful. Before coming to Africa, I had met with some of the rebel leaders in Washington, D.C. They had solicited the meeting, and what was extraordinary was that they were reaching out to let a journalist know that they planned to take every precaution to protect the gorillas at Karisoke. A variety of motives prompted the Rwandan Patriotic Front to reach out in this way: Karisoke was among Rwanda's biggest earners of foreign exchange, and the rebels knew that they would need this cash cow once they took over. They also needed support from the West, and public support would be more likely if they were viewed as protectors rather than destroyers of the world's last remaining population of mountain gorillas.

Talk is cheap, though; what was extraordinary was that they kept their word. As documented by Bill Webber and Amy Vetter of the Wildlife Conservation Society, the gorillas survived not only this civil war but also the 1994 Rwandan genocide, which killed 800,000 of Paul Kagame's fellow Tutsis. The Karisoke gorillas have endured through all upheavals since.

As I drove back to Bujumbura with Diane, I told her of my conversation with the rebel leadership back in Washington, and she confirmed that at that point (March 1991) things were going fine, even though rebels were all around the area of Karisoke. Diane had brought along a graduate student who told a hilarious story about the problems a female field researcher faced in keeping a proper distance from her scientific subjects if one of said subjects developed a crush on said researcher. In Martha's case a young male gorilla decided that Martha was really hot, and showed as much by rolling around near her and occasionally dragging her for short distances. Somehow she let the gorilla know that the relationship wasn't going to work out, and he seemed to accept this.

For the rest of the ride we spoke about Diane's research on the ontology of motor behavior and how different great apes move—particularly how chimps first use palmigrade motion before they learn to walk on their knuckles, and how this indicates that knuckle-walking might be a late-developing behavior in the great apes, one that occurred after the split with humans. *Australopithecus afarensis* lived very close in time to the split of hominids from the rest of the great apes 5 million years ago, and there is no evidence that this little fellow knuckle-walked (though, more recently, some paleontologists have argued that other hominids did). Diane related these developments to the environments, feeding strategies and social structures of the apes. I found the subject fascinating, and the time flew.

Back in Bujumbura, after leaving Diane, I reconnected with everybody. Jane (whom I knew from previous encounters) had arrived by then. Geoff and I picked up Jane and took her to see "Herself," as she witheringly referred to the American ambassador, and then headed over to visit a gold trader who had a chimp that was getting too big to handle. The six-year-old female, Cheetah, was best friends with a gigantic Rottweiler guard dog, Simba. I don't think I have ever seen two creatures have a better time playing with each other. Cheetah charged in and grabbed Simba's foot, while Simba play-bit any part of Cheetah he could get hold of. Throughout their tussling Cheetah was practically helpless with laughter, and it seemed to me that Simba was doing the dog equivalent of laughing himself.

That evening I brought Diane and Martha along to meet Jane but was surprised when she gave them a noticeably frosty reception. Mimi extended a sincere invitation for the women to join us for dinner, but noticing the awkwardness, I begged off and took Diane and Martha out for a meal. Later Jane compounded my confusion by telling me how much she liked Diane and Martha. Mimi, who also noticed the frosty reception, speculated that Jane might have been a bit put out because Karisoke's own charisma as a fabled mountain gorilla sanctuary somewhat distracted the focus from Jane's beloved Gombe.

On Saturday Jane, Mimi, Mimi's mother and I drove down south to catch a small boat to Gombe. Lake Tanganyika is huge, blue, pellucid and very, very deep. The trip was beautiful but disturbing. What thirty-five years earlier had been almost entirely forested with what is called miombo woodland was now almost entirely cleared. Gombe itself was an oasis, an island of the California-like mixture of forest and grasslands that once characterized the lakeside before all the cutting and clearing. Still, the air was fresh as fresh can be, and I felt exhilarated the next morning when we went out to search for chimps. I climbed an acacia tree to look out over the green valleys and saw pure water everywhere—a striking contrast to the rot and dankness of the rainforest. Lying in the branches, I watched weather systems form over the lake as evaporation and convection conspired with the mountains of Zaire to compose huge thunderstorms that were in turn dwarfed by the size of the lake.

When we finally saw the chimps, they were off in the distance, arrayed in a field of grass surrounded by protea trees. Jane pointed out a peak to the left where, thirty-one years earlier, she had enjoyed the sublime exhilaration of her first close encounter with chimps. Four months after arriving, she had found her life's work. Later she told me that she thought up the the title of her famous book *In the Shadow of Man* (1971) while driving across Uganda with her husband, Hugo. When it came to her, she gave a shriek. Alarmed, Hugo said, "What's the matter?"

"I've got the title!" she responded. Once she had the title, Jane told me, she knew that she could write the book.

Chimps are indeed in the shadow of man. There are only a few isolated and doomed populations of chimps between Gombe and the 400 or so hanging on in Mohale, the Japanese-run research area in the south.

When we caught up to part of the Gombe group, they were all in an mbolo tree. There, scattered through the branches, were chimps whose names I had known for more than a decade—Goblin, Everett, Faustino, Prof. Goblin had been top dog for nine years, but now had a low yet special status because he was best friends with Wilkie, the current top-ranking male. When chimps from the next valley sounded alarm calls, the big males responded with a furious, balletic display to show that they were ready for war. Oddly this was the time of the buildup toward the ground war in Kuwait, after weeks of preparatory bombing. Jane had been following events in the Mideast closely and had been talking of little else.

When we moved off, the chimps swung past Jane almost in a procession, and then we followed. Mimi led her mother back down the hill, while Jane, the tracker and I headed off through dense undergrowth to keep up with the little folks knuckle-walking ahead. Jane had a little trouble getting through the thickets and remarked that it now took her two weeks to get back into shape, and that she never had two weeks in Gombe. No excuse was necessary, since at fifty-seven she was clearly in remarkable shape. Later Mimi noted that Jane had little tolerance for people with self-indulgent weaknesses like gluttony or drinking, and I understood a bit better why she might have felt obliged to explain her struggles with the underbrush.

There was one extraordinary moment in the dense brush. Prof, whom Jane had known since he was born twenty years earlier, had been feeding on a vine while we watched from a spot on the ground nearby. When he decided to leave, he walked directly past Jane's shoulder and paused for quite a few seconds. I thought he was waiting for Jane to groom him. Jane just sat quietly, and after a moment he moved on. She explained that she did not think that he wanted to be groomed, but was rather acknowledging her return to Gombe. Whatever the reason, it sent a tingle down my spine. This moment of recognition with mutual respect seemed so perfectly right to me, just the way it should be between apes and humans.

After Prof climbed up a tree to eat palm pith, Jane looked at her watch. It was 11 a.m., she pointed out—one hour until Saddam's deadline. Shortly thereafter we heard screams in the distance. "Colobus," said Jane. "The chimps are hunting colobus monkeys." Again we heard screaming and then quiet. Jane thought and then said, "The colobus chased them away—that's what blew Christophe's mind." She was referring to Christophe Boesch, who had studied chimp hunting behavior in the Tai Forest in the Ivory Coast. "Anyway," said Jane, "I hate hunting. I like mothers and babies."

Later we walked up to the feeding station, which she'd established nearly thirty years earlier, and where she and Hugo raised their son, Grub. From there we proceeded to a waterfall about twenty minutes from the station. Jane explained that the chimps did the most remarkable display in the waterfall, climbing up vines and swinging into the spray. She added that whenever she was asked whether chimps had a religion, she thought of how they reacted to the spray and also the wind and the rain, and all the other magical, essential elements of nature, and how they had no means of sharing their primal response to these forces. She was convinced that what she was witnessing in those scenes was the stuff out of which religions were formed, a pantheism that dates back millions of years.

Back at camp we discovered that a group of potential donors had arrived by seaplane along with a huge shipment of food. This was most welcome, since we had eaten nothing but cheese and bread for the past four meals. Gita Patel turned out to be a nice fellow who was captivated by chimps. When he heard that Jane's guesthouse had been ransacked by thieves and wrecked, he offered to build her a new building and replace all the stolen items. This was not an atypical reaction to Jane. That night we spread out a tarp on the beach and had a barbecue. It was a perfect evening, and I felt the most relaxed since my arrival in Africa.

The next morning I spent a long time looking out over the pure lake from this beautiful spot. I didn't want to leave, but it was ultimately wearying to spend too much time in the presence of a legend. This was no fault of Jane's—indeed, she was funny, charming and as canny an observer of the sexual politics of research stations as she was of chimps. Still, the gravitational force of celebrity implacably bent everything to Jane, the chimps and their plight, and after a while I felt I needed air. It was time to go.

CHAPTER 10

Listening to Pygmies

In New Guinea, the ornithologist Ralph Bulmer discovered that locals like Saem Majnep could offhandedly tell him things about birds that he might otherwise have spent years trying to discover. In 1991 I had a similar experience involving Pygmies and their knowledge of the forest. But perhaps I hadn't been as open-minded as Bulmer, and I discovered that to benefit from indigenous knowledge, you had to pay attention. When a Ba'Aka Pygmy told me about an extraordinary behavior his father had observed, I at first dismissed it as unverifiable. I should have given him more credence.

About ten years later science finally caught up with what Pygmies knew all along. This is a story about what we can learn from listening to those who live in the forest. It is also a story about how little we still know about our closest relatives. As noted earlier, what is a cultural holocaust for indigenous people at the ragged edge of the world has reified into a literal holocaust for the great apes. Even those chimps that have survived in a few isolated enclaves still risk losing their culture. At the eleventh hour for these apes, we are finally discovering how rich their own culture is.

During my travels in the Central African rainforests, the Pygmies told me many stories about chimps and gorillas, which ranged from the same behaviors observed by scientists to the truly extraordinary. A story recounted by Bakombe, a Pygmy who worked with Andrea Turkalo, fell into the former category. He spoke of how his father had told him once that he saw chimps dancing around a tree while making pleasure grunts and "having fun." This corresponded somewhat with Jane Goodall's account of seeing chimps perform what looked like a celebratory dance during a rainstorm.

It was possible that Bakombe was accurately reporting what his father saw, but I had no way of knowing.

The Pygmies had no problem acknowledging kinship with chimps. Said Teti, another of Andrea's guides, "Chimps are like us. They eat like us; they eat honey like we do." He then described how they would take a stick to enlarge a hole in a tree and then put their hand in to remove the honey. Teti said that he had never seen a gorilla use a tool. All the Pygmies I spoke with argued that chimps were far smarter than gorillas.

Then there were the more fantastic stories, some subsequently verified and others yet to be confirmed. Teti had said that gorillas and chimps don't get along, and to illustrate the bad blood he mentioned an encounter he had witnessed when he was out in the forest with his father as a boy. He said that he saw a battle between chimps and some gorillas, and that the chimps won, perhaps in part because they used sticks as weapons.

If confirmed, this would have been astonishing. The literature on chimp "warfare" is large, but I hadn't come across any accounts of fights between chimps and gorillas. Gorilla social structure, organized around a silverback and his harem, is not nearly as complex as chimp society. I didn't know of any examples of gorillas cooperating in warfare, so in theory at least, I could imagine that an organized group of chimp males might have an advantage over a silverback-led group, despite the huge gorilla advantage in size and strength. Chimps are well known to use sticks in threat displays, but no one had ever reported on chimps using sticks purposefully as weapons either in competition with other males or in battle. Finally, chimps and gorillas are typically not in proximity to each other. So to believe what Teti described, I would have had to suspend disbelief about an increasingly incredible series of behaviors.

A year later, when I was on another trip into the forest, another Pygmy guide shared an account of chimps using sticks to do battle with gorillas, likewise citing this as evidence that chimps were smarter than gorillas. Once again I figured that he was confusing a threat display with actual weapon use. Once again I did not think the story worthy of mention in the article I was writing on apes and humans. Once again I may have been wrong.

In 2000 I ran into Richard Wrangham, one of the world's leading experts on chimpanzees, at an interdisciplinary meeting on animal intelligence convened by the Chicago Academy of Sciences in honor of the thirty-fifth anniversary of Jane Goodall's establishment of the Gombe Stream

Reserve. I knew Wrangham from interviews I had conducted during the reporting of my story on apes and humans for *National Geographic*. He was cautious but excited when he passed along some news: Two of the researchers at his study site in Uganda had witnessed chimps using weapons to beat other chimps. His caution was merited because of the paucity of data. With such a small database, the behavior might be the product of anything, including happenstance.

Still, I instantly remembered what Teti had told me years earlier. I also knew that I had to get to Kibale, Wrangham's research station, and the opportunity presented itself a year later when I received an urgent request to go to Nairobi, Kenya, in the summer of 2001 to do some last-minute editing/ rewriting of a United Nations paper on desertification. It was just a brief flight from Nairobi to Entebbe, and I figured that after my work was done, I could take on a trip to Kibale before flying home. Because of the imminent deadline I booked my flight to Kenya for the very next day, and so I immediately called Wrangham, who graciously agreed to contact the two American researchers then in residence and let them know that I would be stopping by. As for directions, he might have been guiding me to the local Starbucks: "Get to Fort Portal," he said as though this were the easiest thing in the world, "and then find the cab stand near the post office. They all know the way, and the trip takes about forty-five minutes." This was not a lot to go on, but I did not have time to worry about details.

I was set, or as set as things ever are when a trip in Africa is involved.

━━━

Wrangham, who is an expert on chimp warfare, established the research program in Kibale in 1988. He began his work at Jane Goodall's Gombe Stream Reserve, and in the course of one of his studies of intergroup raids discovered that during them chimps show none of the restraint that mutes the consequences of fights to improve status within a group. Sometimes raiding groups will hold an enemy chimp down while others try to rip him apart.

Wrangham argues that this rare natural instance of intraspecies warfare is, for better or worse, one piece of evidence of the extremely close links between humans and chimps. He believes that the shared trait of conducting warfare suggests that human proclivities to wage war predate the dawn of the hominid line. Wrangham developed this argument in *Demonic*

Males: Apes and the Origins of Human Violence (1996), which he coauthored with Dale Peterson.

Some studies have shown that as many as one-third of all male chimps die at the hands of other chimps. With that kind of kill rate, who needs weapons? Hence, I was simply fascinated when Wrangham first told me about what his researchers had seen in the forests of Uganda.

The writing job in Nairobi was intense, but it went well, and after I finished I took the short flight to Entebbe. I arrived at the Grand Imperial Hotel in Kampala at about midnight, and its name proved to be quite accurate, since the sprawling building had clearly seen its best days when Uganda was part of the British Empire. My plan was to get up early, hire a reliable car and driver, and head out that morning. To get to Fort Portal, we would have to traverse the entire width of the country, but Wrangham had said the trip could be done in six to eight hours. With any luck I would arrive in Fort Portal before sunset, and with any luck we could get directions to the research site, and with any luck Kathi Pieta, who ran the chimp station, would have received my message and not turn me away. (I'd sent an e-mail, but Wrangham had said that the staff collected e-mails only intermittently when they made trips into town.)

If my journey was successful, I would get up early and tag along if someone was planning to follow the chimps. I've visited most of the major great ape research stations over the years and am fairly familiar with the etiquette of following chimps, gorillas, bonobos and orangutans in the wild. After interviewing as many of the researchers and field assistants as I could fit into this short schedule, I planned to have my hypothetically reliable driver pick me up and take me back to Kampala. Faced with a plethora of other deadlines, I had to get back to the United States quickly.

The plan contained more ifs than Rudyard Kipling's poem, and enough hope to loft a dirigible. In fact it was preposterous. In a country where reliable cars are as rare as rhinos, where the roads have one of the worst accident rates in the world, and where you never know what various armed guerrilla groups are up to, I was leaving myself no margin for error. It would have been absurd for me to try to limit myself to one day's reporting had this research station been in the Catskills, but it was little short of lunacy trying to do so halfway around the planet in one of the more remote corners of Africa.

Sometimes you have a feeling about these things, though, and when my plane landed in Entebbe without incident, I felt I was off to a good start. The feeling continued the next morning when the hotel concierge found me a car and an affable driver who said that he could take me across the country and back for a reasonable fee, plus gas. (I asked the man his name three times, but he was so shy and his accent so thick that I heard only a murmur that sounded like "Marcel.") I took a long look at his run-down Toyota. It seemed okay, and indeed, but for a persistent and ultimately maddening pinging that accompanied us all 900 kilometers of the trip, the car ran fine.

Marcel said that the direct road between Kampala and Fort Portal was bad, so we took a circuitous route south to Mbarra and then up through Kasese. Once outside Kampala we did not encounter a single traffic light during the entire trip. Marcel kept the speedometer needle pressed close to 120 kilometers per hour except on those occasions when we passed through villages, when he dropped to 100 kph.

If Uganda vies for superlatives in any category in Africa, it has the best shot at the title for the most dangerous roads. The problem is that they are just good enough to encourage extreme high-speed driving. On the other hand, there are no traffic lights or other controls whatsoever. During my trip to Kibale, 3.3 percent of the nation's sportswriters were killed in just one head-on collision, according to the *Monitor,* a lively tabloid. The only real limit on the death toll seems to be the price of gas, which keeps most vehicles off the road. As it was, most of the cars we encountered seemed to be official vehicles of one of the myriad organizations attempting to better the lives of Ugandans.

Since I wrote *The Alms Race* in 1976, I have made many trips through the continent. All too often it's been a depressing experience, and this was no exception. Arrayed along the road were village after village, indistinguishable from those I had passed on my first visit to East Africa in 1974. The only difference now was that there were more villages and fewer forests. Growth without development has been the central narrative of sub-Saharan Africa.

At some point it became clear that Marcel didn't know where we were going, so we started asking for directions in Kasese, 70 kilometers to the south of Fort Portal. As it turned out, however, when we finally did arrive, Wrangham's suggestion did the trick. In rundown Fort Portal, we found plenty of cabbies who knew the station, but none who could explain how to get there. Everybody kept saying, "Turn right up ahead," but we suspected it was more complicated than that. We hired a kid on a motorcycle to lead the way.

We arrived at the station just as the sun was setting. I gave my driver some money for a room and meal back in Fort Portal, and then introduced myself. At the station were Kathi Pieta, who ran the station while completing her studies for the University of Vienna, and Kim Duffy, who was doing research as part of her graduate work at UCLA. Naturally, they had no idea I was coming, but to my relief, they knew who I was from my earlier writings on apes and were quite hospitable. At Richard's suggestion I came bearing gifts—some food and, more important, wine.

In terms of amenities the camp itself was in the midrange of research stations I've visited. The buildings were solid, the latrines well designed, and there was even water for washing up. We enjoyed our dinner out on the camp's simple porch. The camp cook had died two weeks earlier of AIDS, so Kathi worked up a nice meal of rice and sauce spiced by some sardines I had brought along and accompanied by a Wente Cabernet Sauvignon. Kim, fighting some tropical bug, passed on the food but joined the conversation, and the two graduate students told me a bit about the Kanyawara community of chimps.

The group then consisted of about fifty chimps, including about ten adult males, seventeen mothers in three different geographic groupings, and assorted other infants, adolescent males and nonreproducing females. The Kanyawara chimps don't seem to hunt as much as other chimps in the region but will go after red colobus monkeys when the opportunity presents itself.

Farther up the mountain slopes lay the Ngogo Primate Project run by John Mitani of the University of Michigan and David Watts, who began his work with primates at Karisoke. Hunting figures far more prominently in the Ngogo chimp community, with prey that includes black and white colobus, mangabeys, duikers, and red tail monkeys, as well as red colobus. (The Ngogo chimps apparently also had epic confrontations with neighboring chimp communities, with up to forty male chimps squaring off against one another in battle.)

In the Kanyawara community, Imoso was then the top dog. Described as young and very aggressive, he had seized the dominant spot in 1998 when the former alpha male, Big Brown, found himself hampered by a snare caught on one hand that forced him to carry around a big log until he eventually got free of the wire. Imoso did not seem to be a popular leader, among either the chimps or their human observers.

His reputation did not improve among the researchers with the discovery that he was a wife beater. As Carole Hooven, the researcher who first saw the behavior, described the attack, Imoso had been trying to get at Outamba's infant. Perhaps afraid that Imoso intended harm (there have been cases of infanticide in the Kanyawara community), Outamba fended off his efforts. This seemed to enrage Imoso, who began kicking and punching Outamba, who exposed her back to Imoso while she cradled and protected the infant.

Carole took notes in her neat, precise handwriting, and then prepared a summary of the attack for Richard Wrangham. As she described what happened next: "MS [Imoso] first attacks OU [Outamba] with one stick for about 45 seconds, holding it with his right hand, near the middle of the stick. She was hit about 5 times with the stick. My notes read that he beat her 'hard.' (The stick was bought down on her in a somewhat inefficient way—if I were to hit someone with a stick, I'd raise a bent arm, holding the stick at an angle to the object I was hitting, and swing the stick down. MS seemed to start with the stick almost parallel to the body and bring it down in a parallel motion. There was a slight angle to his motion, but not the way a human would do it for maximum impact.) During this first beating, she was also punched and kicked several times."

After resting for a minute, Imoso resumed the attack, this time with two sticks, again held toward the middle of the stick. The assault continued with Imoso hurting Outamba in a number of creative ways, once hanging from a branch above her and stamping on her with his feet. To Carole the attack seemed "interminable." Throughout the beating, Outamba protected the infant, and indeed, toward the end, her three-year-old son, Tenkere, gallantly rushed to her aid, pounding on Imoso's back with his little fists.

Imoso may have started a new trend in Kanyawara. Johnny, his best friend, was the next to beat up poor Outamba in the summer of 2000 during the fruiting season of the *Uvariopsis* trees, which provided a favorite food for the chimp community. Again, Outamba's infant daughter seemed to figure in the attack. Kathi was observing Outamba when, seemingly for no reason, Johnny attacked the youngster. Outamba again attempted to protect her offspring, whereupon Johnny turned on her. He tried to hit her, and immediately she became submissive.

Johnny was not to be appeased, however, and after first stepping on Outamba, he picked up a big stick and started hitting her. Excited by the commotion, two other young males came galloping over, displaying, at which point Outamba seized her opportunity to escape and fled to a tree. The whole attack lasted perhaps three minutes. After a short while in the tree, Outamba came down and acceded to Johnny's invitation to copulate. He left the stick on the forest floor. After the chimps moved on, Kathi Pieta retrieved the stick, which is now at the Museum of Anthropology at Harvard.

After the encounter, the humans were stunned, knowing they had witnessed something important but, again, not quite sure what it meant. You don't launch a study based on two observations, but the researchers did start paying attention to the ways in which chimps used sticks.

I was to learn more about the niceties of sticks as weapons when I woke at 4:45 to meet up with Kathi; Donor, the head tracker; and another tracker, Francis Mugurousi, to go in search of Johnny, Imoso, and their beleaguered wives. We left at 5:30 and after a vigorous walk reached the area of a fruiting ficus tree where the chimps had built their nests the previous evening. At 6:30 we heard the first pant hooting, and by 6:50 the chimps were already feeding in the ficus down the trail.

Johnny was there, as were Mokoko and a number of other chimps. Imoso had not been seen for several months. As we watched, a little three-year-old female was struggling to get up into the ficus. The trunk at the base was far too large for her to grab, so first she tried climbing a neighboring sapling. Finding the gap too wide, she carefully jumped to another, closer tree. No luck here either, so the determined toddler tried a third tree. Success! She managed to transfer from a branch of this sapling to a part of the ficus trunk that she could grasp. Donor applauded. He was a good-humored man who clearly was very fond of the animals he tracks.

Donor and Francis brought with them "urine sticks," which had an absorbent sponge on top that they used to collect urine samples from leaves when the chimps above peed. The samples were used for genetic testing and for monitoring hormone levels. As he took a sample, I asked Donor for his thoughts on why Imoso had attacked Outamba. "Imoso is just a mean chimp," he replied, adding that he knew he was witnessing something extraordinary when he saw the beating, but his excitement was tempered by his sympathy for poor Outamba. Donor also confirmed that the chimp's hitting stroke was not particularly efficient if he was trying to inflict maximum damage. "It was not like a man hitting another with a stick," said Donor.

Francis had viewed his share of beatings as well. He saw Imoso beat one female after inspecting her and discovering she was not ready for copulation. In this instance, he picked up one stick and beat her, then dropped it and picked up another to continue the beating.

While all the instances thus far observed had involved males hitting females, Francis and others had observed male chimps threaten other males with sticks. Francis noted that Johnny attacked one male named Stocky in 1998. After screaming, Stocky picked up his own one-meter-long stick. Seeing this, Johnny stopped his attack and ran into a tree. On another occasion, during a charge Imoso picked up a half-meter-long stick and threw it at another male named Tofu, but missed.

The attacks raise many more questions than answers. Is this a new behavior, or merely the first observation of one that has persisted for thousands of years? Why is it that the chimps seem to use sticks more often against females than males? Is it because the stick as weapon is a new technology and the risks are lower testing it against females, who are no physical match for the males? When I spoke to him on my return to the United States, Richard Wrangham noted that male-male attacks have such high stakes that few males would risk trying out a weapon before they were certain that it would work.

On the other hand, no one knows what chimps do during the 99 percent of the time that they are out of sight of humans. If they ever develop an efficient swing, they could, with their incredible strength, do real damage to each other and to other species. Wrangham also said that maybe one out of a hundred sticks lying around in the forest might be robust enough to withstand a blow delivered by an adult male chimp.

After a while the chimps moved off. We followed, Kathi occasionally jotting in her notebook. The blond graduate student had a diffident manner, but she moved with easy confidence in the forest and didn't miss a thing. We had not gone far when the chimps simply melted into the thick undergrowth, providing an excellent demonstration of the virtues of knuckle-walking in such areas. As they disappeared on what seemed like a very deliberate route, I asked Kathi which of the chimps made the plan for the day. "Johnny thinks he does," she said with a laugh.

The preliminary evidence of weapon use may be an exciting discovery, but the last thing these and other chimps need is another way to hasten their own extinction. The Kanyawara chimps already have plenty of external threats to cope with. Apart from intermittent guerrilla activity, there are poachers who set snares to catch whatever comes along. Even if the chimp manages to get free of a wire, it often loses a hand. One chimp, Nectar, eventually lost both hands and starved when she could no longer climb, according to Kathi. The station now has two full-time employees dedicated to finding and destroying snares.

After failing to reestablish contact with Johnny and his chimp gang, we made our way back to the station, where I had further discussions with Kim Duffy and other trackers who stopped by. Then my driver arrived and, again accompanied by the incessant pinging in his car, we made our way, at insane speed, back to Kampala.

———

Back in New York, exhausted, having flown straight from Entebbe, I experienced that inevitable sense of relief that comes from leaving an impoverished, disease-ravaged region that bears the scars of war and returning to the relative safety and comfort of my home just outside New York City. I returned on September 8, 2001, three days before the airplanes crashed into the World Trade Center, horribly underscoring our superiority over chimps in the development and use of weapons.

Still, we don't really know what we don't know about what chimps do in the wild. Absence of evidence is not evidence of absence. In the meantime, researchers continue to ponder the mysteries of chimp weapons in a type of *CSI Chimpanzee*. For instance: Why sticks, not rocks? Chimps do use rocks in food gathering and, in the Tai Forest, to smash nuts. At Gombe chimps have used rocks in hunting. In one documented instance, a male threw a rock at an adult forest pig in order to separate it from a piglet the chimps were hunting. A chimp could mortally injure another chimp by hitting it with a rock.

Both Richard Wrangham and Carole Hooven speculate that this might be one reason for the preference for sticks: Their intention is to inflict hurt rather than serious injury. Most of the attacks have been directed at sexually active females, and while the males might intend harm to the babies, they have nothing to gain by killing their mates. Brutal as it seems, is it possible that the use of sticks is an indicator of restraint rather than a chimp arms race?

It's also possible that chimps are simply more familiar with sticks. They use them occasionally to scratch themselves, and, more to the point, they will sometimes throw sticks at mangabeys to chase them away from fruits that the chimps covet. I had wild chimps throw branches at me, but this was clearly for show, as the branch fell harmlessly to the ground. They also use sticks as props during threat displays. A male wants to look as big and threatening as possible during a threat, and he will seize on anything to help it do so. (One intriguing development observed since the first attack has been instances in which young females carry sticks. In this case, however, the females hold the sticks more like dolls than weapons, sometimes even placing them in little nests.)

Perhaps the use of weapons grew out of threat behavior, but there are many other possibilities. Carole wonders whether Imoso might have gotten the idea from seeing farmers who have invaded the park brandish sticks and machetes at the chimps when they stage crop raids. Wrangham doubts this, but whatever the origins, Uganda is a fitting locale for the first observation of a primate using a weapon against one of its own.

But this was not to be the last word on chimpanzees using weapons. Six years later, in 2007, Jill Preust of Iowa State University announced her findings that savannah chimps in Senegal fashion sticks into spears, which they use to hunt small primates called bush babies. We are likely to learn more about chimps and weapons, as one of the noteworthy takeaways of chimp research over the past four decades is that observers continue to find evidence of new behaviors in well-studied populations of animals.

"New" in this case means new to science, and not necessarily to chimp behavior in general. For instance, since the 1980s Swiss scientist Christophe Boesch has been observing chimps using granite stones to crack panda nuts in the Tai Forest in the Ivory Coast. (The chimps place the nuts on flat wood or a rock and then use the stone to break open the nut.) When I went to visit Christophe there in 1990, no one knew how long chimps had been using these stone tools. Then, in 2007, Julio Mercader of the University of Calgary uncovered ancient nut-cracking stones in Tai that dated back 4,300 years—even before early Africans started using agriculture in that region. The discovery underscores the point that chimps could do something in proximity to humans for thousands of years before the behavior was first discovered by science.

The other lesson of these discoveries is that "new to science" also does not mean new to the Pygmies who have lived in the forests for thousands of years as well. Testimony of Pygmies about chimp and gorilla behavior has often turned out to be a long-leading indicator of what scientists eventually see for themselves. That productive synergy will last only as long as Pygmies continue to go into the forests, there are forests for them to go in to, and there are apes in the forests to be seen.

But all that may not be the case for much longer. A few years after I visited the Tai Forest, an Ebola epidemic decimated the colony I had observed, wiping out twenty-five chimps in a population that numbered just a few score. A few more such outbreaks or a poaching massacre, and there might not be chimps to pass on the knowledge of how to use stones to crack panda nuts. Whatever forest peoples visited the Tai Forest vanished long ago, and the forest itself has only a fragile purchase in an increasingly desiccated (in the time Christophe has been studying the Tai Forest, it has already lost one of its two rainy seasons) and deforested surrounding landscape.

The Central African rainforests, where Teti the Ba'Aka Pygmy claimed to have witnessed chimps battling gorillas, have a better chance of persisting, but there are no guarantees that if they do, they will be populated with chimps and gorillas, or that Pygmies will maintain their unsurpassed knowledge of the terrain and its animals. I have no idea whether Teti was being honest about his accounts or simply pulling my leg, trying to see how far he could go in spinning tales for gullible visitors. His tale certainly strains credulity, but so did the now-confirmed assertion that chimps use sticks as weapons.

If these interspecies battles are confirmed sometime in the future, it will be very good news—not because it will mean that another species besides humans uses weapons in organized warfare, but because it will mean that there will be chimps and gorillas still living their lives in their natural habitats.

PART V

THE ANTIPODES: THE LONG REACH OF HUMANITY

CHAPTER 11

Unfreezing Time

Humans cannot really live in Antarctica except for a few brief months during its summer, and then only with precautions similar to those one might take in preparing to live on the moon. That said, humanity is having a profound impact on the vast continent. Thanks to our meddling with the chemistry of the atmosphere, we have pulled off a necromancer's trick: We have unfrozen time.

On the great ice sheets at the southern end of the earth, the far past and the present meet daily. The past rises from the depths of the sheets in the form of temperature changes in the ice that are ghosts of climates long past. In other parts of Antarctica, time doesn't stop, but rather walks in place. Antarctica is an illusionist itself, and its conundrums are but one aspect of the continent's personality. It also presents a face of haphazard ferocity, where nature is in charge. The ocean surrounding Antarctica is the stormiest on earth; its storms are the strongest. Antarctica is earth's highest continent, with an average elevation of roughly 7,000 feet, but also the lowest, since the actual land surface is about 1,600 feet below sea level. The enormous weight of two miles of ice compresses the very crust of the earth. In some places Antarctica's beauty derives from its immense scale and extremes, in others from its purity, and in others from its colors.

Antarctica is an alien icebox, isolated from the habitable world by ramparts of ocean and air currents. Those who make the trek to this antipode venture into a redoubt where the normal rules don't seem to apply. In fact, much of the strangeness one encounters there results from the simplicity with which the workings of geophysics play out in the slow-motion world of extreme cold without the interference of biology. The consequences can be magical. Scientists report seeing icebergs and islands hovering upside down on the horizon. Through the mechanics of physics, Antarctica can confer on a dead seal the splendor of Arthurian burial rites.

Let's say, for instance, that a seal dies in shallow waters. The corpse will quickly freeze to the bottom of the ice at low tide, and rise slowly to the top as ice forms below it and evaporates above. Once it has made its way to the surface, the seal's body rises onto a pedestal as it insulates the underlying ice from the sun. Eventually the ice breaks up, and the seal, now mummified by the sun and dry air, drifts out to sea. If cold air is flowing down from the ice sheets, the refraction of the sun's rays will create a mirage and it will appear as if the seal is standing as it sails off toward its icy Avalon.

In other parts of Antarctica, dead seals experience perpetual resurrection as a result of the interplay of sun and ice in an environment that never changes. For instance, a short helicopter ride from McMurdo, the main American base on the continent, lie the Dry Valleys, so named because they are free of ice. Scattered through these valleys are frozen lakes fed by runoff from the scores of glaciers that hover at the edges of the valleys. Seals occasionally wander into these valleys but quickly die of the cold (the average annual temperature is 20 below Celsius) or starve—the valleys are so devoid of any form of life that a surgeon could operate on a patient lying on its soil without fear of introducing an infection.

Some of these ill-fated seals end up on the ice on top of Lake Hoare, deposited there by a glacier that abuts one end of the lake. The lake ice averages 15 feet thick. During the Antarctic summer, the dark fur of the freeze-dried seals absorbs sunlight, and the slightly warmed bodies gradually melt the ice around them. In the process they might sink several feet into the ice until they reach an equilibrium point where the sun's rays no longer deliver enough heat to melt the surrounding ice.

Then the processes that give other seals Arthurian burial rites come into play as the lake ice evaporates from the top and freezes from the bottom. Eventually, the seal carcass starts rising, pushed up from below by the newly frozen ice, and as the body approaches the surface the ice evaporates above it. The process continues until the seal reaches the surface, but unlike the seals shipped out to sea by calving from the ice shelf, these freeze-dried mummies are unable to leave the lake. And so the whole cycle begins anew. From the perspective of puny human time scales, this extremely slow-motion bobbing can go on forever.

In 1996 I visited the Dry Valleys as part of a National Science Foundation fellowship program that brings writers and artists to Antarctica. "Dry" is an understatement—it's likely that it hasn't rained there for more than 2 million years. There's precious little precipitation anywhere on the continent, and the valleys are the driest place in Antarctica. Almost all of what meager water vapor gets picked up from the Ross Sea has been wrung out of the air as it travels over the enormous East Antarctic Ice Sheet before it gets to the Dry Valleys.

The valleys form a basin, and tiny amounts of meltwater flow—if that's the word—into Lake Vanda, the lowest point in the area. Most of that flow comes from the Onyx, Antarctica's mightiest river. Crossing the river during "flood" requires one large step for most adults, and the river flows only a few days each year.

The trip to the Dry Valleys was perhaps the most memorable part of my itinerary, which also took me to the edge of the Ross Ice Shelf, a research station on the West Antarctic Ice Sheet, and the South Pole. As always in Antarctica, I was bundled up in clothes issued by the NSF reflecting the latest thinking of their cold-weather specialists. Apart from multiple windbreaking, thermal and insulating layers, I also wore a balaclava and hard-shelled "moon" boots designed for extreme cold. It was a bit cumbersome but effective.

Clothing merits a short digression, because strict rules concerning it are the visitor's first indication of the extremes to be encountered in Antarctica. The National Science Foundation insists that visitors wear NSF-issued clothing and adhere to its rules on how it is to be worn. Some of the most frightening nonfiction writing available comes from the drily written guides supplied by the NSF for visitors to the continent, which methodically cite the dangers that lurk—ranging from being flash-frozen by a ground blizzard to losing limbs to helicopter blades—should one be so foolish as to fail to dress properly for the weather or to ignore safety precautions.

The resident scientists treat the cumbersome bureaucratic procedures as a necessary evil. When I asked for some paper prior to my trip out to the Dry Valleys, one scientist joked, "Oh, you have to fill out a 1047-3 requisition form," while another chimed in, "And be sure to take the paper-cut training course."

I was lucky enough to escape any truly bad weather during my visit, but some of my fellow travelers did not. When I visited a camp on the West Antarctic Ice Sheet, the weather was sunny and the wind low. A producer from the BBC told me that when she went to the same site a week later, her hands froze to the point that she couldn't zip up her pants following a trip to the latrine. Another journalist recalled his latrine experiences when he went to Meteorite Alley, a place so scoured by the howling winds that geologists go there to collect meteorites deposited millions of years ago. He said it was so frigid that a trip to relieve oneself was a highly choreographed affair, during which the principal actor waited until the point of peak urgency before making a mad dash to the latrine and consummating the transaction in a matter of seconds. In Antarctica even the simplest bodily functions require planning and involve risk.

My luck with the weather held when I went out to the Dry Valleys, although this was not that surprising since, by its very nature, the area is spared some of the sudden and dangerous storms that appear out on the ice sheets. The valleys rank among earth's simplest ecosystems.

In an unfortunate parody of the slogan "What happens in Vegas, stays in Vegas," the Dry Valleys are so simple that a visitor can retrace the paths of expeditions from the 1950s simply by looking at the ground. What the Dry Valleys get, the Dry Valleys keep, and that includes footprints and trash. The NSF realized this years ago and instituted a strict carry-in/carry-out policy that applies to everything, including sewage, although the scientists I spoke to complained that their efforts to keep the region pristine were regularly undermined by tourists flown in from Russian cruise ships who traipsed around, heedless of the extraordinary vulnerability of the area.

Still, the resident scientists try their best to tread lightly on the land. Those who stay there for the scientific season, the summer, make do with an absolute minimum of material comfort. Setting aside the cost of having goods delivered, if the rest of the developed world lived like scientists in the Dry Valleys, the price of oil would probably be $2 a barrel, and no one would be worried about running out of resources.

The Dry Valleys are frozen in time. About a hundred glaciers poke their noses into the valleys, but that's as far as they get, as all are frozen solid to the earth beneath them. Ice is pushed forward into the valleys over the frozen base, but an exquisite balance of precipitation, melting and evaporation keeps them almost exactly in place. With the bottom of the glacier stuck, the incoming ice folds over the top. An ultra-slow-motion camera would show the glacier to be "moonwalking," à la Michael Jackson.

I saw dramatic evidence of this when I went into a tunnel that a glaciologist, Howard Conway of New Zealand's University of Auckland, had bored into the base of the Meserve glacier. Meserve has been stuck in roughly the same position for a million years. At the base of its terminus is a roughly 20-meter apron of ice that consists of shards shed by the hill-like front face of the glacier. Conway remarks that the spot at the edge of the apron is roughly where the glacier terminated 15,000 years ago as the last ice age wound down. A little farther out is a moraine that contains volcanic ash dated to 3.7 million years ago, and not far beyond that is another moraine that is even older. This moraine is so ancient that its boulders have been pulverized to gravel solely by the action of the wind.

Conway dug his tunnel in 1995. All glaciers have dirty layers at their base, as the mass of ice picks up detritus from the earth, and lower layers of the ice fold as the glacier makes its slow progress. Conway wanted to look at the dynamics of this folding in part so that scientists who drill holes in glaciers and study ice cores for clues to ancient climates could have a better idea of whether and how folding skews the record of the past as the coring samples are taken from ice closer to the bottom. (If the ice has folded over itself, for instance, the ice core record would produce what looked like extreme gyrations in climate when none in fact took place.) Because of the extraordinary stability of the Dry Valleys, Meserve offered a perfect site for Conway to examine this problem.

Conway's experiment was as simple as the valleys. After digging a tunnel into the base of the glacier (not without risk, because the face is constantly shedding huge blocks of ice), the scientist drove a series of bolts into the side of the tunnel in a straight vertical line from bottom to top and left them for a year—until about the time of my visit.

Conway himself wasn't there the day I came to the valleys, but his colleague Charles Raymond from the University of Washington took me to the tunnel. Charlie, as he is called, is a grizzled veteran of many seasons in Antarctica. He has long gray hair and an affable disposition. It seems as though there is nothing he'd rather talk about than ice.

The walls on the side of the tunnel showed a relatively clear bottom layer, followed by a layer of amber-colored ice (discolored by dirt picked up from the bottom), and then clearer ice above that. As for the bolts, the bottommost series of bolts remained nearly vertical—confirming Conway's supposition that the cold (-17°C) bottom ice was frozen to the underlying ground. The amber layer had moved out toward the edge a bit, while the upper layer was still closer to vertical. Conway interpreted this to mean that the amber ice was folding over the base ice, carrying forward the amber ice on top of it. Picture the way thick molasses would move if its bottom layer were stuck to a tilted pan. As for the clear ice on the bottom, Conway's explanation was that this was ice that had fallen off the edges of the glacier and then become squeezed solid as the ice mass moved over it.

So there it was, the image of how a glacier moves. In some respects, it is like moonwalking; in others, like molasses. Perhaps the most apt image, however, is that of a very large and very slow amoeba that extends a pseudo-podium of ice and then advances over the slick surface.

After we exited, Charlie filled me in on some of the properties of the thousand feet of ice that was massed above us when we were in the tunnel. Ice moves in response to a variety of forces, dominant among them gravity. As the ice in a glacier thickens, the weight and composition of the ice itself create stresses and strains. At about 400 meters thick, the ice is subject to 1 bar of stress, a bar being equivalent to one atmosphere or the pressure under 10 meters of water. Charlie explained that once the stress rises above 1 bar, the ice begins to deform, thinning and spreading out rapidly. Though the action is imperceptible to impatient humans, glaciers and ice sheets are alive with movement, belying the static implications of the word "frozen." Big masses of ice don't just fold and spread; there are streams of ice that move through them, sloughing off excess accumulation when they reach the terminus.

Paul Langevin, who studied the Canada glacier that flows into the valleys, has also monitored the forces maintaining the stability of the area. Because the area surrounding the Dry Valleys is a desert, there is very little accumulation of ice each year, while the sun melts between 20 and 50 centimeters of ice annually (depending on the angle of the sun as it hits the face or top of the glacier) through sublimation, as ice evaporates here without ever becoming water. The glacier is also flowing forward a few meters a year, but it never advances because the sun hits its face and because the front is continuously calving ice. Because of these relatively rapid movements, Langevin believes that the ice in this glacier is only thousands, rather than hundreds of thousands, of years old. So, even though a million-year time-lapse film of the glacier would show extraordinary stability, the ice of which it is made is constantly changing.

The great glaciers of Antarctica convey solidity, permanence and awesome scale, but the geology of the Dry Valleys also reveals how much more vast the continent's ice sheets once were. Looking at the bare, flattened, 8,000-foot-tall mountaintops that surround the valleys, it's possible to envision the scale of the massive ice sheet that once extended over what is now the one ice-free spot on the continent. Seeing those flattened mountaintops is a reminder that change does come to the Dry Valleys, though on unimaginably long time scales. The last time these valleys were wet—about 13.8 million years ago according to recent studies—was several million years before ancestral forms of humans started trying to figure out how stone tools worked. Four and a half million years ago, there were two very large lakes in the valleys, of which the twenty or so much smaller present-day lakes are remnants.

Now, like some geologic-scale Rip Van Winkle, the lakes have begun to awaken and change again.

While the rest of the world began warming at an accelerating rate in the 1980s, for the most part Antarctica stayed on the sidelines. Perhaps the warming strengthened the Antarctic vortex, the air currents that encircle the continent, further insulating it. Or perhaps something else was at work since there is no more complex system than climate.

In recent years, however, the effects of warming have been creeping into Antarctica, most notably at its edges. The Antarctic Peninsula, which once reached like an umbilicus toward South America and now juts out beyond the protective cordon sanitaire established by the Antarctic vortex, has warmed dramatically in recent years. As temperatures have shot up on the peninsula, ice shelves, some of which had been in place for thousands of years, have collapsed. In the case of the Larsen B Ice Shelf, the collapse took just a few weeks and was captured by satellite imagery. Similarly, on April 6, 2009, the 40-kilometer-long ice bridge that tethered the Wilkins Ice Shelf to the Antarctic Peninsula disintegrated, making the Wilkins the tenth major ice shelf to collapse in recent times.

While the warming of the peninsula is understandable, even if it is not reassuring, changes within the vortex are more disturbing. It's been snowing a bit more at the South Pole, for instance, a place conventionally thought to be beyond the reach of changes in the weather. Just before my visit, it rained at McMurdo Station, something never before documented in a place that previously encountered precipitation only in the form of snow. And then, a few years after my visit to the Dry Valleys, the area experienced what was described as a "flash flood."

This occurred during the summer season of 2001–2002. Only in the

Dry Valleys could the several-inches-deep flow of water that resulted from the warm temperatures that year be called a flood, but in a place where the weather never changes, change is highly noticeable. Accounts from that season report that the Onyx got so deep, scientists were forced to wear hip boots to wade across. Cracks appeared in the ordinarily smooth surface of the tops of the glaciers, providing more surfaces exposed to direct sunlight (the sun is always low in the sky at that latitude) and furthering melting. Temperatures rose as high as 10 degrees Celsius, and some veteran scientists ignored NSF guidelines and roamed the area in shirtsleeves.

While the flood provided them with a fabulous opportunity to study how a simple ecosystem responds when change comes (the lakes became less saline, algal mats were washed away, nematode populations exploded), it also raised questions. Was the warming part of some natural cycle, or was it evidence that human-caused changes in the atmosphere were beginning to penetrate Antarctica's formidable defenses against the rest of the world?

While the Dry Valleys provide a sensitive indicator of what might be happening in Antarctica, a large cohort of scientists is monitoring Antarctica's vast ice sheets, where any change would have global implications. The East Antarctic Ice Sheet dominates the continent, but the smaller West Antarctic Ice Sheet (WAIS) has been getting the most attention. "Smaller" is a relative term. To put it in perspective, consider that the melting of all the world's mountain glaciers would raise sea level by less than a foot and a half. If the WAIS disintegrated and slipped into the sea, it would raise sea level by 16 feet. (For the East Antarctic Ice Sheet, the number would be 170 feet.)

As is the case with a glacier, the outward stolidity of an ice sheet conceals a great deal of turmoil beneath the surface. Streams of ice move through the sheet, pushed and pulled by various forces within it, including gravity. When I was there, a number of scientists were trying to determine whether these streams have sped up. At that point, there was interest but little real anxiety that this vast mass of ice might collapse on a time scale meaningful to anyone living today. Now, thirteen years later, there is genuine concern that this might happen.

An analysis of temperature data taken from various points in Antarctica and published in *Nature* in 2009 provides "robust" evidence that the West Antarctic region has been warming significantly—not as fast as the peninsula that juts outside the Antarctic vortex, but still more rapidly than eastern Antarctica. Moreover, some of the ice streams that dump ice into the water near Pine Island are moving ever more briskly. This is alarming because the ice shelves surrounding Pine Island serve as a kind of doorstop, preventing the more rapid flow of ice into the sea. As we have seen in recent years, the breakup of ice shelves can be quite rapid.

As this has focused the mind, one unresolved issue has gained the status of an interesting question: When was the last time the ice sheet disappeared? When I spoke with glaciologist Ian Whillans (he died in 2001, and an important part of the West Antarctic Ice Sheet now bears his name), he noted that the positive feedbacks that turn a slow decay into a rapid disintegration are very difficult to model and that "this gets you nervous about predictability." Another ice sheet specialist, Reed Sherer, told me that the most surprising thing about the WAIS would be if it was much older or much younger than everybody thinks. If it turned out to be younger than 100,000 years old, it would make everybody extremely nervous. If, on the other hand, the WAIS was older than 10 million years, we might breathe easier, because that would imply that it survived through the last protracted warm period, 400,000 years ago. (To put in perspective how warm that period was, the polar front retreated to 58 degrees south, versus its present variance between 48 and 52 degrees.)

Sherer then went on to answer his own question by finding diatoms in an ice stream dubbed Upstream B that strongly indicated that there was open water under that region 400,000 years ago. He could date when the diatoms were laid down by comparing their chemical composition with that of other diatoms, a process called biostratigraphy, which is analogous to matching tree rings to calibrate dates. The discovery that a great ice sheet like the WAIS might collapse during an interglacial warm period is not reassuring, particularly since we are now busily engineering our own warm period.

Our hope is that the longer wavelength phenomena of the overlapping time scales at play in the workings of the ice sheet will prove to dominate in the struggle of forces that determine when the ice sheet might collapse. If it can take 10,000 years for a pulse of warming entombed in the ice to make its way from the bottom of the sheet to the top, then maybe a collapse will take place in slow motion as well. Unfortunately, that remains only a hope, not a confident prediction, and that hope is challenged by the increasing drumbeat of disintegrating ice shelves as well as an alarming shrinkage in the Greenland ice sheet in the north.

Change in Antarctica is already taking its toll on creatures that evolved to withstand the harshest imaginable conditions. The maturation of emperor penguins, for instance, has evolved in precise coordination with the breakup of sea ice during the Antarctic summer. When I visited Antarctica, Gerald Kloyman, a biologist who has devoted his career to studying the birds, told me that the ice that year broke up two weeks early, forcing the young to dive into the Southern Ocean before they were ready to cope with its many dangers, dooming most of the fledglings.

Outside of the vortex on the Antarctic Peninsula, changes have been equally dramatic. The area covered by sea ice has shrunk dramatically, and along with it the krill population (which depends on algae trapped in the sea ice). The peninsula penguin populations have begun to swing wildly, with Adélie numbers plummeting, while open-water-favoring penguins such as chinstraps and gentoos do better.

While a few might still question whether the climate changes in Antarctica are part of a natural cycle or the result of human activities, virtually no one disputes that the ozone hole that appears annually over the continent is a curse resulting from generations past when humanity used chlorofluorocarbons in refrigeration and spray cans. Initially CFCs were hailed as miracle compounds because they were supposedly harmless. (Their inventor, Charles Midgely, used to drink Freon to demonstrate its safety.) Though they might be benign here on earth, they wreaked havoc once they floated to the upper atmosphere, where it was discovered that tiny amounts of CFCs could act in concert with sunlight to destroy the ozone layer that protects life on earth from lethal cosmic radiation. Though CFCs are now banned, those already produced have a lifetime in the atmosphere measured in several decades. As a result, the ozone hole continues to reappear each year.

Because of the vast number of interrelated moving parts involved, it is practically impossible to predict how our alterations of the atmosphere will play out, particularly since damage to the ozone layer is taking place at the same time that humans are otherwise changing the chemical balance of the atmosphere through the release of greenhouse gases. We are going to have to wait and see the results of this real-time, inadvertent experiment with the fundamental recipe for life on earth.

In the meantime, the fractured, disintegrating, and disappearing ice is telling us that we are unfreezing time. Who knows what monsters will now awaken, and what they will bring with them as they lurch to life?

CHAPTER 12

The Arctic

I love the Far North. For many years I made it a point to try to get somewhere in or near the Arctic during the summer. Often these trips were put together at the last minute, and never was the call more last minute or more welcome than in July 1999, when I was driving back from Cape Cod to New York with my wife, Mary, and our then very young children. It was about 100 degrees, the kids were fighting and squalling in the back, and we'd just heard from friends staying at our house in Nyack that the one working air conditioner had broken and the house was an oven. Then my cell phone rang. It was my editor at *Time*, Charles Alexander. I'll re-create the key part of the conversation from Mary's point of view as she was sitting next to me in the car.

> EL: Let me get this straight: X [another *Time* writer] has dropped out, we've already paid for the trip, and you're asking me to leave for the Bering Sea in two days?
>
> EL: [listening]
>
> EL: Okay, hold on while I check with Mary.
> [I relay the request, stressing that I'm being asked to do this for the team. Mary stares at me with a look of disdainful skepticism that a prosecutor (she's a lawyer) might use to convey to the jury that the witness is the lowest form of life. I take this as assent.]
>
> EL: [back on phone with Charles] I think it'll work.

Three days later I was in the Pribilofs, shivering on St. Paul Island, directly in the middle of the frigid Bering Sea. "Forlorn" does not begin to describe this windswept landscape, where the sun may shine one day out of every two weeks. The vegetation is sparse and low, a result of the harsh climate and winds. Decades earlier the Coast Guard had planted a "national forest" as a joke in front of its station, and the scraggly evergreens were still just a few feet tall.

But take a trip to the island's cliffs, and an entirely different world unfolds, as I discovered when I rented a bicycle and rode out one day. (The island is only five miles long.) The islands are volcanic, and St. Paul's basalt cliffs rise over 1,000 feet from its rocky shores. There are no guardrails, of course, and you are on your own to trust that the crumbly soil and rock won't give way as you peer out over the edge, but your judgment, or luck, will be rewarded with one of the most spectacular sights you've ever seen.

Before getting to that, it's important to set the context. The Far North is very different from the Antarctic, and it is different in ways that leave its adjacent landmasses very sensitive to change. Antarctica has land on which to build an ice sheet, and a strong vortex that makes it easier to store cold. The North Pole is situated on an ocean, and there is water under and around it for 10 degrees latitude in all directions. This makes it easier for the north polar regions to shed cold, and also for heat from the south to penetrate northward. Sea ice and permafrost amplify and broadcast these heat transfers, giving the northern polar regions a disproportionate influence on the adjacent latitudes.

It all adds up to making the Far North something of a first responder to global changes. Over the years, I've witnessed these changes during several trips to Alaska and the Inside Passage (the island-sheltered seaway between Washington State and Alaska), visits to the Arctic coastland of Yakutia in Russia, and sailing trips in the seas north of Iceland, as well as trips to various points on Hudson Bay. Most of my trips, however, took place on either side of the Bering Sea, an area called Beringia.

Beringia's most noteworthy feature is the Bering Strait, a vital passage that now divides continents and connects oceans, but that once connected continents and divided oceans. This watery corridor separates the landmasses of Eurasia and North America and connects the vast waters of the Pacific basin with the frigid world of the Arctic seas. Beringia froths with life, as birds, whales, fish and other creatures are funneled by the converging continents through one narrow gateway during their seasonal migrations.

In bygone times, however, so much of the world's water was locked up in continent-sized ice sheets that sea levels dropped and the strait became a land bridge that enabled the ancestors of the Amerindians and great herds of mammoths and other beasts to trek from Eurasia to the Americas.

If the cold of the Antarctic preserves time and mummifies the dead, the remoteness of the north preserves life. Long after mammoths died out in the lower latitudes, they persisted in places like Wrangel Island, which lies about 90 miles north of the Russian Far East at about 71 degrees North latitude. In the 1990s paleontologists found bones of a dwarf mammoth that dated as recently as 3,600 years ago, several thousand years after other species of mammoths disappeared from the continent. Dwarf species like this raise profoundly intriguing questions in biogeography, a topic I'll address in a later chapter.

The southern border of Beringia is formed by the necklace of the Aleutian Islands, which extend so far to the west that the International Dateline has an indentation to accommodate them so that adjacent islands within eyeshot of one another aren't living simultaneously on different days. The Pribilofs lie in the middle of the sextant-shaped Bering Sea, 600 miles south of the Bering Strait, about 200 miles north of the Aleutians. The archipelago is so remote that the seafaring Aleut Indians never colonized it, despite their 10,000-year history in the area. Not until the eighteenth century, when Russian sealing vessels brought Aleuts to the islands to help them hunt the world's largest fur seal haul-out, did these natives first settle in the Pribilofs. Once sealers found the Pribilofs, they hunted the animals to within an inch of extermination. The decline of seal numbers became so alarming that an artist and Treasury Department special agent named Henry Wood Elliott began a campaign for protection that ultimately led to the 1911 North Pacific Fur Seal Treaty, the first international agreement to protect marine mammals.

While the Pribilofs are home to hare and arctic foxes (introduced, not native), life really begins at the water's edge. The cliffs are a birder's paradise, with horned puffins, murres, murrelets, auklets, cormorants, and other diving birds contributing to a 2.5-million-strong population of seabirds, one of the largest in the North Atlantic. While I watched from the cliffs, every few seconds a bird would take off and I'd be treated to a hunt, during which a puffin or murre would dive into the water far below and whirr like a torpedo after its prey. Once, as I was looking down, a Stellar sea lion, looking as big as a white whale, glided by. On the other side of the island, the largest fur seal colony in the Bering Sea was in full mating session, with unchivalrous 660-pound males tossing 110-pound females around as if they were beach balls.

As has been mostly the case during my career, I came to the Pribilofs not because everything there was going well, but because the region was under threat. At that time the Bering Sea was earth's only great fishery that was not in some stage of collapse, but there were troublesome portents, including a dramatic decline among Stellar sea lions—an 80 percent drop in their numbers since the 1970s—that suggested that all was not well. The fishery was and is huge, producing about 4 billion tons of bottom-dwelling pollock a year—the largest whitefish fishery in the world. Much of that catch ends up in frozen fish sticks or in meals served at Long John Silver's or Burger King.

Suspicion fell on overfishing because Stellar sea lion populations fared much better in places in southeast Alaska where there was no commercial fishing for pollock. Moreover, even if the total amount of fishing could be sustained relative to reproduction, conservationists were concerned that commercial fishing near the nurseries where the sea lions raised their young might still devastate populations.

The decline in numbers was a crisis for the Stellar sea lions of course, but equally bad news for every other creature in the food chain, starting with the orcas that feed on them. Orcas are very adaptable and resourceful creatures. With the disappearance of 2,500-pound male and 770-pound female sea lions, the orcas needed to find a substitute and began catching and killing sea otters to fill out their diet. Since the otters only weigh between 50 and 75 pounds, the orcas would have to eat a great number of them to keep up their weight. This may explain why otter numbers, too, have dropped (by 90 percent) in the past decade.

Since my visit in 1999, a number of scientists have filled out this picture. Jim Estes of the University of California, Santa Cruz argued that by reducing sea otter numbers, the orcas indirectly contributed to an explosion of sea urchins (the otters' primary food). That in turn led to the devastation of kelp forests, which serve as nurseries and protection for myriad fish and crustaceans.

Subsequently, other scientists explored this web of connections even further. Alan Springer, one of the scientists I spoke with during my trip to the

Pribilofs, wondered whether orcas had shifted to Stellar sea lions because an even larger potential food source—whales—had been depleted by whaling in the decades before a moratorium was put in place. This chain of logic is a hot topic for debate, in part because whale populations have since recovered, but there is not a lot of evidence that orcas have shifted back to hunting them.

And then there is the question of the role of global warming, which has dramatically shifted northward the southern edge of the sea ice, as well as the duration of the ice during the winter. This has had an entirely separate set of repercussions. It retards the blooming of the algae that form one pillar of the Arctic food chain; it deprives walruses, seals and seabirds of platforms to give birth and rest; and the warming waters penalize some of the sea creatures while rewarding others. In attempting to describe how these various forces have weighed on the Bering Sea, Alan Springer used an analogy: Imagine that a puppy is swimming across a river with a knapsack on its back. As it makes its way people keep dropping pebbles into the knapsack until, weighted down, the puppy drowns. "Which stone killed the puppy?" asked Springer.

The western border of Beringia is formed by the Russian Far East. In the summer of 1995, I spent several weeks traveling by plane, helicopter, boat and truck over 8,000 miles through this vast territory while reporting for my *Time* cover story "The Tortured Land." This was Russia just past the peak of its post-Soviet, outlaw days. Traveling was not easy, and every day brought a surreal experience, whether it involved an otherwise sensible scientist telling me that the neighboring Chinese were sending in infiltrators who had been taught to make themselves virtually invisible as they darted from tree to tree, or hiring a large Russian military helicopter in Kamchatka to convey me and the photographer, Tony Suau, up to the Valley of the Geysers—only to discover that the pilot had invited thirty friends and relatives along (and probably charged them, too). In the course of my travels, I encountered gorgeous lakes with floating boulders, and a perfectly preserved baby mammoth, frozen in the (fast-melting) permafrost. The most memorable part of this trip, however, was my journey to the mouth of the Kolyma River, where it flows into the Arctic Ocean.

Tony; Andrei, Tony's longtime in-country facilitator in Russia (formerly in Russian army intelligence); and I flew from Yakutsk, the capital of Yakutia, up to Cherski, a small port town about 100 miles upstream from the mouth of the Kolyma. I'd already done a series of interviews with various Russian scientists and environmentalists, and Cherski and the extreme Far North played into my story in a number of respects. For one thing it offered the chance to meet with some of the Far East's indigenous peoples, such as the Yukagirs and the Chutskis, but I was also intrigued by the possible impacts of the opening of the Northern Sea Route as global warming dealt with the traditional barrier of sea ice.

Yakutia is vast, empty, yet still grievously polluted. Imagine a republic seven times the size of California, with a population of only about 1 million, most of them residents of the capital, and many of them suffering from environmentally caused illnesses characteristic of unregulated industrial centers. The pollution comes from near and far. When I had earlier met with Vasili Alekseev, then Yakutia's minister of ecology, he matter-of-factly ticked off the astounding array of insults visited by air, water and land on this otherwise empty landscape.

For years diamond and other mines simply dumped toxic wastes in rivers. When the authorities flooded a wooded area as part of a plan to build an electrical-power-generating plant, they left behind a million cubic meters of wood to rot, which released phenol into the water during decomposition. Agricultural contaminants are released as well, and because all of Yakutia is covered by permafrost, pollutants stay on the surface and accumulate.

Then there were the nuclear tests, several of which released radioactive debris into the area. Alekseev told me that levels of plutonium 239 and 240 in parts of Yakutia rivaled those in the soils adjacent to Chernobyl for contamination. Finally, there is the curse called the Arctic Front, an artifact of geophysics that defines the boundary between polar and subpolar climate zones. It is the product of global air currents that collect contaminants from throughout the Northern Hemisphere and pool them over the polar region during wintertime. Its role in the distribution of toxics came to light in the 1970s, when an American scientist taking air samples discovered to his amazement that at certain times of the year the remote Far North has worse air pollution readings than many cities in the United States.

The contaminants condense and fall with snow, and then during the spring melt they enter the tundra food chain, where they are taken up by animals and plants and the people who eat them. Men, women and children living thousands of miles north of industrial cities carry mercury in their hair and blood and carcinogens in their fat, and often suffer cancers and other afflictions more commonly associated with jobs in factories and mines. Alekseev casually enumerated the burden that both local and distant pollution places upon isolated Yakutia: high rates of cancer, gastrointestinal illnesses, kidney problems, and opportunistic infections that take advantage of weak immune systems.

Cherski was a run-down port town that had lost half its population over the years. Huge cranes—the Russians have a thing for enormous equipment—stood idle everywhere. As I was to discover, the river between Cherski and the Arctic Ocean had not been dredged or charted in many decades. The one anomalous note was a number of fit young men wearing track warm-ups, the uniform of choice for hit men. Andrei told us that the town is a "riverbed," a place where mafia hit men chill out between jobs. Our local contact, Olga Kulishova, said she didn't mind the presence of the mafia, because the bigger criminals kept the local thugs in line, and because the mafia supplied the police department with cars and equipment.

Between them Andrei and Olga lined up a boat to take us up to the Arctic Ocean. It was a Russian-government pilot vessel, over a hundred feet long and with a crew of ten. (In those days, almost anything was available for rent in Russia.) With nothing else to do, the captain, Vladimir, was happy to charter it to us for the three-day trip up and back for $500.

We set off, and not too far north of Cherski we ran aground on a sand bar for the first time. After some rocking we were off, and then about an hour later we ran aground again. In the course of the trip this would recur over a dozen times, with subsequent delays ranging from a few minutes to three hours. It was all too clear that the Russian coast guard could have used some updated charts. During our enforced idleness we watch a pirated version of the original *The Poseidon Adventure*.

Gradually making our way farther north, we came upon a tiny native settlement and were invited into the main, reindeer-skin tent-house, which had an open fire burning at its center. The chief, Slava Kemlil, wiry and weathered, told us that there were about thirty Chukchi elders in this community. With the collapse of the Soviet Union, he explained, they had been left alone, not that they'd had much contact with officials before. "Nobody brings us anything," he said, "and we were the last to be supplied, anyway. Now we are absolutely independent, and it's better. No chiefs order us around."

The Chukchis are probably the most isolated group in the Northern Hemisphere. While the Soviets might have wanted to bring them under their influence, they probably had a hard time finding anyone willing to take on the task of riding herd on these reindeer hunters. They live in the coldest place in the Northern Hemisphere, scraping out a life despite constant howling winds. Even in the summer, bone-chilling fogs sap the joy from the long days. In my notebook, my notes read, "coldest fog imaginable!"

Not everyone in the room agreed that things were better now. One pointed out that only when a Chukot named Nikolai held a position in government had any attention been paid to their needs—mostly medical— but then admitted, "After him, nobody cared." Another pointed out that in some of the other villages, people had not received any payments from the government in six years.

What little cash this settlement, called Yaronga, received came from the sale of caribou meat. They devised their own system of income distribution: half to those who did the work and half to the community. Given the importance of community to each member's survival, the system had a brilliant simplicity.

In certain respects this village was closer to its traditional roots than were the Penan villages. The people were quite hospitable, ceremoniously inviting us for tea. As Slava told it, they lived a mostly barter existence, living on caribou and fish, and hunting polar wolf and polar bear for skins to make clothes. Without elaboration, he said that they still practiced their traditional religion, and that the entire group joined in songfests—traditionally, they compose a song when each child is born, mentioning every member of the baby's extended family. The firstborn takes the surname of the father, the second born that of the mother. Slava then added, "And so on," though I had no idea what that meant for the third, fourth, and other successive children.

My first impression was that these natives had a truly miserable existence, but as I listened to Slava's common sense and tried to get Olga to translate the matriarch's witty interjections, that initial notion gave way to one of respect. These were relatively happy people. After a mild comment about the bureaucracy in Yakutia, Slava said, "We know it's a sin to complain—if we want to make things better we should work." I can't remember the last time I heard a remark like that in the developed world. That sentiment may have been a legacy of having survived a regime where a complaint could land you in the gulag just downstream, but the Soviet Union had collapsed several years earlier, and more likely it reflected the ethos of an ancient people whose survival depended on what they did, not good intentions.

Where the Chukchis make their living is where Stalin sent his imagined enemies to die. The Russian leader paid his respects to the harshness of life on the edge of the Arctic Ocean by sending political prisoners to a place where the extraordinarily harsh environment provided security and the weather did his killing for him. From 1938 until 1953, tens of thousands were sent to Ambarchik, a bleak, flimsy encampment hard by the Arctic Ocean, where very few survived. Most were fit for work only for the first three months from their arrival, after which the combination of cold, starvation, abuse and hard labor mortally sapped their will to live.

After leaving Slava, his nineteen grandchildren and their warm fire, we picked our way down to Ambarchik. Even in August, a couple of hours outside were barely tolerable. The pathetic fallacy was alive and well in Ambarchik, as we disembarked amid windblown fog so frigid that it was as if a cold ghost were invading your body core. Here and there we could see human bones sticking up through the soil. We could also see the remains of the wood lattice that made up the walls of the barracks that housed the prisoners, providing little protection against the elements. Slava and his family were far cozier in their animal-skin tents than any prisoner in Ambarchik. Stalin's loathsome minions succeeded in turning housing design into an instrument of murder. After touring this place of sorrow and death we headed back toward the relative warmth of Cherski and Yakutsk, again running aground constantly.

Yakutia's blood-drenched history and toxic legacies from the USSR notwithstanding, the republic still holds great promise. With good government, its tiny population might prospect the fantastic riches Yakutia contains in the form of diamonds, gold, base metals and minerals. That said, the vast country is also part of an Arctic time bomb that threatens the entire world. All of Yakutia lies on permafrost, and the permafrost both traps and caps enormous amounts of methane, a greenhouse gas with roughly twenty times the potency for warming of CO_2. Much of the methane is trapped in a permafrost structure called a clathrate, a cagelike structure that traps the gas in a lattice of frozen water. If the lattice melts, the gas is released, and there are an estimated 400 gigatons of methane contained in permafrost clathrates.

Throughout the Arctic, permafrost is proving less permanent than the name implies, which establishes the potential for one of those ugly surprises that could act as rocket fuel for global warming. As melting permafrost releases methane, for instance, it enhances warming, which in turn reduces the duration and extent of reflective snow cover, which further enhances warming, which speeds the melting of permafrost, releasing more methane, and on and on in a vicious circle. The nightmare scenario is that at some point this process could become out of control, or nonlinear, as scientists drily describe it, resulting in a sudden massive release of methane, either from the Arctic or perhaps from deep under the ocean. Such so-called methane burps are suspected as the cause of massive climate disruptions such as the Paleo-Eocene Thermal Maximum of 55 million years ago, and also as contributing to the greatest known extinction event at the end of the Permian epoch, 251 million years ago.

While it may someday kill us all, the melting permafrost is in the meantime performing one helpful, unexpected service—urban renewal. The hideous Stalin-era construction in Yakutia was built on top of permafrost. As it melts, many of these eyesores are beginning to lean and sometimes topple. The Sakha Republic may one day be able to invest some of its windfall from diamonds and minerals into replacing these derelict monuments to despair with better-designed, better-constructed buildings.

Climate change figured only indirectly in my trips to Beringia and Siberia, but it was the main reason I returned to the Arctic, or more precisely the near Arctic, in 2000. Much has been written about the ways in which the warming Arctic is affecting the web of life, but no one story more exquisitely frames its impact than the plight of the polar bear. Of all the polar bear populations throughout the Northern Hemisphere, the most vulnerable are the bears of Hudson Bay, whose existence depends entirely on the extent and duration of the winter sea ice.

The polar bear is a magnificent predator. It can swim over a hundred miles at a stretch, and the males can grow to 11 feet long and 2,000 pounds. (Not having to deal with gravity for a significant portion of your day removes one of the impediments to growing to enormous dimensions.) In Hudson Bay the bears get almost all of their sustenance by hunting ringed seals in a delicately balanced system: The seals use the sea ice as a platform from which to hunt capelin, an Arctic fish, and the bears use it in turn as a platform from which to hunt seals.

Currently, Hudson Bay is the southernmost limit of polar bears. During the Little Ice Age, a series of cold periods that is commonly dated from about the beginning of the fourteenth century to the beginning of the nineteenth, they did move farther south. The French explorer Jacques Cartier wrote about sightings of polar bears in the St. Lawrence River in the 1600s, something that hasn't occurred since. In July 2000 I flew up to Churchill on the western shores of Hudson Bay in the Canadian province of Manitoba, taking a room, appropriately enough, at the Polar Motel. As a town Churchill consists of a charmless strip of sheds and tilt-ups, but it draws tourists by the thousand due to its being the polar bear capital of Canada, thanks to its location on a peninsula that is directly in the line of the annual migration route cycle on and off the sea ice. If the ice freezes early—say, late October or the beginning of November—the bears, traveling north on the western side of the bay, will walk out onto the ice south of Churchill, but the later the freeze, the more likely they will pass through town. As the Arctic has warmed over recent decades, the average date of this freeze has moved from November 15 on into December. This creates a problem, because the town dump lies directly in the bears' migration path, and the bears, being opportunistic, will rummage around for food. Such Dumpster diving is dangerous for both bears and humans, and so Manitoba has instituted a policy of jailing bears to discourage the practice.

I had set up a series of meetings with various scientists and officials, and one of the first people I connected with was Wade Roberts, an officer of Manitoba Conservation, whose thankless job it was to jail the thousand-pound predators. As he explained it, the drill is to dart the bears and then place them in the jail's twenty-three specially constructed barred cages for a few days before flying them 35 miles farther north to the ice edge, where they are released. The wildlife officials don't feed the incarcerated bears because they want the experience to be as unpleasant as possible. (In the past they did feed their animal captives, and some bears started trying to break into the jail in search of food.) Bears are smart and quickly figure out that the dump is to be avoided, but as with humans, the young bears are more prone to foolish mistakes than their wiser elders.

Wade has observed that the bears they've encountered recently have been thinner than in the past. Little wonder: In normal times, they would go on the ice and feed until late July or early August before having to leave for their annual summer sleep in peat dens on terra firma. (Ian Stirling, a noted polar bear expert, told me that some of the dens show evidence of having been used for hundreds of years.) The ice now forms later and melts earlier, and summer has lengthened from two to four months. Consequently the bears sometimes don't get out onto the ice until New Year's and then have to come ashore in early June. This means less time feeding and more time burning stored fuel.

This is an entirely different adaptation from that of more northern polar bears. Their strategy is to go onto the polar ice when they mature, and to stay on it, retreating north with it as it melts in the summer. Land is for breeding and rearing the young. Warming has created a different set of problems for these bears. For instance, in the late 1990s the ice retreated north of Wrangel Island before cubs were old enough to go out on the pack ice. This forced mother bears and cubs into close quarters with mating marine mammals, and reportedly created sheer mayhem as the upended cycles of predator and prey left them together when they should have been hundreds of miles apart.

The cold calculus of the lower Hudson Bay bears' adaptation leaves little margin for error. On average a bear loses 2.2 pounds a day once it leaves the ice—not a huge problem for a 1,200-pound male, who might lose 200 pounds during three months off the ice. That same weight loss is very significant for a 300-pound cub or a smaller female with cubs.

Bears are quite adaptable, but the challenge posed by global warming is not a simple matter of finding a new food source. For instance, it takes ten to fourteen days to shut down a bear's digestive system during estivation, the summertime version of hibernating. If the bear starts eating blueberries or scavenging seal carcasses at times when it would ordinarily be estivating, it delays that shutdown, leaving the animal in the worst of positions, as it will continue to lose weight on this low-quality, intermittent diet, while not having the benefit of the 10 to 15 percent daily energy savings it would achieve if it simply went to sleep for the summer. Still, the bears are trying to get by; while in Churchill, I heard reports of female bears hunting during the summer, a behavior that had not been previously observed.

These animals might be trying to adapt, but as of my visit their strategies were not working. The survival rate of cubs had dropped to below 50 percent from nearly 75 percent. Bears that used to breed every two years were now breeding every third year—a reproductive rate more typical of northern polar bears. Brood sizes were smaller as well.

Local entrepreneurs confirmed the grim picture described by wildlife officials and scientists. Mike Macri, who at that point had been running whale-watching and bear-watching tours out of Churchill for thirty-five years, confirmed that bears had started hunting in summer, saying that he had reports of bears killing seals that had become marooned on rocks. He'd also seen bears switching from hunting ringed seals to preying on bearded seals, deep divers that are better adapted than ringed seals to floe ice. The big bears are highly motivated to find a way to survive.

While I was visiting Mike's office I noticed a photograph of a polar bear standing nose-to-nose with a sled dog. It looked as if the huge bear was about to have a snack, but Mike explained that, in fact, the two were friends. The female bear's route onto the ice took her directly past the dog, and the dog had reacted (either stupidly or brilliantly) with a playful attitude, and, incredibly, the wild bear had responded in kind. Apparently the bear would break her trek onto the ice to stop by and see the dog.

Mike had other unusual animal stories. My trip to Churchill coincided with the annual migration of beluga whales up the mouth of the Churchill River. The highly social whales, with their distinctive melon-shaped forehead (essentially a sonar dome), followed the spawning capelins. Mike was taking out a group and invited me to go along.

As we entered the river on his boat, we picked our way past a regatta of brilliant white ice floes and encountered a sea of belugas. Mike lowered a hydrophone into the water so that we could hear the incessant chatter of the whales. He is convinced that the whales are highly intelligent and use their extraordinary communication abilities not just for echolocation but also to convey information. For instance, he believes that the whales had figured out that the watchman at a whorehouse on the coast was alerting hunters to their presence, and they would vacate the river whenever they saw him.

He also told a story suggesting that the whales could distinguish between human friends and foes. Once, when a beluga had become entangled in a monofilament Arctic net, Mike jumped into the water to set the animal free; remarkably it didn't struggle as he cut the net away from its teeth and around its eyes. "If it struggled I would have lost a finger," said Mike. "In fact I have lost two fingers, but that's another story." Once he cut a large enough hole in the net, the beluga swam calmly away. It seemed to know he was being helpful despite the fact that he was approaching it with a large knife. I've subsequently heard similar stories about humpback and sperm whales, so I'm open to Mike's interpretation.

The Churchill residents I spoke with offered varying opinions about global warming. All had noticed a change, but a few wondered whether it reflected normal variations in climate. One group, however—the Hudson Bay Port Company—was prepared to take advantage of the warming. About 600 miles of flat land separated Churchill from Canada's grain belt, and if global warming doubled the window of time during which the port could remain open to shipping, it was preparing to benefit.

I sought out several longtime port employees for their opinion. Allen Johnson fit the bill, having worked in the port for thirty years. He said that he started noticing change roughly around 1980. Churchill's propinquity to the grain belt made it more attractive than Vancouver on the Pacific or Thunder Bay on Lake Superior—but only if Hudson Bay stayed clear of ice during the harvest season, so that shippers did not have to use expensive ships clad to protect against ice. "The harvest comes off in August and September," he said, "so there's a huge advantage to us if the normal shipping season extends into November." At that point the window for non-ice-clad ships was from July 20 to October 31. Johnson also saw great potential for the port in shipping copper, zinc and nickel extracted from Canada's vast interior. He speculated that there would be even bigger opportunities if the Northwest Passage was navigable, which would put Churchill in a very favored position to ship to Asia.

Subsequently, the Northwest Passage has opened up, a development no one would have predicted as recently as 1970. Explorers since the time of Sebastian Cabot have dreamed of a route between Europe and Asia that would not involve a detour of thousands of miles, either around the southern end of South America or through the Mediterranean (with the opening of the Suez Canal). That prize is now at hand, though it is the result of the nightmare of human-caused global warming.

The price of this newly opened route will be steep. Apart from starving polar bears, disoriented birds, scrambled predator-prey relationships, melting permafrost, and innumerable other symptoms of ecosystem chaos, the economic consequences of climate change could overwhelm any narrow geographic advantage that it makes possible. It doesn't really benefit a town like Churchill to be in an ideal place for transcontinental shipping if global trade itself faces collapse.

PART VI

THE NEAR WILD

CHAPTER 13

The Wolf at the Door

Yellowstone Park today is a very different place from the park I trekked through in 1992 looking for wolves. As I write this there are over 1,500 wolves in the greater Yellowstone ecosystem. Since the reintroduction of 66 animals in 1995, after a seventy-year absence, the wolves have had a profound impact on America's greatest wild preserve. Elk, which had become relaxed about most predators before the wolf returned, have changed their behavior, and this in turn has relieved some pressure on seasonal plants. Coyote numbers have been cut in half.

In the fall of 1992, just as the U.S. government was preparing to reintroduce gray wolves to Yellowstone, a hunter shot what looked like a wolf just south of the park. This caused an uproar, not so much because the hunter might have shot an endangered species, but because the very indication of the presence of wolves in Yellowstone would pose a huge bureaucratic problem. If the wolves had indeed managed to make it back to Yellowstone on their own, it mooted an arduously crafted management plan to install a new population of the animals.

I was told about this killing by Renee Askins, who then ran the Wolf Fund, an NGO she had set up to promote the reintroduction of wolves to Yellowstone. Renee is smart, telegenic and very persuasive, and she played as big a role as anyone in lifting the profile of the issue to the point where the government had to act. As for myself, I came to the story agnostic on whether it was better to reintroduce wolves or hope they would recolonize the park on their own, and saw the killing of this particular animal as a perfect opportunity to frame the issues swirling around wolves and Yellowstone. And so in late October, I set off with Bill Campbell, a *Time* photographer with whom I'd done a number of stories; Dan Sholley, the chief ranger of the park; and Mike, his assistant, on a horseback trip into the most remote area of the park to determine whether there was any more evidence of wolves. We found only one ambiguous footprint, but in the course of this trip I made other discoveries, unexpected and inspiring.

At 2.3 million acres, Yellowstone is the largest park in the United States. It's also the centerpiece of the Greater Yellowstone Ecosystem, an 18-million-acre expanse that encompasses six national forests, two wildlife refuges and two national parks (Yellowstone and Grand Teton), as well as Native American territories and some private lands. It is the largest intact temperate ecosystem in the world, though "intact" has become a relative term since a number of invasive species now threaten the region. For instance, its meadows are being overtaken by thistle—an introduced species—and Yellowstone Lake's native fish are being crowded out by lake trout, also introduced.

Yellowstone is also the oldest park in the United States, established by an act of Congress in 1872. It came into existence partly as the result of lobbying by railroad companies. The railroads were looking for attractions (such as Old Faithful) to tempt tourists to travel to the West on their newly laid tracks. The potential park's other big asset, stressed frequently during congressional hearings at the time, was that the land had "no economic value."

The park is indeed remote. A place called the Thorofare (so named because Native Americans used it as a migratory route before the arrival of the Europeans) in the southeast part of Yellowstone is more than 30 miles from the nearest road in every direction, making it the most remote place in the lower forty-eight states. If there exists a part of this country where wolves could live without being spotted by humans, this was it. From a wolf's point of view, finding itself in Yellowstone in the early 1990s would be akin to the first European's discovering North America, a boundless cornucopia with giant trees and limitless game.

Dan set up a route that took us from the Heart Lake trailhead up onto the Two Oceans Plateau and then down into the Thorofare. For Dan, the trip was all business. As chief park ranger, he gets pressure from all sides—from conservationists with conflicting views on how to balance access with the needs of the park's species and ecosystems, from the many commercial interests who make their living off the park, and from outfitters and snowmobilers who covet Yellowstone for very different reasons than the environmentalists do. Dan handled these pressures with diplomacy and humor. He looked every bit the ranger out of central casting—square-jawed and easy in the saddle. Still, this little expedition was anything but casual.

If we did in fact find evidence of wolves, both Dan and the wolves would face a problem. For one thing, the animals would have absolute protection under the Endangered Species Act. While good for individual wolves, this would cause problems for human-wolf relations because the plan worked out for reintroduction of the animals included provisions for killing the predators should they venture off the reservation and start taking livestock. More than any other animal in the American West, the wolf has evoked irrational loathing among ranchers, and this so-called predator paranoia made and continues to make the reintroduction of the animals a matter of delicate diplomacy.

For me the trip was a twofold adventure. On the one hand, I had the rare privilege of traveling through what is arguably the most glorious wilderness in America. On a more personal level, I was about to renew my relationship with horses after a fifteen-year hiatus, and my last horseback outing had not ended happily. I had been riding in Asheville, North Carolina, when my mount decided to bolt. He took off like a rocket, trying to scrape me off by running through an apple orchard. I managed to stay on only by virtually gluing myself to the horse's neck. After that experience I was happy to let horses pursue their thing while I took a different path. Now I was back in the saddle. Sure enough, not an hour into this expedition, Prince (who was anything but) got spooked and took off through the scrub pine of this part of Yellowstone.

This time, however, I was better prepared. I'd been told that the trick was to reach up and grab one of the reins just below the bit and pull the horse's head hard to the left or right. The horse is going to go where his head is pointing, and if that means a sudden turn to the left or right, it's going to slow down. So that's what I did when Prince rocketed through the trees. To my (and probably Prince's) astonishment, it actually worked.

Yellowstone is a place where you feel nature close at hand, its terrain as extreme as the weather. The park has recorded some of the coldest temperatures in the lower forty-eight states. Up on the Two Ocean Plateau, probably the highest plain in the United States, the snow was already several inches deep even though it was only October. Wolves thrive in the snow. Their big feet distribute weight so that they can run on crusted snow without breaking through, giving them an advantage over more heavy-footed prey.

We saw a good deal of wolf food in the form of elk, but the wolves themselves remained elusive—if they were there at all. Among the strongest arguments that proponents of reintroduction had was that, by 1992, Yellowstone had near-historic high populations of elk, mule deer and other ungulates. Wolves could happily eat their way through ungulate populations for a long time, and with elk and mule deer as their food imprint, it was unlikely that they would cast a wandering eye on cattle or sheep. Meanwhile, no other top predator had emerged (there are mountain lions in the park, but not enough of them to have an impact on the browsers) to replace the missing wolves and restore the balance of the ecosystem. Yellowstone, like virtually every other part of the United States, has paid a price for the extermination of large predators. Until the coyote recently colonized the Northeast, white-tailed deer populations were exploding. With unchecked population growth comes crowding, and with crowding come epidemics of new diseases, some of which, like Lyme disease, can jump to humans.

This factor may be the last and best hope for large predators. Once the public recognizes that we actually need wolves, or grizzlies, or big cats, ordinary people might be more willing to tolerate the tiny but real risks that come with living in propinquity to big animals that hunt for a living. Unfortunately, this realization—one that is fundamental to protecting ecosystems—requires that Americans abandon their assumption that a risk-free life is a God-given right.

On that first day, riding through snow on the verge of patchy forest, we saw our first teasing, ambiguous sign of the presence of wolves. It was at 5:00 p.m. at Mile 26 on the trail when Dan spotted a large canine footprint. "That's too big for a coyote," he remarked as he dismounted. It measured 2.75 inches by 2.75 inches, and Dan said that it was fresh since a snowfall yesterday. We couldn't tell, however, if it had been made by a wolf, or whether a smaller animal had left the print, which had then expanded because of melting. Still, the sighting was enough to lift our spirits (mine anyway—finding wolves would spell nothing but trouble for Dan).

As it grew toward dusk, we stopped for the night at the Heart Lake patrol cabin, one of the ranger cabins scattered through the backcountry of Yellowstone. The cabins are simple gable-roofed log structures with a tiny covered porch at their entrance. In front was a small meadow, bounded by lodgepole pines, Engelmann spruces and other firs.

When we entered, our first sight was of the propane lantern and cooking stove, both festooned with wooden matches stuck in every conceivable place. The cooking stove was prepped with wood, tinder and paper, as was the wood stove. The bunk beds were neatly made with six blankets on each, fold facing the door. Dan explained that the rationale behind the provisioning was that a snow-blind ranger should be able to stumble into the cabin when it was 30 below zero and a full-on blizzard, and still be able to find matches and start a fire simply by touch. The blankets were laid with fold toward the door so that the ranger could still get warm in a dry blanket even if the wind or a bear had knocked the door open and snow had blown into the cabin.

The cabins were an exemplar of minimum-impact design. We found matchboxes, jars and cans that had been reused since the 1920s. The next morning we spent an efficient hour restocking the stoves, planting the matches, sweeping the floors, remaking the beds and otherwise making preparations to welcome the next itinerant ranger, just as the cabin had welcomed us. So it had been in this cabin for the better part of a century.

Bill and I felt privileged to be a part of this continuum. Never have I more gladly swept a floor, and indeed, the eye-opening discovery of this expedition was the esprit de corps and quality of life of these rangers. Most of them made less than $30,000 a year, but those who chose this life did so as a calling. Apart from frustrations with budgets and parks bureaucracy, job satisfaction was and is off the charts. Dan and the other rangers we encountered spent their days amid nature at its most glorious and dramatic . . .

. . . and dangerous, for Yellowstone is as harsh as it is beautiful. The next day we continued to make our way toward the Thorofare. After a day spent searching for wolves, we realized that dusk was falling and that we had better find a way down to the Thorofare if we were going to descend during daylight. This turned out to be not an easy thing to do. The plateau is a bit like a steep-sided mesa, and most of the ravines have pitches more suited to bungee jumping than horseback riding. Eventually Dan found a route that was navigable. We maneuvered our way down very steep slopes of loose shale, walking beside our horses rather than in front of them (so that if they fell, they wouldn't land on us), eventually emerging into the ancient and remote passageway of burn areas, wetlands and meadows, interspersed with scattered copses of evergreens.

It was dark by the time we got to the Thorofare patrol cabin, a slightly more elaborate version of the ranger cabin where we'd spent the previous night. In residence when we arrived were two rangers, Mary Taber and Bob Jackson, a veteran Yellowstone backcountry ranger who had made the patrol cabin his seasonal home since 1978. Mary, an attractive and wry young woman, was bemused by the furor about the possibility that wolves had made it back to Yellowstone.

She had her own wolf tale to tell. She and another ranger had spotted an animal that looked like a wolf a few weeks earlier up in the Hayden Valley to the north. Frustrated by their inability to keep the animal in sight, they tried howling to get it to reappear. Apparently they were quite good at it because another agent, Wayne Brewster, heard the howls and reported it as evidence. Somewhat ruefully Mary called in and said, "Umm, that was us."

Bob Jackson was somewhat more detached from the wolf furor, though he did claim to have seen a wolf track in August, a week before the Hayden Valley sighting. His fervor for the Thorofare, however, verged on the rhapsodic. He liked nothing better than exploring its remote drainages, some of which, he believed, had never seen a white man. He spoke of coming upon undisturbed chip piles left by migratory Native Americans fashioning flint arrowheads hundreds of years ago, as well as wickiups—temporary dwellings made of brush and sticks—that were still intact after 400 years. If you were someone who wanted to drop out of the twentieth century, or for that matter the nineteenth and eighteenth as well, the Thorofare was just the place.

Bob's pet peeve was outfitters. While hunting was off-limits in the park, the southern part of the Thorofare bordered the Bridger-Teton National Forest, where outfitters could bring in hunters to shoot elk. "Outfitters fear no regulation," Bob complained, and went on to share a theory he had about a noticeable decline in grizzly bear numbers in the 1990s. He believed that outfitters would encroach on the southern border of the park and lay out salt to attract elk, whose carcasses would attract grizzlies. Hunters would then shoot the bears and bury their carcasses to hide the evidence of poaching an endangered species. According to Bill, this became something of an obsession with Bob, who was outspoken on the subject and became a favorite of environmentalists and the press. His rising profile did not endear him to park service bureaucrats, however, and he eventually left in the late 1990s.

We didn't find wolves on that trip, but it left a profound impression on me, and made even more of an impression on Bill. He and his wife, the author Maryann Vollers, moved to the region in 1997, in large part to follow the wolf story as it unfolded in the years following reintroduction. Bill had enjoyed a career as a celebrated "bang bang" photographer, and had documented many conflicts in Africa. By the time he was in his late thirties, however, he had suffered through so many bouts of malaria and other tropical diseases that his doctor told him that he had the internal organs of a seventy-year-old man. He came back to the United States, his internal organs rejuvenated, and turned his attention to nature and environmental stories.

Moreover, he (and I) could see the writing on the wall. *Time* and other magazines were shrinking along with their budgets, and Bill began turning to producing and filming documentaries. His PBS documentary *Wolves in Paradise,* narrated by the folk singer Tom Rush (Renee's husband), explores, in a finely nuanced way, the tensions that have arisen due to the very success of the wolf reintroduction program, as the packs have ventured beyond the borders of the park and occasionally killed livestock.

What's wonderful about this film is that it does offer an answer to the dilemma of whether a modern society can live with big predators like wolves. The owners of the Sun Ranch, in the Madison Valley just north of the park, are trying to do just that, and in a most ingenious manner. When a wolf pack migrated out of the park and started to prey on livestock, it forced an anguished decision among the nature lovers who staffed the ranch to kill some of the members of the pack. But rather than continuing to exterminate raiding wolves, they are hoping to find a solution to such incursions by conditioning a pack to the notion that preying on livestock is a losing proposition for them. Their reasoning is that if a pack does get habituated to this idea, then they might pass it on to their offspring (just as the fear of humans gets passed on), and, even more important, they will defend their territory from invasion by new packs radiating out from the park, which might have other ideas about the wolf-livestock relationship.

Other ranchers, with far less sympathy for wolves, are working with wildlife authorities and environmentalists to find other nonlethal ways (such as rubber bullets or volunteer patrols) of letting these intelligent, social animals know that while humans will tolerate their presence outside the park, that toleration comes with rules. As someone who has spent a career studying animal intelligence, I've noticed that animals can be more punctilious about honoring human rules than humans themselves are. Whether or not any of these approaches ultimately bears fruit, it is an encouraging development that ranchers, whose antipathy to wolves and other predators runs deep, are trying to find a practical entente.

PART VII

SURVIVORS

CHAPTER 14

The Lost Worlds of Cuba

Coloring many of my travels has been a sense of urgency to encounter cultures and places before they are lost or transformed by the grim cultural entropy of modernity. Tourism's hyperbole to the contrary, there are very few "timeless" places left on the planet. Almost any area with cultural, physical or natural significance that is lucky enough to have avoided the "extractive industries" still has a clock hovering over it, ticking out the days in an accelerating countdown before it is "discovered." At that point the travel industry and assorted hangers-on will work their magic, until whatever charm the place once had exists only on postcards and in the tightly cropped images of tourist brochures, which leave out the high-rises and slums. When I first visited Tulum, it was an isolated Mayan ruin on a quiet Mexican coast. Now it's part of a marketing concept called the Costa Maya, essentially a theme-park version—"Hey, there's the sacred *sinote,* right by the Taco Bell!"—of its former self.

The countdown for Cuba can be measured by the remaining heartbeats of Fidel Castro, and this EEG has been registering tachycardia. Cuba is perhaps the most remarkable place remaining on the planet that has not yet suffered the deracinating makeover that heralds the arrival of the ragged edge of the world. Despite the fact that it lies closer to Miami than does Georgia, Cuba remains isolated by quirks of politics.

On the one hand, anti-Castro Cubans remain an important though rapidly aging constituency in Florida, and Florida remains crucial to the ambitions of American presidential candidates. On the other, Fidel Castro is (as of this writing) the only surviving unreconstructed, charismatic Communist revolutionary still influencing the fate of a nation. Thus, Cuba has

been both victim and beneficiary of a fifty-year standoff that has starved the
country of American investment and, with the collapse of the Soviet Union,
of Russian subsidies as well. (Russian officials, however, have recently been
making unwelcome statements about reestablishing ties—the Russians
have a genius for doing the most irritating thing at the most inopportune
time.) The result of this situation is that Cuba remains a living relic of times
past, and, because it has had to sustain itself without access to fossil fuels
or trade with its natural partner to the north, Cuba simultaneously offers a
proleptic look at what the rest of the world may face as oil supplies dwindle.
Sometimes it's good to have a superpower as an enemy.

There seems to be no end to the contradictions that characterize the
island. While capitalist countries have wreaked havoc on their natural resources, communism has been far worse. Russia and China have so
despoiled their landscapes that many generations will pass before they
recover, if they do recover. Yet Cuba, perhaps one of the most repressive
communist regimes of them all, has nearly 22 percent of its territory under
some form of protection, and sports a proudly dedicated cadre of park professionals and biologists.

There are other places on the planet where development has yet to take
hold, but almost all of them are failed states that have made no effort to devise
a modern economy. Cuba represents a unique attempt to devise an economy
based on extreme fossil fuel scarcity. Some might argue that Cuba is a failed
state as well, but it has harnessed the ingenuity of its people and the formidable power of a first-rate education system to try to find a way to make do
without money or oil. While stipulating that economic hardship and the rig-
ors of a police state have inflicted untold hardship on Cubans, it remains the
only geographically accessible tropical island in the world that has escaped the
curse of ribbon development, with stores and homes strung alongside roads.

While it would be absurd to justify the repression and lack of freedom
imposed by the Cuban government, it must be recognized how well positioned that nation finds itself going forward. As the rest of the world begins
to grapple with a fossil-fuel-constrained future, Cuba has the advantage of
years of trying to come to grips with the problem through trial and error.
Maybe the last shall be first, as the Bible avers.

It's not the way we'd like it to be, but good can come out of bad and suffering. Just as the Nicaraguan civil war limited logging and left the nation
with the healthiest ecosystems in Central America once hostilities ended

(an opportunity for sound policies that Nicaragua immediately set about squandering), so have the costs of Cuba's harsh dictatorship and isolation left the nation ideally positioned to improve the material well-being of its people without repeating the ecologically and culturally catastrophic errors of every other emerging nation. Given the depressing history of environmental degradation that has characterized development, it's fair to say that Cuba's future represents the world's best and perhaps last chance to find a balance between material improvement and the needs of nature.

Here is Cuba, a nation bottled up in a time capsule for fifty years and only now beginning to emerge from isolation. But Cubans have been able to witness what has been going on in the outside world, even as they have been condemned (some would say blessed) to remain in the past. Cubans have had fifty years to figure out what aspects of modernity are truly beneficial and which ones represent a poisoned chalice. If Cuba with its stable population and highly educated workforce can't turn this into something workable, there is faint hope for the rest of the world.

If this were the only reason Cuba caught my attention, the stakes would justify any amount of effort to try to bring this slowly unfolding test of Cuba's moral fiber to the world's attention. But there is much more to Cuba than its de facto status as an experiment in post-fossil-fuel sustainable living. It's a fascinating island in a biogeographic sense, and its ecological history offers a glimpse of what we might expect for the world in the future in the realm of ecology. Cuba exemplifies the fascinating transformations that islands work on various life forms, most notably the proliferation of giant and dwarf variants of various species in the wild. What has happened in Cuba is now happening everywhere in the world, for as humanity colonizes every habitable hectare of the globe, it is transforming formerly vast and interconnected ecosystems into an archipelago of biologically isolated islands.

———

I knew I had to get to Cuba, but it took several years for me to find a publication that was willing to send me there. Finally, in the fall of 2002, I got the chance when *Smithsonian* magazine agreed to give me an assignment. (As an aside, I'm sure that some readers wonder why I didn't just go there on my own. The reason was simple: Cuba is a police state, and I needed official credentials to get access to the park officials and biologists I wished to interview. I didn't want to show up to be detained in Havana.)

I set up the trip with the help of Mary Pearl, then executive director of Wildlife Trust, and Luis Gomez-Echeverri, who was then director of the UNDP mission in Cuba. Between them I ended up with a spectacular itinerary that took me through the parks, coastline and towns of Oriente and then down to Zapata Swamp. Mary Pearl's group has been working in Cuba for years, providing support and expertise for Cuban environmentalists. She had superb contacts among its biologists and ornithologists and gave me an insightful overview of Cuba's importance to the Caribbean and regional ecology. Luis agreed to cooperate in part because Cuba was one of the few nations that actually took the United Nations–sponsored Rio Earth Summit of 1991 seriously, and he thought the country exemplified the crucial concept that protecting nature does not first require that a nation be rich.

I flew to Cuba via Cancún on October 20, 2002, and was met at the airport by Alberto Perez, an information officer from the UNDP, an affable sixty-something who remained a fervent supporter of Fidel Castro. Alberto brought along his ten-year-old son, who sported a tattoo on his arm. We drove to Havana through a huge downpour. There were few cars on the road, but those we did encounter represented every vintage American car imaginable. "There's a Torpedo," said Alberto, pointing out a futuristic car from the 1940s. "There's a '56 Bel Air like mine!" And so on for the entire drive. He was as passionate as a birdwatcher, annotating every observation with a comment. Some of the cars we encountered were immaculate, others barely moved. I asked how people found parts, and Alberto explained that they made them, scavenged, or used substitutes. "Our mechanics can fix anything," he said with pride. Because of these alterations, few of these vehicles would be candidates for an American vintage car show. Many of the cars also now had diesel engines. I mentioned to Alberto how many Americans long for the Caribbean of forty years ago, and how this could be a selling point for Cuba as it opens. "Sixty years ago!" he replied with incongruous pride, given that he also presents himself as a fervent supporter of the changes of the Castro years.

Alberto dropped me off at the Hotel Nacional in Havana, a gracefully crumbling but still glorious colonial wreck, where I spent the night before meeting up with Luis the next morning. Luis had arranged for us to fly to Holguín in Oriente, and then drive through much of the region before flying back from Santiago de Cuba. Our group consisted of Luis; Antonio Perera, a former parks official who was instrumental in setting up many of

Cuba's protected areas; and Alberto. Perhaps I should feel guilty for saying this, given the economic privation I witnessed, but this trip was one of the happiest I've ever taken, at least once I safely disembarked from the rickety Russian Yak plane that took us to Holguín.

As we drove away from the airport, the cavalcade of cars from days long gone continued. We passed Studebakers, Packards, Willys, DeSotos, Nashes and Diamond Trucks, some dating back to the '30s. I couldn't help remarking on each one, and neither could Alberto. When I finally asked him why he still showed such enthusiasm in identifying these living relics, he simply said, "These were the cars of my youth." This remark was the closest Alberto came to showing any wistfulness for the old days, when his family owned sixteen homes.

Not long after leaving Holguín we entered the Cuban time warp. The empty roads were litter-free and lined by thatch-roofed houses, villagers sold fruit and sugarcane juice along the way, and neat hedges of euphorbia completed the image of the Caribbean of a half-century earlier. Everyone we encountered was relaxed and cheerful. I can't help but say it: But maybe the best word to describe the feel of this sleepy part of the island is, in fact, "timeless." That may account, at least in part, for why I felt so happy—at least for a few days, I couldn't hear the beat of the metronome. I kept thinking of the notion of "sunk costs," which was immediately followed by another thought: *This place has a chance.*

After going through small villages immortalized by the late Campay Segundo of Buena Vista Social Club fame, we headed for Alejandro de Humboldt National Park on the northeast coast. At 300 square miles, it would be considered enormous in any country, but on an island Cuba's size it is truly remarkable. The park is essentially a roll-up, combining prior protected areas with some added lands. To some degree it's Antonio Perera's baby. I've spent a great deal of time around hard-core conservationists in every corner of the globe, and Tony has all the hallmarks of the species. He's intense, uncompromising, highly intelligent and straight talking, and he radiates conviction. He explained that the park grew directly out of the Convention of Biodiversity, which, anemic though it was, represented one of the few concrete achievements of the Earth Summit.

The park is big, beautiful and wild, but, best of all, much of it is inaccessible. We drove in, fording streams, and then Tony and I hiked a bit to a vista point where we could look into the interior. On our hike we encountered patches of mariposa, the national flower, which has a delicate, seductive fragrance. From our vista point, we could see a high plateau with waterfalls streaming down its steep face. Tony said that much of that plateau was unexplored. Among the wonders that may await biologists there is the ivory-billed woodpecker, which was thought to have gone extinct in the 1950s until a pair was sighted in Cuba in 1987. More recently, ornithologists made credible recordings of the bird in 2005 in the Cache River National Wildlife Refuge in Arkansas.

The discovery of the pair of birds in 1987 was one impetus for formalizing protection of the area that was to become Humboldt National Park. The bigger question, however, is why there was a push for protection at all, particularly since conservation was the last thing on the minds of most Communist leaders (at least until Mikhail Gorbachev took over in Russia). The answer had to do with an accident of fate.

As luck would have it, the illiterate farmer Guillermo Garcia Frías, who saved Castro's life when he came ashore from the yacht *Granma* on December 2, 1956, happened to be a nature lover. Batista's troops were waiting when Castro arrived, and his ragtag group scattered during the ensuing battle. Commandante Garcia (as he came to be known) found Fidel, his brother Raúl and some others and took them to the Sierra Maestra, which ranges along the southern coast. The forces regrouped, and Garcia ultimately led Castro's Western Army and became a member of the Central Committee and Politburo.

Throughout the campaign and afterward Garcia retained, as Tony put it, a "naïve" love of nature and particularly of the Sierra Maestra. In the 1980s he created a technical group to, as Tony described it, "put a little science and technology" into the design of protected areas. Tony was part of this group and worked closely with Garcia. More important, Garcia's political clout provided cover for the nurturing and development of an entire generation of conservation biologists and parks planners who now held senior positions in the government. Later, Luis told me that there were two people in the Cuban government who could get anything done they wanted. One was the man in charge of the restoration of Havana, and the other was Garcia.

After our brief hike, we returned to the main road and made our way to Taco Bay, a rare place on earth where pines and mangroves grow side by side. We stopped at the park station to meet up with a ranger, Durán

Oliveros, and take a tour of the bay. Near the headquarters of the park is a statue of Humboldt, the German explorer who lived to be ninety (dying in 1859), and who was the first to map Cuba accurately. The bay is fed by three rivers and has one small outlet to the sea. We putt-putted around in a small boat powered by an impossibly small outboard (yet another reminder that fuel was scarce and expensive) and looked for manatees. We didn't see any but explored a few inlets into the mangroves that can only be described as tunnels, since the mangroves formed a closed canopy over us. We went ashore on the far side of the bay and hiked up to the ruins of the villa owned by two Americans, known only as "Mr. Mike" and "Mr. Phil." The roofs were gone and strangler vines were cracking the walls as the jungle reclaimed the formerly elegant estate.

That image provided a metaphorical reminder that nature had come back, at least to some degree, in Cuba. When Christopher Columbus landed in 1492, the island was about 90 percent forested, according to Tony. By 1812 only half the trees remained, and by 1959 forest cover was down to 14 percent and declining fast. Now it stood at 21 percent, and if people like Tony Perera had their way, that number would rise even higher.

As we toured, Tony kept up a running patter on some of the animals native to Humboldt that we weren't encountering. One was the bee hummingbird, the world's smallest bird, and the smallest frog in the world, *Eleutherodactylus iberia*. Then there was the largest insectivore in the world, the soledon, and elsewhere on the island, the smallest scorpion. Cuba also has one of the smallest owls (and once had the largest owl), as well as both tiny and giant bats. All of which raises the question: Why does nature go for extremes on islands?

Biogeographers and ecologists have been pondering this for many decades. In the early 1960s, J. Bristol Foster of the University of British Columbia theorized that reduced predation and competition on islands allow some species to expand into niches that would on the mainland be occupied by other species. In general there is less diversity on islands—they're often harder to reach—and over time that diversity diminishes through extinction until it finds an equilibrium with in-migration from the mainland. This was one of the conclusions of the great biologist E. O. Wilson, who with R. H. MacArthur published *Theory of Island Biogeography* in 1967. Curious about this phenomenon, I contacted Foster, Wilson and other biogeographers after my trip. As Wilson summed it up, the lack of diversity on islands "opens the door for ecological opportunity" for the resident species. Something like this happened on a global scale some 65 million years ago, when mammals invaded every niche formerly occupied by the giant herbivore-eating dinosaurs, according to a study published in *Science* in 2010.

What this means is that the factors that keep small animals small and big animals big may no longer apply. Another scientist I spoke with, Mark Lomolino, who with James H. Brown coauthored the classic work *Biogeography,* noted that among island mammals, large animals tend to get smaller, while small animals tend to get larger, with the tipping point being creatures about the size of a red squirrel. He suspected that given the absence of predators and the uncertain food supply of islands, the smaller offspring of large mammals such as mammoths survived better, eventually driving the mammoth on the island of Crete down to the size of a Great Dane. The absence of predators and competitors, meanwhile, enabled small animals to grow larger to take advantage of new food sources.

Thus Anguilla once was home to a 300-pound rodent dubbed *Amblyrhiza*. Consider this rodent together with the Cretan mammoth and, presto, you can see the magic of the island rule: rodents larger than elephants.

While there may be powerful advantages to being the biggest or smallest—an exceptionally large animal may have the edge in competing for a wider variety of resources or in surviving during lean times, while a small one may best elude predators—either extreme involves fateful tradeoffs. The bee hummingbird may have few enemies, but with a heartbeat roughly twenty times that of a human, it has a nonstop need for energy; a person with an equivalent metabolism would have to consume 100 pounds of food a day. Such specialization makes these species extremely vulnerable to ecosystem disruption. In Humboldt, Tony pointed out a plant called *Dracaena cubensis*, which is so closely linked to the rocky, magnesium-rich and nutrient-poor local soil called serpentine that botanists haven't been able to grow it in Havana.

The absence of predators affects animals in other ways besides size. In Humboldt Park, for instance, Tony said there is a snake called *Alsophis*. On the mainland the snake's near relatives are poisonous, but while the variant on Cuba has sacs to produce venom, it has lost the ability to inject the poison. Testimony to the absence of predators is the fact that there are no poisonous snakes on Cuba.

Another life-form seizing the brass ring of ecological opportunity has been the lowly snail. Colorful tree snails of the genus *Polymita* snails have proliferated wildly in Cuba, particularly in the hills of Pinar del Rio, where they use the limestone to build their shells. Humboldt has *Polymita* snails as well, including one species that occurs in three colors, yellow, red and green. The pretty shells are in such demand (we passed vendors selling them beside the road) that the snails have become endangered, and in turn, the snail hawk (more formally, the hook-billed kite), which feeds exclusively on this one species of snail, has also become critically endangered.

Which brings us to the larger point of this exercise. There are no large mammal predators on Cuba, except for one that arrived a mere 7,000 years ago: *Homo sapiens*. Humanity's relatively recent appearance on the island may explain why some animals persisted longer there than on the continents. The giant sloth, for instance, vanished from the South American mainland roughly 11,000 years ago, presumably hunted to extinction, but survived for another 5,000 years in Cuba. Humans probably did in the giant owl that once ran around the island as well. Before our arrival it had no need to fly, and whether or not the giant owl realized the fatal error of this evolutionary choice, it could not rediscover the ability to do so.

As an aside, when I first heard about the discovery of the bones of tiny *Homo erectus*–like hominids on the island of Flores in 2004, I immediately thought of this aspect of islands. Dubbed *Homo floresiensis* and nicknamed "hobbits," these little people stood about three feet tall, had heads the size of a grapefruit, made stone tools, and cohabited on Flores with the typical assortment of island giants and dwarves—including a pony-sized elephant, a rat the size of a dog and giant Komodo dragons—until about 12,000 years ago. The remains of several hominids of all ages were found in a limestone cave called Liang Bua.

If the hobbits did represent the last living examples of *Homo erectus,* they lived past the species' extinction date by some 90,000 years, which would be astounding in itself. Some critics of this hypothesis claim that the hobbits were merely a dwarf family of modern humans, the result of random mutation that spread because of the isolation of this family. But is it possible that the hobbits were a result of the same processes that produced Flores's dwarf elephants and giant rats? If so, from what original form could the hobbits have derived—*Homo erectus* or *Homo sapiens*? I doubt these questions will be settled anytime soon, but recent analysis of the bones supports the mindboggling possibility that the hobbits were indeed a relic of the deep past. For instance, an analysis of the hobbits' long, flat feet suggests they had more in common with early bipedal hominids, who had yet to develop a foot that facilitated long-distance running. Regardless, the hobbits stand as the most intriguing discovery of this century thus far.

The peculiar patterns of islands may seem like curiosities, but they have great relevance today, argues Mark Lomolino. For one thing, the destruction of mainland habitats due to agriculture and urbanization is turning many continents into a series of islands, and Lomolino wonders whether, for instance, the disappearance of large predators in nature reserves is having the effect of replicating the process of dwarfism on the mainland. Wilson agrees and notes that our understanding of island evolution can help us understand how to preserve natural systems everywhere. More specifically, because island species tend to be so exquisitely adapted to particular circumstances, and because they evolve in isolation from predators and parasites on the mainland, they are particularly vulnerable to disruption. That's why, says Wilson, most of the major extinctions caused by humans have occurred on islands.

Following our stop in Humboldt we made our way east and then south, first to the exuberantly tropical city of Baracoa, and then past Guantánamo to Santiago and Granma. It's a stunning drive, through rainforests and past waterfalls and the deep limestone gorge of the Yumuri River, with cliffs towering hundreds of meters high. Along the way we saw someone at the side of the road offering a Cuban parrot for sale. Tony didn't want to stop, because the parrot is endangered, and if we did stop he would have felt obligated to denounce the man and have him arrested, and he didn't want to spend the rest of our day dealing with the bureaucracy. From the look of the parrot, the species should be the official mascot of the revolution, as its olive-green feathers make it look as if it were copying Fidel's combat fatigues to demonstrate solidarity with the revolution.

Once we passed through the divide on the Nipe-Sagua-Baracoa Mountains, we descended toward the south coast, and the climate dried out noticeably in a matter of miles. On the coast we encountered thousands of melon cacti. As we drove past the DMZ that divides the American-controlled portion of Guantánamo from Cuba, Alberto helpfully provided the Cuban perspective on past American meddling in Cuban affairs. Tony wryly remarked that the 1-kilometer-wide zone, with its fences and land mines, was "the most protected place in Cuba." He also described the Cuban city of Guantánamo as the "ugliest" in Cuba. The tamarind-lined boulevard leading up to the city, however, was quite lovely. Farther on, another boulevard was lined with *Guaiacum* trees, whose precious wood contains oils that protect it in seawater and make it an ideal material for boat rudders. In town we looked for a *paladar* (a private Cuban home that offers meals) for lunch, but settled for pizza. I noticed a number of cafés billed as vegetarian restaurants, another example of the Cuban tendency to make a virtue of necessity, as there was little meat, nor much of anything else, in Guantánamo.

The southeastern coast of Cuba has to be one of the most beautiful in the Caribbean. There are formations called marine terraces in Punta Caleta, easily visible from Parque Nacional Desembarco del Granma (which commemorates Castro's landing). Some 500 meters high, with twenty-four stairsteps, each dozens of yards high, these terraces provide a dramatic record of past sea-level rises and falls. Lifted from the sea courtesy of plate tectonics, they offer paleontologists a perfect site to study past climate change. In a 1999 UNESCO report, Jim Barbarak called the terraces the most impressive coastal cliffs on the east coast of the Americas from the Canadian Maritimes to Tierra del Fuego.

The beaches are pristine, the waters clear, and the occasional lagoons rich. We stopped at Daiquiri Beach, supposed home to the drink that was made famous by the Floridita in Havana. We passed through spotless and delightful-looking towns such as Imías.

The only reminders that there was more to this tropical paradise than met the eye were the occasional billboards exhorting revolutionary fervor (the island's inhabitants don't look particularly fervent), and Alberto's continuing monologue on the revolutionary history of the island. It turned out that Alberto had traveled extensively for the regime, and, amusingly, we discovered that we might have been in Vietnam at the same time, though I was in the south reporting and he was in Hanoi doing God knows what.

It was eerie but pleasant to listen to the two running commentaries. While Alberto recounted in detail every significant event of the revolution—"Here in Granjita Siboney, Castro holed up in a safe house on the twenty-fifth of July, 1953, and then attacked the barracks on the twenty-sixth, upon which Battista strafed the house"—Tony filled in the biological significance, noting that the caves at Siboney Justisi contained a Cuban boa that sat at their mouth and caught bats as they flew in and out. (Both

Siboneys are named for the aboriginal hunting and gathering tribe that set-tled Cuba roughly 4,000 years ago.)

We stopped for the night in Santiago in another charming colonial wreck, the Casa Granda. The hotel sits right off Cespedes Square, named, as Alberto informed me, for the "father of the country, who in 1868 set free the slaves and initiated a war with Spain." Santiago is known for its music, and indeed, the city fairly vibrates in the evening. I stopped by a couple of clubs and was immediately mobbed by beautiful young *giniteras* (girls, often with college degrees, who moonlight as call girls). Surprisingly Alberto defended the practice, noting that each *ginitera* could support four people, but, as I was married with children, I decided that I was not going to make this particular contribution to the Cuban economy.

Our visit to Granma Park the next day prompted another history lesson from Alberto and some reminiscences from Tony. He had fond memories of climbing Mount Turquino, which is connected to the coastal park by a corridor, as a rite of passage when he was a high school student. The moun-tainous terrain is covered by a beautiful evergreen forest, which has the feel of a dry tropical forest on the lower slopes and gives way to a cloud forest in the upper elevations. Granma extends 17,500 hectares, and Tony hopes that it will be joined with the 30,000 hectares of neighboring Parque Nacional La Bayamesa to form a 50,000-hectare park.

On the way back into town, we stopped at a stunning vista point. I remarked that if I were the hotel-building type, this is where I'd site my resort. Tony amiably replied, "In that case, I'd be fighting you." He went on to note that he had already won a big battle by halting a plan to dynamite the cliffs and straighten the road.

On the way back we stopped for lunch as Los Galleanos, an immaculate small resort hotel perched on a cliff and connected to the beach by a 200-step stairway. There were few tourists, and Tony remarked that what build-ing had taken place in the area was more preparatory to an expected tourist influx than a response to current demand. That demand will come, and I only hope that Cuban officials open the valve in a cautious way that pre-serves the wonderful purity of this part of the island. Christopher Colum-bus is said to have observed when he landed in 1492, "This is the most beautiful land that human eyes have ever seen." It still is.

After traveling back to Havana, I met, at the recommendation of Mary Pearl of Wildlife Trust, with Orlando Torres, a distinguished zoologist from the University of Havana. Short, balding and exuberant, Orlando was impossible not to like. Back then he made about $23 a month, but he was a living embodiment of the truth that if you love your work, everything else will fall into place. He offered to take me up to Zapata Swamp National Park.

If Alberto's obsession was cars, Orlando's was birds. As we entered the Ciénega Zapata, he became visibly excited. Ciénega Zapata is not only the largest municipality in Cuba, it's also the least populated, with only 9,000 permanent inhabitants. Our first destination was the Hatiguanico River, which runs westward, start to finish, through Zapata. We met up with Cesar Fernandez, the local park ranger, and hopped into a small outboard to explore the park. Cesar's park office was solar-powered (again the scarcity of fossil fuels being the driving force), and was connected to the river by a canal. Orlando proudly claimed that the Hatiguanico is one of the few rivers in the world that has no human influence for its entire length.

I could believe him, seeing how cool, delicious and absolutely clear its water was. This was as close to a wetland Eden as any place I've been since the Ndoki. At 50 by 60 miles, Zapata Swamp is the size of Delaware and is the largest wetland in the Caribbean. Orlando said that Zapata is a bit like the Everglades in structure, meaning that it is really a broad, shallow sheet of slowly flowing water. Here again, the economic crisis had protected the outer part of the swamp, as Cuba now used 50 percent fewer chemicals in agriculture, further reducing the already small burden coming from the rice fields outside the park.

As we made our way a constant parade of herons, egrets and kingfishers passed ahead of us. Orlando counted twenty-five species of birds in the first hour alone. We stopped at a deep pool, the site of one of the river's tributary springs, and I dove into the shimmering, cool water. Like the river, the pool teemed with fish. I held my breath and dove down, but it was pointless trying to find the bottom; Orlando said that scuba divers had gone down as far as 200 feet and still not found the inflow point.

The next day we returned to explore a different part of the park. We entered at Salinas, formerly a commercial salt flat that has been returned to nature, and then went toward the beach at the Bay of Pigs. While the day before we had been surrounded by lush vegetation, today we were closer to the ocean, where it was drier. Once again Orlando began calling out birds he spotted. "There's a pewee . . . a black hawk! . . . a West Indian woodpecker . . . Wilson plover! . . . green woodpecker." We were then joined by a guide named Osmani—"The best in the park!" boasted Orlando with his irrepressible exuberance.

Osmani tried playing a tape of the trogon, the Cuban national bird, with its long scalloped tail, blue-green back, red belly and white front, but had no luck in attracting any. We headed farther into the swamp, where Osmani seemed to be looking for something particular. He led us to a stand of dead palms and, peering around, found the one he wanted and began scratching its trunk. After a moment he heard something. "She's coming up," he whispered in Spanish.

A moment later a tiny suspicious head appeared at the top of the hollow trunk. While trying not to scare the bird, Orlando could barely control his excitement. "This is the bare-legged owl [properly *Otus lawrencii*]!" he whispered. "It's a very good record." Trying to convey the significance, he explained, "If sighting a trogon is worth a dollar, the bare-legged owl is one million dollars!" He went on to say that only the Cuban pygmy owl is smaller; it might actually be the smallest owl in the world.

We then headed deeper into the swamp and toward the Bay of Pigs. Orlando said that he has documented 115 species just along this road. As we drove I spotted a tall bird with a white chest perched on a stump in the wetland. I tried to point it out to Orlando, but it flew off before he turned around. With typical exuberance he thrust a bird book into my hands, and I riffled through, trying to find a match. When I did, both he and Osmani laughed, as I was pointing to the ivory-billed woodpecker. Count this as a dubious and unconfirmed sighting.

As shallow ponds proliferated we began seeing more and more stilts and other wading birds, their legs almost impossibly thin to enable them to stand more easily in flowing water. We finally reached Playa Largo, the beach at the bottom of the Bay of Pigs and the site of the abortive CIA-sponsored 1961 invasion. Setting aside the question of whether the Cubans had been tipped off to the plan, by simply wading out I could see that this was a terrible place to launch a major offensive. I could walk out hundreds of yards, and still the water was barely knee-deep, meaning that any landing craft would have to disgorge its soldiers far offshore, and they would be terribly exposed as they made their way in.

Clearly Zapata is better suited as a refuge for migratory birds, American crocodiles, whistling ducks, iguanas and hundreds of other species than it is for invasions. Earlier I'd spoken with Martin Acosta, another Cuban ornithologist from the University of Havana. He described how Zapata and other wetlands in Cuba are vital as a refugium for the whistling duck, the pink flamingo, the wood stork and many other birds that are under severe stress elsewhere in the Americas. As much as the world needs Cuba as a laboratory for sustainable living in a post-fossil-fuel and economically constrained world, it also needs Cuba's ecosystems as a haven for animals, birds, plants and trees that are under siege everywhere else.

What will happen to Cuba after Fidel dies is unknowable. Ironically, there is faint cause for hope in the strict adherence to ideology of Cuba in contrast to the Soviet Union. There the so-called *nomenklatura* and KGB were corrupt and self-seeking by the time of the collapse, and they promptly set about divvying up the spoils as communism gave way to cowboy capitalism. While ruthless, Cuban intelligence officials are more idealistic, and if nationalism rather than greed prevails as Cuba opens, there's hope for Cuban nature.

And so I left this place, a place that is so beautiful and yet has endured so much pain. I left feeling elated, and even six years later, I can't think back upon this trip without smiling. Whatever happens after Fidel and the countdown end, I hope whoever is in charge realizes what priceless treasures the nation possesses in both its ecosystems and in such protectors as Antonio Perera, Orlando Torres and Martin Acosta.

CHAPTER 15

Midway

O n a beautiful warm January evening on Midway Atoll, which sits smack dab in the middle of the Northern Pacific at the extreme western end of the Hawaiian chain of islands, I stood with Stuart Brown and Stacy Koslovsky, two Duke University graduate students, on a small bluff, beyond which lay a perfect white sand beach that ended at the atoll's lagoon. The spot we'd chosen was next to one of the many impromptu runways that Midway's millions of albatross use for takeoffs—a stretch of sand that ran downhill between two clumps of beach shrub toward the lagoon. As the day moved toward sunset there was a noticeable uptick in activity, and we prepared for the best show in town. Laysan albatross (the most numerous species on Midway) are rather clumsy on the ground but magnificent in the air. Built for gliding over thousands of miles of the Pacific, they need the long runways to get enough lift from their six-foot wingspans.

Albatross waiting to take flight formed a rough line at the beginning of the runway. When a bird's turn came to take its shot, it careened down the path, feet flapping as it tried to get airborne. Birds would occasionally wander across a runway during a takeoff, leading to graceless collisions and many near misses. Every so often, an albatross would abort its attempt and end up in a face-plant in the sand. Young albatross seemed to be hanging around the runway, and Stu and Stacy speculated that the juveniles considered it a good place to pick up mates. (Because the birds mate for life, they tend to be very choosy, as is evident from their elaborate courtship rituals.) Some confirmation of this hypothesis came in the form of a couple of albatross performing the Laysan's courtship dance just off to the side of the runway. The dance looks like a variant of "Hand Jive" from *Grease,* although performed with the head and neck rather than the hands. Stu, who had been coming to the spot for several days, shook his head sadly, observing, "Relationships formed near the runway tend not to last."

If albatross takeoffs are nerve-racking, landings are even more fraught with peril. As I walked back to the former officers' quarters where I was staying, I watched the birds come in. For an albatross, every landing is an emergency landing. Finding a spot to land is difficult enough, since every available bit of land on Midway seems to have a nest. Unless there's a stiff wind to land into, they have to put on the brakes immediately on touchdown, and quite often this, too, ends up in a face-plant.

The whole panoply was endearing, even heartwarming, not least because the albatross now own Midway. There's a lot of tragedy at the ragged edge of the world, but the story of Midway suggests that every now and then tragedy can set the stage for something wonderful.

Nearly a century ago, the apostate Russian revolutionary Leon Trotsky quipped, "You may not be interested in War, but War is interested in you." The reductio ad absurdum of this insight applies to Midway Atoll, which existed as a largely ignored and very remote republic of seabirds before it was swept up by the gathering storm of World War II in the 1940s. The unlucky fate of this subtropical atoll was to figure prominently in the strategic plans of both Japan and the United States.

If Japan was either to invade the United States or set up a buffer to protect its shores, its military needed a foothold in the North Pacific. Conversely, unless the United States had a major airfield and naval base well west of Hawaii, it would de facto cede most of the Pacific to Japan, and at the same time leave U.S. western shores vulnerable to surprise attack. Thus did an atoll whose previous human visitors had been egg and feather collectors (who in short order killed off most of its birds and turtles) find itself at the epicenter of one of the great conflicts of the twentieth century.

Now, almost miraculously, Midway is once again a republic of birds. I've been to a number of places where wild animals are trusting of humans, but perhaps none so unlikely as Midway Atoll. After more than a century of abuse at the hands of man—first being slaughtered for their feathers by hunters, then being paved over by Seabees, then shelled by the Japanese during World War II, and finally Osterized by the engines of the planes of the U.S. Strategic Air Command during the Cold War—the albatross and other birds don't seem to bear a grudge. Maybe that's because they've won.

Albatross have succeeded where the Japanese military failed and have successfully taken over the island. And they did so in a way that Mahatma Gandhi would applaud—through passive resistance. It's only fair that they are now dominant, given that they have ancestral rights to Midway, but it's still both eerie and wonderful to see how the birds have been able to enforce an avian eminent domain and build their nests on every available open space, including the middle of the island's paths. It's no mean trick for a bird to domesticate a superpower. Even more touching has been the gracious way in which we humans have surrendered control of this much-fought-over place. The story of Midway shows that sometimes it's good to have a superpower as a friend.

I got the chance to visit Midway in January 2008, when I was invited to accompany a group of graduate students from Duke University's Nicholas School of Environment on a research trip to the atoll, where they would pursue their studies of marine and coastal issues. My invitation came from Bill Chameides, an atmospheric scientist who had recently taken over as dean of the school. Bill had had to cancel the trip at the last minute because of a bad case of the flu, and so the faculty duties fell to Andy Read of Duke and Dave Johnston of the National Oceanic and Atmospheric Administration and the University of Hawaii, both highly regarded experts on marine conservation. Also offering insights to the students (and me) were the wildlife biologists; the refuge manager, Barry Christian; and park rangers stationed on the atoll. The graduate student contingent consisted of eight young women and one young man.

For me the students were like a jolt of vitamin C from the moment I met up with them at the University of Hawaii. I've given lectures at a number of campuses and occasionally taught courses over the years, and I've come to the conclusion that one of the greatest compensations of teaching is the sheer surplus energy of intellectually curious young minds. Forget about elixirs and fountains of youth, the concentrated energy of the young—if they are engaged in something that excites them—is a proven tonic.

Our point of departure was the Honolulu airport. From the outset it was obvious that Midway was governed by a different set of priorities. We had to fly in by night, for instance, and the 1,250-mile trip was made doubly long because only propeller-driven planes are permitted to fly into the atoll, and then only once a fortnight. The inconvenience for humans is all part of concierge-level service for the birds. The logic is that the millions of birds that nest on Midway are mostly settled in by night and therefore less likely to have encounters with planes during takeoffs and landings. Moreover, prop planes are more maneuverable and require less runway on landing, which also serves to minimize bird deaths. Just before we landed, a fire truck came out to run interference in front of the plane and encourage sleepy albatross to move out of the way.

We flew to Midway on a chartered Gulfstream G-1 that had been making the round-trip to the atoll for decades. During the five-hour flight, Dave Johnston gave me the amusing history of how these stringent restrictions came about.

With the end of the Cold War, the fate of the necklace of atolls that linked Midway to the Hawaiian chain moved into conservationists' field of vision. Heedless development, tourism, and both witting and unwitting introduction of exotic species had already wreaked havoc on the ecology of the main islands. With no human inhabitants, the Northwestern Hawaiian Islands offered a tempting opportunity to set up a refugium for some of the chain's many indigenous species.

Discussions about the fate of the islands got going in earnest after 2000, and the very surprising hero of the second battle of Midway was none other than George W. Bush, a consensus pick as the president with the worst environmental record in American history.

Bush's executive order establishing Papahanaumokuakea Marine National Monument can only be described as wonderful. The Northwestern Hawaiian Islands already had some protection—presidents have recognized that Midway is a special place since the era of Teddy Roosevelt—but when Bush gave Midway and adjacent atolls monument status, he also imposed protective measures developed by the U.S. Fish and Wildlife Service that were strictly focused on preserving the ecology of the marine preserve.

The story of how this protection came about offers a glimpse of how Washington works. As was the case with Yellowstone Park in the nineteenth century, Midway's ace-in-the-hole was that it had no economic value. At 28 degrees North latitude, the atoll is subtropical, and while air temperatures in January are pleasant, the water is cool (Midway represents the northern limit of coral), making the atoll less attractive as a winter retreat for human snowbirds.

Every conservation victory needs a champion, and from what I can gather, a key player in establishing the monument was Laura Bush. Through meet-ings with former Coast Guard admiral Roger Rufe (then with the Ocean Conservancy and now with the Department of Homeland Security), the first lady became interested in marine issues, particularly the fate of the North-western Hawaiian Islands. A screening of a National Geographic documen-tary about the islands was arranged at the White House, and the president remained for the subsequent presentation by Jean-Michel Cousteau.

Bush was taken with the idea of establishing the world's largest marine sanctuary around the islands and atolls that link Midway to the main Hawaiian chain. His interest astonished many in the environmental com-munity. David Helvarg, for instance, executive director of the marine group Blue Frontier, quipped, "Perhaps he thought the monk seals were an oppressed Christian group."

In any event, Bush decided to go ahead. As Andy Read explained it, the Fish and Wildlife Service was charged with drawing up a set of rules to gov-ern access to and use of the area. Assuming that this would be a protracted negotiation, the wildlife service came up with a very strict wish list, in the belief that some of these rules would inevitably have to be given up. But then Bush decided that it would be easier to designate the region a monu-ment, which he could do by executive order. Rather than spend time devel-oping a new set of regulations, he directed the involved agencies to use the rules that the wildlife service proposed. Thus Bush created the largest marine protected area in the world, governed by the most conservative and conservation-minded set of regulations yet imposed on a U.S. site.

This decision garnered so much positive publicity for the beleaguered president that he set in motion plans to establish a number of other monu-ments in the final year of his administration, protecting Palmyra Atoll and the Marianas Trench, among other marine treasures. Helvarg believes that this late-developing interest in monuments exactly recapitulates President Clinton's flurry of monument designations at the end of his second term. In Clinton's case, it was Bruce Babbitt who planted the idea that through execu-tive orders and the establishment of monuments, he could protect more land than Teddy Roosevelt. Arguably, protecting isolated parts of the oceans is easier, but it is also arguable that the oceans are most in need of protection.

That became obvious once we began to tour the island.

But first, a little background.

When it emerged from the sea some 28 million years ago, Midway was situated where Oahu now stands. Continental drift has been moving the Pacific plate slowly northeast ever since. Within Midway's encircling coral are three islands. At 1,200 acres Sand, the only inhabited island, is the largest, followed by Eastern at 334 acres and then Spit, which at 6 acres is a mere dot.

The atoll almost, but not quite, qualifies as a Pacific tropical paradise. It has the requisite white-sand beaches and achingly blue lagoons, and when the weather holds it's pleasant enough. In winter, however, the northern Pacific's big storms regularly march through. Midway also has more infrastructure than the stereotypical paradise. Sand and Eastern still bear the marks of the war, including miles of runways in various stages of decomposition. (Only the main runway on Sand, where we landed, is maintained, since it provides the sole emergency landing strip for large planes in the northern Pacific.) Aprons, hangars, fuel depots, pillboxes, barracks, sheds and other legacies of past wars and struggles also cover the land. There are older ruins as well, such as the decaying remains of the veranda-skirted cable station built in 1905 for employees of the Commercial Pacific Cable Company, the enterprise that built and maintained the transpacific portion of the world's first round-the-world communication network. (No trace remains, however, of the posh hotel built in the 1930s by Pan Am to lure notables like Ernest Hemingway and John D. Rockefeller.)

Much of what remains is gradually returning to nature, and there is actually a good deal of charm in the sun-bleached, slowly slumping structures left behind. War has left a more lasting imprint on the ecology of the island. For instance, the Navy dredged a channel to accommodate big ships and built a sea wall, both of which affected the water flow in the lagoon. The iron in the sea wall fertilized algae growth. This and other changes fostered the invasion of the ciguatera dinoflagellate, a toxic, single-celled plant that accumulates in fish and leaves them inedible for humans. (My wife, Mary, got as sick as she's ever been in her life after getting ciguatera poisoning from sushi in San Francisco.)

Left to its own devices, nature could probably accommodate the lingering impact of war, but it's having a harder time dealing with the by-products of peace and prosperity. Walk anywhere on the runways on either Sand or Eastern Island and you will see scattered skeletons containing boluses of fiber and plastic, the remains of young albatross who ingested one too many plastic lighters, pens or other trinkets the birds picked up on the open ocean. In fact, plastic lies everywhere on Midway, and virtually every bit of it has been transported there in the stomach or beak of an albatross.

All that plastic serves as a reminder that we can run but we can't hide from the detritus of the consumer society. There is nowhere more remote from the making or use of plastics than Midway. No matter, it makes its way there, courtesy of ocean currents. Midway has the misfortune to lie in the sweep of one of the great gyres of the North Pacific.

The North Pacific Gyre is a wind-driven current that is strongly influenced by the spinning of the earth, as is the North Atlantic Gyre, halfway around the globe. As the current slowly rotates clockwise across thousands of miles, it collects floating debris dropped from ships, dumped into rivers, or otherwise discarded, often many thousands of miles away. Geophysics thus conspires to collect and concentrate this garbage in a giant floating patch on the ocean, an area larger than Texas that lies in the Pacific between Hawaii and California. The Hawaiian chain has the ill luck to sit precisely in the middle of the lower arm of this gyre, and, as Dave Johnston puts it, the islands act like a "comb," trapping a good deal of the junk as it is swept past.

For wildlife, the tragedy is that the same forces that concentrate floating garbage are also vital to the food chain. While the vast expanse of the ocean seems to offer unlimited supplies of food, most of that water is nearly sterile. As Dave explains it, the oceans are dilute, so that anything that concentrates prey is important to marine mammals, birds and other predators that live off the ocean's productivity. This means that albatross, monk seals, whales and big fish look for the fronts that form boundaries between water bodies, such as the boundary between an ocean current and the surrounding water.

Albatross, for instance, look for markers like smooth surface waters, which signify a down-welling, or for choppy water, which marks the shear point where moving water meets the larger ocean. At such boundaries the differing movements of surface waters bring up nutrient-rich waters from the depths, which fertilize growing plankton, which then attract squid, which in turn feed the albatross and a host of other animals. These boundaries and convergence zones, however, also collect surface trash. The big seabirds evolved to find these zones and pinch food from the surface, and when they are feeding they don't always discriminate between a squid and a bright object like a lighter.

This became clear when Marc Romano, a Fish and Wildlife Service biologist, gave the grad students an assignment. If Midway does not exactly conform to the Michener ideal of a tropical paradise, from the point of view of a migratory bird professional like Marc, the atoll comes pretty close.

Ninety-six percent of the world's black-footed albatross and 99 percent of the world's Laysan albatross breed in the Northwestern Hawaiian Islands, two-thirds of them on Midway alone. The sight of hundreds of thousands of nesting birds brings up surprising emotions, possibly because such immense concentrations of life also remind us of how much has been lost elsewhere. Birds were literally everywhere, and either never developed or had forgotten any fear of humans. This means that they only grudgingly gave way when we walked or pedaled about the island. Indeed, they seemed sociable and curious (though not so curious as penguins, which can't get enough of people watching).

In fact, walking among the albatross is an ego-enhancing experience. Their most common vocalization is a clacking, and when that is multiplied by many thousands of birds, the resulting background noise sounds like polite applause, which gradually swells as you pass. Notwithstanding that the clacking is probably an expression of annoyance, we all got to feel like rock stars as we moved about.

To give the students some hands-on experience with the plastics threat, Andy, Dave and Marc sent them out to collect the stomach contents of dead birds. Once gathered, the contents were dumped on a table and itemized. In bird one, a plastic comb; bird two, a lighter, bottle caps, and a stopper; bird six, a plastic spoon; and so on. One bird had dental floss in its stomach, another monofilament (which Marc says attracts fish eggs, which in turn attract albatross). The plastics are mostly a threat when the birds are young—older, more developed, animals can regurgitate their stomach contents. Younger birds can survive one ounce, but two ounces of plastics crowds out food, and they starve.

Despite plastics and other threats like the stray fishhook, albatross have better chances than most of earth's species. Marc said that the northern species of albatross had the highest survival rates of any species of bird. One study of a colony documented a 94 percent survival rate year after year for adult albatross. (This compares with 70–80 percent for puffins and 30–40 percent for waterfowl.) Wildlife officials started banding albatross on Midway in 1952, and some of those original banded birds still turn up.

Further proof of the birds' low mortality rates is their leisurely approach to breeding. Many don't breed until after they are five years old, and some start as late as thirteen. If a species has a high infant mortality rate, evolutionary forces favor those that breed early and often. Marc explained that once a bird reached adulthood it really didn't seem to age any further. What must it be like to be an albatross and feel no sense of aging or loss with the passing of the seasons?

This longevity also could be taken as proof of the benefits of a virtuous lifestyle. In fact, there's something for everyone in the albatross's approach to family life. Feminists would have a hard time taking issue with the males, who pitch in and take over child rearing immediately after the babies hatch. Albatross may be one of the few species in which fathers are an asset rather than a clumsy menace around newborns. On the other hand, the "values" crowd might find inspiration in the birds' commitment to monogamy and their practice of mating for life.

Nutritionists might learn from the birds' healthy diet: squid and fish. Exercise buffs would approve of the albatross's willingness to cover large swaths of the planet just to find a good patch of squid. And in this day of scarce, expensive oil, energy-efficiency experts can marvel over the albatross's parsimonious energy use. Their graceful, tapered wings can lock in gliding position so that with favorable air currents an albatross can traverse huge distances with very little effort. They exploit the energy of storms and will ride the winds to fly 800 miles north—flying twelve hours at a stretch—to points just south of the Aleutians, where an underwater seamount causes an upwelling of the Kurosawa Current, which brings masses of squid to the surface. Once there, the albatross will bulk up before flying back to feed the chicks.

Biologists have succeeded in placing tracking devices on albatross. One bird covered 15,000 miles in 120 days, venturing as far as Japan. A computer-generated map of another bird's route near the Aleutians revealed that the bird followed the exact same path as one favored by long-line fishing boats in the area, which had the benefit of radar and sonar. For all the endless expanse of the Pacific, there turn out to be very few places to get a good meal, and so birds, humans, whales, seals and, for that matter, predatory fish all converge on the same places.

On Midway the three species of albatross coexist amicably. Laysan albatross are by far the most numerous, followed by the slightly larger black-footed albatross. There are also a few short-tailed albatross, the largest of the northern albatross species, distinctive because of their golden heads. After watching a mating dance of the black-footed albatross, Stu dead-panned: "Well, the stereotype holds. The black-footed birds are definitely better dancers."

In our wanderings we came across black-footed and Laysan albatross cohabiting. Andy was amused and speculated on how these couples came about: "It was late. . . . I had one too many squid. . . ." No one seems to know whether these mixed families work out.

One of the pleasures of Midway is that there are almost no motorized vehicles. The tiny island is ideally suited to bicycles, and that's what we used to get around. One of the group, a poised young woman from the United Arab Emirates named Suaad Alharthi, had never learned to ride, unfortu-nately, and so for the first few days she used a cumbersome three-wheeler. Since we were on what is possibly the best place on earth to learn to ride a bike—a flat piece of land with no cars and vast empty expanses of pavement for runways and aprons—I took it upon myself to teach her. There was never a possibility of driving off the road, so the process took about twenty minutes. All she had to do, after all, was learn to turn into a fall if the bike started to lean over.

Islands tend to attract eccentrics. The management of the island infra-structure has been outsourced to Chugach McKinley Inc., a Native American–owned company. Our administrative contact was a cheerful Inuit woman named Darlene, and at first it was a bit startling to be dealing with an Eskimo on a subtropical island. Darlene, however, is an unusual Inuit, professing to hate the cold—"I was always freezing in Alaska!" She doesn't like fish, moreover, or birds, for that matter. She seemed to like us, though, and cheerfully joined us for meals and the occasional beer at the Captain Brooks (named for the sea captain who stumbled on Midway in 1859), a small, airy bar built on the low dunes on the north beach.

Part of the study routine was to take trips out to various parts of the atoll. John Klavitter, the resident ranger, took us out to Eastern Island, a virtually featureless patch of deteriorating runway, sand and brush, to see Laysan duck and some of the other exotic birds that make it their home. Though the Laysan duck was once widespread through the Hawaiian Islands, hunting and habitat loss had reduced the world's population to a mere eleven members in 1911, before efforts to protect it began. A century later it remains the most endangered duck in the Northern Hemisphere.

It's easy to see why: The bird adapted to conditions without humans and, indeed, without mammal predators. Over the millennia the birds grew to prefer duckwalking to flying, and even lost some of their primary feathers. Before the appearance of humans and introduced species like rabbits (which eat the vegetation that sustains the bugs that sustain the ducks), the only real hazard for the ducks was curious albatross, which occasionally picked up chicks, trying to figure out what they were. Dave Johnston said that the ducks have learned to bark to scare off approaching albatross. As part of a recovery plan, a number of ponds were dug on Eastern Island, and the ducks were introduced. The effort has been incredibly successful, with up to 200 nesting pairs happily snapping up brine flies.

We got a full dose of Midway's other avian species—noddies, boobies, tropic birds and terns—as we explored Eastern Island. White terns, also called fairy terns, hovered around us. Andy told us that if we were patient and held our hands in the air, the fairy terns might land on them. Some of the group tried this, although I didn't hear of any success. One of the students, Leah Medley, who often seemed to be enjoying a private joke, looked at me seriously and announced, "I've decided that if a fairy tern lands on my hand, I'm going to make it my favorite bird."

Midway also serves as a refuge for a number of other endangered species. Monk seals and green sea turtles haul out on the beaches, acrobatic Hawaiian spinner dolphins fly through the lagoons, and fish that have become rare elsewhere, such as giant trevally, are common here.

Almost every species on the island has some human agency or agent studying it and protecting it. On Midway, at least, each animal has a guardian angel. And while all this scientific firepower and goodwill has definitely improved the prospects for the local species, it may not be enough.

Despite endangered species protection and the security of the Midway Atoll refuge, for instance, Hawaiian monk seal numbers are not really recovering to the degree that Dave Johnston and other marine mammal specialists have hoped. There are about 1,300 monk seals left in the world, 60 of which make Midway their home. Monk seals are vulnerable to many threats, including plastics, but their plight may also be an indicator of a force that threatens every corner of the earth: global warming.

As Dave explained it, monk seals, like seabirds, look for boundaries and transition zones in the ocean for feeding opportunities. While albatross use their eyesight from far above, marine mammals have to find these zones from below, using their hearing, their senses of taste and touch, and their sonar. They listen for bubbles produced by turbulence, they use their sonar to detect changes in the thermocline (the boundary between warm surface water and cooler waters below), they taste the water to determine its salinity, and they use their whiskers to feel currents and track fish wakes.

Monk seals deploy all these abilities to find what is called the Transition Zone Chlorophyll Front (TZCF), a 200-kilometer-wide transition zone that separates the relatively sterile subtropical gyres in the North Pacific from the chlorophyll-rich sub-Arctic gyres. As the front moves north and south with the seasons, it fertilizes massive stretches of the ocean by bringing south nutrient-rich waters from the north, as well as by stirring up nutrients through its eddies. Apart from monk seals, white sharks, sea turtles, seabirds, and northern species like elephant seals and orca all join the party.

This moveable feast tends to hover between 22 and 30 degrees North in the fall and spring, said Dave, and then moves north of 40 degrees in the summer. Midway lies at 28 degrees North, so monk seals don't need to venture far to get a good meal when the front's nearby. Some years, though, the front does not come down as far as Midway, and that can have fatal consequences for seal pups within their first two years of life. In 1999 the front never fell below 32 degrees North. With no injection of nutrients, the pups born that year had a low survival rate.

Johnston stressed that the monk seals evolved to deal with climate variability, but he believes that their high mortality is a function of cumulative human impacts. For instance, in the deep past the seals might have migrated to the main islands of the Hawaiian chain in times of stress, but most of their haul-outs there have long since been given over to tourist development.

With their enormous range, albatross have far greater flexibility in seeking out feeding grounds, but they still need land to build their nests and raise their young. Unfortunately, almost none of the Northwestern Hawaiian Islands are more than a few feet above sea level. Dave ticked off the likely losses under very conservative sea-level-rise assumptions in this century: French Frigate Shoals would lose 43 percent of its area; Pearl and Hermes Reef, 31 percent; Midway, up to 67 percent; and so on.

On balance, Midway is a happy story, a story of humans atoning for past sins, of bloodshed giving way to life, of nature's resilience, of the exhilarating freedom of the albatross and their admirable lives, of a safe sanctuary on this beleaguered planet. But, like every story at the ragged edge of the world, it is a good story in the sense that a story of heroism and selflessness during a war is a good story: humans undertaking something elevating, but within a context of fear, death and destruction.

CHAPTER 16

In the Forests
It's Good to Be a Pygmy

I 've had the privilege of traveling with Pygmies in the African rainforest on several different occasions. From my first encounter I felt a bond that went beyond mere respect for the preternatural skills they displayed in the forest. Almost invariably Pygmies have proven to be good company, possessed of an easy sense of humor, and completely devoid of the passive-aggressiveness that all too often characterizes encounters between locals and expatriates in sub-Saharan Africa. When I was in the Ivory Coast, hostility toward whites bubbled just beneath the surface, and in both Francophone and English-speaking Africa, undercurrents of tension and resentment tended to make official and social encounters forced and exhausting—probably for both sides. With Pygmies, however, racial politics never intruded on any encounter.

Mike Fay, the explorer-botanist, has probably spent more time with Pygmies in their element than any other American during the past several years, and he, too, has noticed the absence of resentment. Fay's opinion is that the Pygmies' confidence in their forest skills makes it easy for them to approach expatriates on their own terms. Pygmies admire the white people's ability to navigate the modern economy, Fay once told me, and their attitude is, "You whites are good at certain things that we aren't good at, and we Pygmies are good at certain things that you aren't good at."

The key to their confidence lies in an important qualifying phrase—"in their element." Their element is the rainforest. Pygmies encountered outside of the rainforest all too often come across as pathetic displaced people displaying all the pathologies of the dislocated, including heavy drinking and the breakdown of family and social structures. In the forest, however, these same people thrive. Fay has seen this many times, and I've witnessed it as well.

The intractable problem facing Pygmies is that all the things they excel at take place in a setting that is vanishing by the minute. Pygmy culture endows its people with extraordinary knowledge about the workings of the forest and the habits of its creatures, but those who have acquired these skills from their elders have fewer and fewer places to deploy them.

My first experience with Ba'Aka Pygmies was on my initial forays from Bayanga in the Central African Republic. With Andrea Turkalo and Nick Nichols, I went into the forests around the town with a Ba'Aka Pygmy named Teti and some of his confreres. Andrea relied upon the Pygmies in her research on trying to determine what forest fruits, berries and nuts the gorillas ate, and how their diet overlapped with that of human hunter-gatherers. Pygmies have to be familiar with these foods as a source of nutrition, and they need to know how to recognize seeds embedded in scat in order to know what animals have been passing by and what they have been eating. When we came upon a pile of dung near a tree, Teti casually remarked, "Leopard." When I asked when it had been there, he replied, "Last night."

Although Andrea had by then studied 1,100 samples of gorilla dung, her specialized point of view had its drawbacks. On a trail, when we came upon a seed, she would recognize it only when Teti mentioned its name. "I'm more used to seeing these seeds coming out than going in," she remarked.

Another, more impressive display of Pygmy knowledge came just a few days later. On another of my trips out of Bayanga I went to visit Bai Hoku, a clearing near where gorilla researcher Melissa Remus had set up a research station, again accompanied by Andrea, Nick and Andrea's Pygmy assistants. Before setting off, Bakombe, one of the Pygmies, spied an assortment of seeds that the researchers had collected and arrayed on top of a stump. He instantly started to identify the trees from which each seed had come and what creatures had eaten it. The assortment was supposed to be limited to fruits consumed by gorillas, but Bakombe picked up one and, speaking Lingala, said that only people ate it. Andrea confirmed that Bakombe was right, and the seed should not have been included.

During our exploratory hikes we got a taste of how the Pygmies used their knowledge of gorillas' eating habits. Teti pulled some *mosabe* berries off a branch by the trail to see if they were ripe. If they were, gorillas were more likely to be in the area. Off the trail we came upon the fruit of *taebor montannu;* one of our trackers picked it up, identified it as gorilla food and gave us its Pygmy name, *mogaminza.*

While the average Pygmy's knowledge of the forest dwarfs that of all but the most erudite tropical biologists, and while they respect the forest for its bounty, few have any sense that the rainforest can be depleted or have any particular passion for protecting it. As we hiked we passed a five-foot-thick tree that other Pygmies had cut down to get at a honey-filled hive in its upper branches—about as wasteful a use of the forest as one could imagine. Pygmies don't see themselves as having the capability of killing off the forest, and at least the Pygmies I met had not yet realized that others might have that power. Throughout the Congo logging opens the forest to poachers, who quickly kill off game, but even though the Pygmies depend on hunting, those I spoke with did not make the connection of the inverse relationship between their livelihood and logging. One, when asked whether logging ruined the forest, shrugged and replied in effect, "We're just working for the white man." Another, thinking of the cash that loggers bring, quipped, "We eat money very well."

Make no mistake, though—none of the Pygmies I encountered showed any interest in seeking out opportunities to get regular jobs, settle down and raise the kids in the suburbs. The men loved money, but used it mostly for drink. What's remarkable is that while a number of Pygmy villagers have been in contact with Bantu villagers and expatriates for generations, periodically earning wages working as poachers, guides and porters, almost without exception the typical trappings associated with development haven't crossed the boundary between Bantu and Pygmy encampments. To be sure, the Pygmies have been persistently cheated and taken advantage of, but meager compensation does not explain the almost complete absence of modern material goods in the Pygmy villages I visited. Drink does, however, since it can consume a great deal of money and leave no trace except for the ruination of the families involved.

Mike Fay argued back then that, in a perverse way, the exploitation of the Pygmies and their binge drinking actually helped maintain at least part of Pygmy culture, since the only way they could get money was to use their native skills in the forest. Mike noted that they had lived in proximity to Bantu agricultural villages for over a thousand years, and that in all likelihood, the villagers had been exploiting them throughout that time. There had to be some benefit to the Pygmies to continue that relationship, since otherwise they could have easily vanished into the forest. Mike suspected that the lure of the villagers was that they offered access to manioc, bananas, taro and other foods. Since access to such carbohydrates was the biggest problem for Pygmies in the forest, they were locked into a devil's bargain that required that they stay relatively close to Bantu villages.

Perhaps one reason Pygmies don't seem interested in the trappings of modern material culture is that they are so good at making things on the spot. On our hike, one of the Pygmies picked up a nut from the ground, split it with a machete, and quickly fashioned a pick that he used to get out the meat. Whenever it started to rain, the Pygmies would almost instantly construct a domelike shelter out of broad leaves, supple branches and vines. Long before Pfizer began marketing Viagra, Pygmies with flagging sex drives were using *konssou,* a fruit that they described as a "male hospital." They find the fruit in the forest and trade it with villagers, who sell it to Arabs for a good deal of money.

As we continued our hike, we passed a trophy-sized bongo just off the trail. In other parts of Africa orthodontists from Texas would pay upward of $15,000 to shoot a specimen like this. Teti, who dealt with such white men, asked if we wanted to shoot it. When we demurred, he then offered to get any nearby gorillas to charge us by imitating the call of the females.

Pygmies tend to have strong stomachs. On one of our hikes we passed the rotting carcass of a dead elephant. The smell of decay was overpowering, and a sea of maggots rippled on the exposed innards of the long-dead animal. It takes a long time for a creature as big as an elephant to rot, and I was told of instances where Pygmies had come upon week-old elephant carcasses and then crawled into the infested body cavity and cut through the rotting meat to get to flesh that had not yet begun to spoil. We hastened past the dead animal before any of the Pygmies with us got the idea to do that.

———

While my journey to the *bais* of the CAR gave me a taste of Pygmy knowledge of the forest, I was to have an immersion experience nine months later when I joined up with Mike Fay for a trip into the Ndoki. As I noted in Chapter 7, my initial reaction upon hearing about this pristine forest was to resist the urge to visit it, and leave it in obscurity for its own sake. Subsequent to my visit to Bayanga, however, Mike contacted me and informed me that logging concessions were encroaching on the area, and that if something wasn't done to let the world know what was at stake and arouse public support, concessions would surely be granted in the Ndoki itself.

It did not take me long to set aside my misgivings. If the Ndoki needed to be introduced to the world, I wanted to be the one to do it. *Time* saw the potential of a first-person account of a visit to this extraordinary place, and I arranged to meet up with Mike Fay in Ouesso in June 1992.

The Ndoki lies in the extreme northwest corner of the Democratic Republic of the Congo. Entering overland from the north would require a long trip through wilderness with little access to water. (On its three other sides, vast swamps protect it.) The easiest entry point involved trekking in from Bomassa, a Pygmy village on the Sangha River. In 1992 there were two ways of getting to Bomassa. The easiest was to travel downriver from Bayanga, but that involved either a cumbersome search by untrustworthy border officials when crossing into Congo from the CAR or an undocumented border crossing. The other way was to fly on one of Congo's rickety jets up from Brazzaville to Ouesso, and then take a motorized canoe up the Sangha to the staging point. I took the latter route.

Ouesso's airport served as a mute emblem of the economic schizophrenia of Africa's resource-based economy. Landing, I noticed at least two half-completed terminal buildings. As it was explained to me, one requirement of the logging concessions was that the companies were obliged to contribute to a public-private partnership to upgrade the airport facilities. They discharged this commitment by building their section of the terminal on at least two separate occasions. Both times, however, the government reneged on its part of the bargain, leaving the city with a series of Potemkin-like facades for a terminal.

Ouesso itself was a dump, a growth of unplanned sprawl encircling what was once a colonial enclave set up to administer the area. Joining me on this trip was Karen Lotz, later the editor of *The Parrot's Lament*. The role she assumed for this trip was photographer. Although she had no prior experience, she's a quicksilver-fast study, and *Time* ended up using a number of her photographs. On arrival we connected with Mike Fay, and after a night at the run-down but once gracious villa rented by the Wildlife Conservation Society, we took a motorized canoe for the nine-hour ride upriver.

On the way we passed Kabo, the center of operations for Nouvelle Bois

Sangha, the logging company whose concession extended over much of the territory south of Bomassa. Mike said that the area on either side of the river was largely devoid of game. Hunters and poachers had been using the logging roads cut by the company as a way of gaining access to the forest. He also told us that there were hundreds of shotguns in the area, and that typically, the Bantu owner of a shotgun would hire a Pygmy, who would then go into the forest and hunt for him.

For Mike the pernicious ecology of logging was that it greatly extended the poacher's ability to enter the forest. He had done a study that showed that all game tends to be shot within a day's walk of the nearest road. The many roads built by loggers extend like capillaries into the forest, opening it to hunters, and, in many places, to follow-on colonists who then cut the secondary growth and establish farms. In this sense logging was a crucial first step in the process by which a great forest was destroyed.

Mike was casual in the extreme about his expeditions, and consequently we had gotten a late start out of Ouesso. This meant that we had to pick our way upriver by flashlight for the last several miles of the trip. Because we couldn't see the sandbars, we ran aground several times. This was not to be the last time we would find ourselves traveling by flashlight.

Bomassa lies about 25 kilometers south and west of the Ndoki River, across which lies the enchanted forest that time forgot. In Bomassa a small, spare set of cabins had already been built in anticipation of ecotourists who might someday visit carefully monitored parts of the forest. Mike Fay and others believed it would be necessary to open a small section of the Ndoki to carefully controlled numbers of tourists in order to help the local economy, whose support would be necessary if a larger, inviolate part of the area was to be preserved. Mike was well aware of the curse of ribbon development, and the last thing he wanted was for Bomassa to become a magnet for migrants. So he and his colleagues took pains to bring in workers on temporary contracts rather than enlarge the settlement.

After we settled into the camp for the night, Mike sent out word to the surrounding Pygmy villages that he was looking to hire trackers and porters. The next morning a group of Pygmies showed up, and if we had been hiring on the basis of first impressions, we would have sent the whole lot packing. Most were dressed in ragged clothes. More to the point, they were all drunk. Since it was morning, I had to assume that their response to the news that work had arrived had been to launch an all-night celebration.

Mike showed not the slightest concern, however, and hired two trackers he'd worked with before, Ndokanda and Joachime, on the spot. He also selected as cook a Bantu named Seraphim, whom he had also used before and who had proved to be reliable and good-natured. Mike then laid out all of our food and camping gear so that he could estimate how many porters we needed to hire. His method was to examine the goods and say, "That's half a Pygmy; that's three-quarters," and so on. Most of us would have counted the backpacks and used that as a base, but I was to learn that there was a purpose to this method.

Instead of putting on a backpack and adjusting the straps, for instance, the Pygmies would pick up a pack and then tie it to other packages, the whole of which would be exquisitely balanced. By using this method, they could carry staggering amounts of weight, especially given their diminutive size. The BaNgombe and BaNbengele Pygmies are taller (just under five feet) than most other Pygmies, but still tiny compared to us. The only one who carried just one backpack was the unfortunate given the job of carrying a single 132-pound backpack. During this repacking, we discovered another casualty of Mike's *que sera, sera* attitude toward jungle treks: We'd left our recently purchased supply of eggs (which last long and efficiently supply nutrients), chocolate and batteries back in Ouesso. We could get by without the food, but the batteries turned out to be an important oversight.

On Sunday morning at 7:30 Mike sent the Pygmies off toward the Ndoki. Ndokanda had gone with Mike into the Ndoki a few years earlier and knew the way to the first camp on this side of the river. It was 15 miles to the crossing point of the Ndoki River, and a good deal of the trek consisted of making one's way through swampy quicksand. With an early start, Mike entertained hopes that we could make it to the crossing point in one day, rather than stopping at a former research site called Djeke. Our hopes were dashed, however, when we set off an hour later and found our men drinking in a Pygmy village just a few hundred meters up the trail from Bomassa. Mike had to threaten to hire new porters to roust the crew, and then made a theatrical show of storming off, with Karen and me following.

By one o'clock we made it to Djeke camp, which had been established by Masazumi Mitani and Suehisa Kuroda in 1987. These legendary Japanese field researchers had been the first to explore the Ndoki, and just those few years earlier it had taken several days to get from Bomassa to the river crossing. Since then the researchers had cut a rudimentary trail and also driven

posts into the quicksand so that it was possible to pick your way through
the swamps by feeling for the sticks with your toes and thus get to the river's edge without sinking to your thighs with every step.

Two hours later the Pygmies finally showed up. Mike figured that they
had purposely stalled so that it would be impossible to get to our destination by nightfall. We had a pleasant dinner of soup, salami and cookies, and
as Karen and I settled in to sleep in the tent at about 8:00, I began to wonder whether Kuroda, who had described traveling in the Ndoki as "very,
very difficult," had intentionally overstated the hardships.

Just as I was drifting off to sleep, I felt something on my hand. I flicked
it off, only to feel something else crawl on me. Whatever it was that I had
flicked didn't like it, and decided to bite me. I woke Karen, who thought I
must be having a nightmare, but a second later I heard a strangled cry from
her. Suddenly bugs began dropping on us from every direction. I scrambled
to find the flashlight, and when I finally got it on, the light revealed that our
tent was filled with ants—by now to a depth of several inches. By slapping
at them, it seems, we have released some signal for the other ants to attack,
and suddenly we were being bitten by hundreds of them at once. We raced
out of the tent, stumbling over roots and a massive column of ants, tearing
off our ant-infested clothes as we frantically looked for the river—my reasoning being that we could hold our breaths longer than the ants could. As
we ran, more ants dropped on us from the trees.

We finally found the stream and, not really caring what might be in it,
jumped in, keeping only our noses above water. This did the trick. Eventually we emerged and, shaking out our clothes, got dressed and tried to
rouse Mike. He sleepily appeared at the front of his tent and, the soul of
sympathy, noted that driver ants could kill a tethered goat. He went back
to sleep, but the Pygmies, who had by now also awakened, were clearly
amused by the entertaining spectacle of our frantic dash. The ants unaccountably didn't seem to be interested in them.

I got hold of two simple hammocks we'd brought along and set them up
in the nearby forest, away from the ants' path. In doing so I drove a spiky
vine clear through my thumb, releasing a gusher of blood to entice God
knows what other predators that might be hanging around. Then it started
to rain. When the weather cleared, I heard a leopard cough. So much for
our first day.

The next morning we begin crossing the swamps that guard the Ndoki.

At one point I missed a post and sank in the muck to my chest before I managed to grab a root. As we moved through the swamps we began to approach the maze of oxbows and secondary channels of the Ndoki River.

The river itself is unnavigable. Channels become swamps become dead ends; fallen trees and branches are everywhere. Kuroda and Mitani had found a relatively narrow spot where they could cross the deepest part of the water in a small pirogue. We headed there and spent the next couple of hours ferrying ourselves and our bags across.

It was while out on the river that I finally realized how close to paradise our hike had brought us. The day was bright and dry, and soft breezes carried fragrant pollens. The water was absolutely pure. The only sounds were the rustlings of animals and insects. Mike had described the crossing into the Ndoki as a trip back to the Pleistocene, a time before humanity began reshaping the planet to its short-term needs. He was right, and it was the best feeling in the world.

When I first wrote about the Ndoki, my reporting that people had not been in the area had been greeted with widespread skepticism. Indeed, one of my *Time* colleagues insisted that Pygmies had taken him through the region some years earlier. When I brought this up with Mike Fay, he said that the man must have been confused about where he'd been, because the Pygmies were terrified of the place, and there was no evidence that they had ever ventured in before Kuroda entered the forest in 1987.

The neighboring Pygmies had no songs or stories about the region, and if they had actually ever been in the Ndoki, Mike argued, that would not be the case. The night before we crossed, Mike said the Pygmies had been talking about going into the area inhabited by Mokeli Mbembe—a monster of Pygmy lore that lives in the open areas. Mike suspected that the creature was actually a black rhino, an animal that Pygmies would not otherwise have encountered in the forest. (Years later Richard Carroll of the World Wildlife Fund confirmed this when he showed a rhino footprint to a group of Pygmies, who identified it as the track of Mokeli Mbembe.)

The physical barriers of the Ndoki also created a practical impediment for the Pygmies. Killing animals there would have been the easiest hunting any Pygmy had ever done, but getting the carcasses out would have been all but impossible. The river could not be crossed without a pirogue, and even if the resourceful Pygmies could have solved that problem, carrying the meat across miles of swamp would have presented a formidable challenge. The combination of superstition, physical barriers, and the availability of ample game outside the Ndoki protected the place for at least several hundred years.

The most dramatic evidence of the absence of humans, however, was the behavior of the local animals themselves. Once we crossed the river and began hiking toward Mbeli Bai, where we were to spend the night, we began to encounter animals, glorious numbers of them. When we came across a troop of red colobus monkeys they jumped a bit upon seeing us, but made no effort to flee. The same thing happened when we saw gray-cheeked mangabeys. Our first gorilla bellowed and did a false charge, but then, instead of moving off, he simply stopped and stared at us. All of these creatures would have fled immediately had we encountered them just 20 miles away. Their lack of fear was a poignant indication that they knew nothing about humans.

One of my concerns about this expedition had been that, even though my trip had been motivated by a genuine desire to help save this forest, I might inadvertently contribute to its destruction. The most obvious way this might happen would be by demystifying the region for the Pygmies. As game disappeared from the surrounding forest, the temptation of healthy, well-fed animals that took no fright at the presence of hunters might prove irresistible for them, Mokeli Mbembe or not.

So far, with one exception, that hasn't been the case. The one exception is somewhat surprising, because the man who brought a group of Pygmies into the Ndoki on a hunting expedition was not a local bush meat entrepreneur or trophy hunter, but Louis Sarno, a supposedly enlightened expatriate and the great champion of Pygmy culture. Apparently, at one point when game was scarce, Sarno went with a group into the Ndoki from the north (the one place where it is not girded by swamps). When the depredations were discovered, however, Sarno was chastened and has not taken Pygmies into the forest since.

In years prior to our expedition, Mike Fay himself had thought it acceptable to hunt in the Ndoki for scientific purposes. His argument was that it was not possible to carry enough food for an extended expedition through the forest and that the trivial amount of game that would be hunted would have no impact on the ecosystem. Mike is a passionate guy, and he was scornful of the naïveté of bleeding hearts who were absolutist about hunting.

When he shared his thoughts on the subject, my reaction was that he might be right in practical terms, but wrong in all other ways. Here was an opportunity to see animals as though humans were not on the planet. Why change that by showing them that we were killers? Surviving animals, at least the smarter ones, would quickly learn to run away from humans when they were hunted, which would mean that subsequent researchers would not have the advantage of studying naïve creatures.

More to the point, I argued that it would make it even more difficult to convince the Pygmies that hunting in the Ndoki was improper if they saw that it was permissible when they accompanied white researchers. And, although I did not say this to Mike, I simply felt that it was just wrong to introduce hunting into one of the only places on earth where animals were safe from guns, traps and poisons. I guess that made me a bleeding heart.

By the time I went into the forest with Mike, however, he, too, had decided that the Ndoki should be kept safe from hunting, even if done by researchers for the most noble reasons. I don't know who convinced him, but it wasn't me.

During this first day in the Ndoki, Karen and I had a vivid demonstration of the difference between Pygmies and all other peoples in the forest. We were hiking in a couple of different groups, and, for a time, Karen and I separated from the main group accompanied by our one porter, who was Bantu. He billed himself as a tracker and had spent a good deal of time in the forest, since he was married to a Pygmy woman and lived in a Pygmy village. We were not unduly concerned about being separated, because at that point we were generally following the river. Within fifteen minutes of parting company from the Pygmies, however, we were lost, and it was quite clear that our tracker was guessing where we should go. Eventually, one of the other Pygmies tracked us down and showed us the way. When I asked him how he knew where he was going, he pointed out a broken leaf along the trail. Amid this ocean of green, it was like picking out a particular grain of sand on a beach.

After we set up camp for the night, the Pygmies became somewhat withdrawn. Mike sat down to talk with them after dinner to see what was wrong and discovered that they didn't want to go any farther. I almost laughed, since I had never expected to be living out the cliché of every B movie about exploration—"At one point the porters refused to go on!" It turned out that they were afraid of this forest not only because of Mokeli Mbembe. The word *ndoki* means "sorcerer" in Lingala, and the Pygmies, peerless masters of the forest, were reluctant to find out whether their fears were justified. With the help of Ndokanda, who had accompanied him on a trip into the Ndoki some years earlier, Mike was able to convince the rest that their fears were unwarranted. I had mixed feelings about this victory. Without the Pygmies it would have been exceedingly difficult to continue, but if they overcame their fear, the forest's security would rest on human vigilance alone—a far more porous defense than religious terror.

Ndokanda had an interesting history. He was born across the Sangha River in Cameroon, and by turns had worked for a coffee plantation, for a logging concession and as an elephant poacher before Mike Fay hired him to help stop poaching. As we hiked it was Ndokanda who led the way. When I asked him how Ndokanda knew where to go, Mike replied, "He's probably following our tracks from 1990" (two years earlier). Little did he know then how true that statement was.

The next day we set off into what Mike jokingly called "the unknown." The Pygmies now became reluctant to take the lead. Given the loads they were carrying, it was an entirely reasonable position, since taking the lead also meant hacking a path with a machete. It promised to be an arduous hike, since we would have to leave the broad elephant trails and bushwhack through dense brush. Our goal—and Mike's ostensible reason for this expedition—was to find a clearing that he and Ndokanda had come across during an expedition two years earlier. Poring over satellite maps, Mike picked a path that would take us through uncharted forest. I'd brought along some good cigars, and I offered Ndokanda one if he was willing to cut the trail.

"You bet!" he said in Lingala, but after just forty minutes of work, he sat down. Mike, getting impatient, made a show of taking the machete, in part to goad the Pygmies. As we headed off he remarked, "The one thing Pygmies can't stand is for a white guy to lead in the forest."

We made our way on a zigzag path, trying to head south and east. Wherever we could we took advantage of elephant trails, which tended to hew to a north-south/east-west grid. Unfortunately, we did not find many east-west trails and Mike finally said, "We've got to head east!" and began hacking through the tree-falls and brush with a vengeance. At some points we were literally tunneling through the underbrush. By 3:30 I was parched beyond all measure. It was unclear whether we would find any water by nightfall, and we were facing the prospect of spending the night dangerously dehydrated. The Pygmies were nowhere to be seen.

As our thirst approached the unbearable, I heard Mike say, "Aha!" He'd spotted a thick vine, and after he hacked off a section at just the right spot, pure water began spurting into his mouth. I grabbed his machete and sliced at the plant called *Sissus danclydgia,* but managed to taste only a few remaining drops.

Here's what happened next (taken from *The Parrot's Lament*):

> As the sun sinks and it appears that we will spend a dry and desperate night, we finally hit sandy soil—a good sign. Soon we find elephant footprints filled with water. It looks pure, and I drink greedily. Fay's hand is so tired from hours of hacking with the machete that he cannot open the water bottle I have just filled.
>
> Just before dark, Ndokanda comes motoring by us. Not bothering to stop, he yells at Fay in Sangho, his Pygmy language, "You fool, I know this place. Right ahead there is plenty of water." Ndokanda is right, of course, and we are left openmouthed, wondering what enabled him to recall this tiny part of a vast forest from a brief foray with Fay years earlier.

The astonishment was, in fact, mutual, as the Pygmies could scarcely believe that white guys could even come close to finding this place. Later, Ndokanda, impressed by Mike's orienteering, offered a condescending and paternalistic compliment: "You are coming along pretty good."

That night I gave the Pygmies one of my precious trove of cigars. Sharing the communal wealth, they passed it around. Despite Mike's warnings that it was not something to be inhaled, each took a deep draw, causing the ash to increase visibly as the cigar passed from man to man. They must have had lungs of leather, since none of them so much as coughed, although one of the group remarked with approval, "That's strong!"

Five minutes later, when they had extracted the last toke (from a cigar that should have lasted forty minutes), Mike asked them whether it would be a good idea to build a road through the forest. He did this for my benefit, to make a point. They became visibly excited at this question, and I could see the scales falling from their eyes as though they'd finally figured out why we were really in the forest.

Samori, one of the most accomplished trackers, was the first to speak up. "Yes, build a road," he said. "It will mean lots of money." Rising to this potential opportunity, he went on, "We'll build it for you. We'll set up camp at Mbeli Bai [right in the middle of the park]; we'll bring our women, and we'll work until 2 p.m." (Apparently this was considered a reasonable workday in Pygmy culture.)

As Ndokanda launched into a long explanation of where he would put the road, another tracker, Joachime, jumped in: "Make it straight," he said, "not that zigzag path you took today."

Samori then piped up, still pursuing his original line of thought. "If you pay us well," he said with the subtly double-edged words of a true negotiator, "the work will go well." Having spent many hours trying to convince the Pygmies of the evils that follow roads, Mike gave me a long-suffering look.

The conversation then turned to elephants. "Good or bad?" we asked the Pygmies. Ndokanda, the former elephant poacher, answered unequivocally. "Good," he said. "This is their village, their real city." He was exactly right. Their grid of paths connected various feeding spots, plazas for socializing, and even health facilities. They used the mud baths, for instance, to get minerals, but also to remove ticks.

When I asked them which was the smartest animal, Somari was the quickest with an answer: "Chimps," he said, echoing what I had earlier heard from Bakombe in the Central African Republic, "because they can kill gorillas." He said they fought all the time. Ndokanda was skeptical, noting that he had never seen such a thing, but Somari insisted that he had witnessed a chimp smashing a gorilla with a stick. Ndokanda arched an eyebrow and, according to Mike, asked in Sangho, "Oh, really?"

For what happened in the days following, let me again quote from *The Parrot's Lament:*

> After a couple of days exploring the area, we set off deeper into the forest. Trips with Fay are a bit like a treasure hunt—if you consider the half-eaten remains of a fruit discarded by a gorilla to be treasure. Fay enthusiastically sampled these fruits, and I tried the juicy kernels of a *Myrianthus arboreus.* This may have been the moment I picked up a mysterious gastrointestinal disorder that took a couple of years of consultations with tropical medicine experts and rainforest healers to cure. Or perhaps I got the bug from the partially eaten *Treculia africanus,* a fruit eaten

by Pygmies, gorillas and chimps, and which, I discovered, tastes a little like peanut.

During these walks we would occasionally stop and ask the Pygmies to call duikers. They do this by holding the bridge of their nose and making a loud braying sound in imitation of the sounds made by these small deer-like animals when giving birth. Other duikers come running when they hear the sound, which makes hunting easy for the Pygmies. Hunting, however, is not our purpose. Among the other creatures attracted by the braying sound are chimpanzees that see this as an opportunity to do some hunting of their own and catch a duiker at a vulnerable moment.

Stopping intermittently to make the calls we attracted several unusual animals, including the rare yellow-backed duiker, an animal whose dull golden patch on its back supposedly gave rise to the myth of the Golden Fleece. Then, pausing for a rest, we hit pay dirt. Fay, Karen Lotz and I were ahead of the rest of the group of Pygmies along with Ndokanda. Ndokanda hunkered down and made the call. This time a group of large animals came crashing toward us, and for a moment I felt the shiver of being hunted.

That feeling vanished as soon as a very large band of chimpanzees appeared from the brush and saw us. They stopped dead in their tracks. Bloodlust gave way to astonishment. It was quite clear that they were seeing something they had never seen before. They began stamping their feet, shaking their arms, calling to one another and, occasionally, throwing branches at us. Little ones ventured bravely toward us, only to be pulled back by their protective moms. In the branches above us, a very old chimp with completely white hair gazed down on us slack-jawed with amazement. I wonder whether the other chimps would later turn to him for an explanation of these otherworldly visitors.

As many as 25 animals screamed at us from all sides as we maintained a studied, casual stance, minimizing jerky movements. Each time we made a move, a new round of calls erupted among the chimps, but they never showed signs of fleeing, and they never attacked. Wild chimps do not react this way to humans in any other part of the African rain forest. For more than two hours, the mesmerized chimps hovered around us, drawing to within a few arm lengths.

Later Mike Fay called this the signal wildlife experience of his fourteen years in Africa. (I'm sure his subsequent adventures eclipsed this moment.) For me it was the experience of a lifetime. For the chimps surrounding us, seeing humans amounted to an ape version of *Close Encounters of the Third Kind.* The ruckus they raised began with threats and distress calls, but some of them seemed to let out the hoots that chimps use to greet one another. I would like to think that at least some of these chimps were welcoming us apelike aliens into their forest.

With every encounter I became further convinced that this forest, empty of humans, is not devoid of intelligence of various sorts. There is the accumulated knowledge of the elephant civilization that gives this forest its distinctive flavor. There are the chimp bands whose members scheme and forge alliances for their own advancement, who make and use tools to get food, and who cooperate with one another when hunting or in conflict with other bands. There are the gorilla families dominated by silverbacks, who must be alert to treachery in their harems and plotting by ambitious young males. There is some measure of awareness in the leopards, who must learn a host of different skills in stalking and killing in their never-ending search for prey.

At some point during these forays I picked up one of the innumerable diseases lurking in the rainforest. It felt as though every bone in my body was broken. Most likely it was dengue fever, though Mike said that it might be any number of what he called "deadly tick diseases." Over the years Mike has come down with so many illnesses that he's rather blasé about anything that doesn't immediately do you in. Since we were more than 30 miles from even the most rudimentary medical help, and since we had no idea whether this disease was going to get better or worse, we decided to try to hike out rather than wait here.

The first day we got back to Mbeli Bai, which was the starting point of our venture into "the unknown." I stumbled along, somehow keeping up. The next morning, June 1, we set out at 7:30, once again a little later than we'd planned. Along the 10-kilometer path that led to the Japanese research camp, we came across five different groups of gorillas. In all we encountered fifteen groups of gorillas during the course of our hikes, as well as buffalo, several species of duikers, forest pigs, chimps, many different monkeys and innumerable birds, not to mention pests like ticks, ants and foot worms (which burrow into you and wriggle their way around until they figure out that you are not an elephant, whereupon they die and rot, leaving behind a nasty infection), as well as the nameless microbe that inflicted misery on me.

We stopped at the Japanese camp, where the lone researcher, Aobe, kindly offered us honeycomb, and then continued our long march. At 1:00 we made it to the edge of the Ndoki River and poled across. By 2:00 we emerged from the swamp, and by 3:40 we were at the camp by the Djeke River where Karen and I had earlier been attacked by ants. Only Seraphim and Joachime kept up with us. Every breath was killing me because of the heart attack/pulled muscle/dengue fever/deadly tick disease, but I didn't dare ask to slow down, because I wanted to get to Bomassa that night.

After a brief stop at the camp, we raced out at 4:15, trying to extract every bit of daylight. Since we had left the batteries behind, we made do with a succession of failing flashlights once the light began to fade at 6:15. By 7:15 we'd groped our way to Wali. During the last few hundred yards of our trek, our only source of light was one of those pencil lights you use to read maps, and finally that failed, too. By this point, though, Mike knew the trail by heart, and we made it to Bomassa in another forty minutes. As we arrived in camp, Mike noted that these nighttime returns (apparently he had had many) were sure to inflame suspicions that he was an ivory trafficker. We'd covered over 30 kilometers that day.

I recovered fairly quickly, but never did get a definitive diagnosis of what it was I had had (and I brought other ailments back with me from the forest as well). It certainly had the symptoms of dengue fever. Or perhaps it fell into the category of Mike Fay's "deadly tick diseases." In any event, this sickness was a very small price to pay for a glimpse of Eden.

PART VIII

INNER WORLDS: MAGIC, PRACTICAL AND OTHERWISE

CHAPTER 17

Shamans, Healers and Experiences
I Can't Explain

One of the more interesting expatriates I encountered during my forays into the Sangha River region was Louis Sarno. A thin, dark-haired mathematician from New Jersey, he had by the early 1990s already lived with various Pygmies for long stretches over the previous several years. He had taken it upon himself to advance their interests as well as record their music, dance and rituals. On the day he showed up at Andrea Turkalo's cabin in Bayanga, however, Louis was not concerned with Pygmy culture—he was starving.

He'd come into town from a Pygmy village, where he said there had been no food, and he had not eaten in a few days. We rummaged around in Andrea's freezer and found a grizzled bit of meat that she speculated was over a year old. No matter, Louis wanted it, and once it was cooked, he ripped into it with feral intensity.

After partially sating his hunger, he offered a few of his thoughts about the Pygmies. He had a somewhat more idiosyncratic explanation of the persistence of Pygmy culture despite the propinquity of modernity in the form of Bantu villages. Basically, he felt that it was their stubbornness that helped protect the traditional forms. And to hear Louis tell it, the culture itself bordered on the magical.

He recalled a recent experience to illustrate the everyday magic of Pygmy life. There was no food in the village, explained Louis, because the Pygmies had stopped hunting, preferring to stay home and smoke pot. It was only when Louis goaded them to go out and get some game that they slowly roused themselves. As a first step the men organized a dance to summon the forest spirits and ask their permission to hunt and collect plants.

The men would go into the forest and return possessed by a forest spirit called Enanyi. They gathered around a pile of raffia leaves on the ground in the center of the village. A young boy walked over to the leaves and held them up to show that there was nothing underneath. Then, however, as the men started singing, the raffia leaves composed themselves into a mask and somehow popped up from the ground.

Louis told this story in all seriousness, and over the years I'd heard many such accounts of supposed magical abilities possessed by indigenous people. In West Africa, Janis Carter, an American woman who spent years trying to teach an American-raised chimpanzee named Lucy how to be a wild chimp, told me of getting lost in the southern Liberian forest. At the precise moment she realized that she was lost (the exact time was later reconstructed), her African guide, who was sitting with one of her expatriate colleagues some miles away, suddenly announced, "Janice is lost," and then went and found her.

I have, in fact, had my own experiences that, at least so far, defy reductionist explanations. The denguelike fever had disappeared by the time I returned from the Ndoki in 1992, but I also brought with me a stomach ailment that defied both diagnosis and treatment. I may have gotten the bug from drinking from the elephant footprint, or from tasting the fruits the gorillas had discarded. Whatever its source, it was now living the high life in my stomach. I first went to Dr. Kevin Cahill, a leading specialist in tropical medicine, who tested me for all sorts of diseases but came up with nothing conclusive. At last he said, "I may not be able to diagnose you, but I think I can treat you." He put me on a course of Flagyl, a very powerful parasite-slaying drug. It helped, but some months later, the ailment returned.

Then, in the fall of 1992, I was invited to meet with two celebrated brothers named Sydney and Tacuma Sapaim, who were shamans from the Xingu tribe in the Brazilian Amazon. They had been flown to the United States by a wealthy student of shamans and healers named Kamal Benjalloun so that they could participate in United Nations events celebrating the "Year of Indigenous Peoples." I'd written a bit about healers and shamans for *Time,* so when I was contacted and asked about whether I'd like to interview the brothers, I immediately said yes, and then asked whether they might be willing to treat me as well. I was told they would, and to bring a $100 bill. (For all its ties to the world of spirit, shamanism has its practical and materialistic side.)

I was eager to see the brothers because I had previously had good experiences with other healers, notably an Israeli named Zev Kolman. Zev called himself a "bioenergist," and to paraphrase Kevin Cahill, while I may not have known what that meant, I did know what it felt like. Zev passed his hands over you, holding them several inches above your body, and at some point you began to feel a very pleasant tingling in your skin, interspersed with what seemed like mini-flashes of lightning between his hands and your body. It felt different from static electricity, and the energy seemed to gravitate to injured or weak areas. Even though I was in good health, I took the opportunity to experience what it was that Zev did. At my first session with Zev, witnessed by several people, my back audibly popped even though I was lying still and his hands were at least a foot above me.

I have had several subsequent sessions with Zev, and I still can't explain what it is that he does. I can rule out chicanery—between patients he does not disappear into a closet to charge up his hands with static electricity. Nor can the energy be explained by some supercharged version of the placebo effect.

I always left sessions with him feeling absolutely terrific, though I can't say whether improvements in the ailments that led me to see him were the result of natural healing or bioenergy. One thing I do have a hard time accepting is Zev's explanation for his powers: He claims that his abilities suddenly appeared after being visited by aliens in the Negev Desert when he was in the military. Whatever the case, I don't have a more logical explanation. He does seem to be a conduit for some form of energy, and I am not one to insist that something doesn't exist simply because I can't explain it.

This attitude left me open to seeing what Sydney and Tacuma might be capable of. We met at an apartment in Manhattan, where the brothers, with broad Indian faces, were dressed in Western clothes—jeans and shirts. I began by asking them—through an interpreter—questions about how they had become shamans. Sydney told the story.

Becoming a Xingu shaman, in Sydney's version, was a case of "don't call us, we'll call you." As a young man he began to have dreams. "Something happened, something special," he said. He smoked a "special" cigarette, and after the dreams he woke up feeling sad and afraid, and worried that he might die. So he went away to think about it. The next night a spirit he called Mamae came to visit him. The spirit instructed him to go to the woods and build a house. Once he was installed in the house, Mamae said, he/it would pay a visit.

After building the house, Sydney was walking in the woods one day when he heard a noise. Thinking it sounded like a machete, he fled. That night the spirit visited him again, and asked, "Why did you run away?"

Then the spirits upped the stakes. Two spirits visited him in his dreams and told him that they could make him a great healer. He recalled that they smoked a long, thin cigarette, and the smoke it produced formed a ball. He inhaled the smoke from each spirit three times. This, he said, sealed his senses and left him in a coma-like state. He said he "stood" for twenty days. It was like being dead, although he also said that the spirit delivered regular, chatty reports on villager reactions to his trance. People thought he was under a spell and the victim of black magic.

His concerned clan members finally went to another village to summon a great shaman to see what was wrong with Sydney. The spirit then told Sydney, "I can't wait to see what this man will say." As the great shaman examined the immobile Sydney, the spirit continued its narrative: "He's smoking; let's see if he can see me." Then the great shaman fainted. Again, the spirit said, "Let's see if he can see me." When the great shaman came back to consciousness he pronounced Sydney the victim of black magic.

The spirit was exultant: "See! He can't see me. He can't see what I put in your eyes, your nose, your ears. . . ." The shaman then tried to heal him. He placed his hands on Sydney's face and chest, but Sydney didn't feel anything. Sydney reported that the spirit merely laughed at the shaman's efforts.

The spirit then told Sydney that he could see that his people were getting worried, and promised that on the next day at 4 p.m. he would allow him to see, hear, and feel again. When he came back to the living, Sydney said, it was difficult to move, walk, or even stand up, but he did feel a deep need to smoke.

He also came back possessed of powers: He could extract things from people's eyes, noses. The clan was amazed; an elder said that the ancients had those abilities, and that Sydney was destined to be one of the greatest shamans. Exhausted, Sydney fell asleep and the spirit gave him further instructions. He was to stay in the house in the woods for eight months and during that time he could not touch his wife. People brought him food, because he couldn't fish or hunt either.

Eight months later he began practicing as a shaman, and his first patient was a young woman who was bleeding from the mouth. He was timid at first, but he was able to capture the disease. In the shaman's universe, illnesses are often malicious spirits, which adepts can capture with their hands. For other diseases he would use plants, and if he did not recognize the symptoms, the spirit would show him what plants to use and how they should be applied. For instance, he claimed that the previous year he had cured a malaria epidemic by preparing what he called *moacap,* a thin-stemmed, long-leafed plant with a huge root like a tuber. For measles he used different preparations taken from a big tree he called *yahu kuitap ariuwap.*

As he talked, I got the impression that he served as a type of National Institutes of Health. The spirit would tell him which plants to use, and then medicine men would come to him and he would pass on the prescription. The spirit was always with him, and he would access the spirit through a waking dream.

After Sydney finished his story, we got down to business. I ceremoniously handed Sydney the $100 bill, and he began to work on me. First he rolled some plant into a fat cigar, lit it, took a deep puff, and blew the smoke into his hands. Then he started moving his hands over my stomach, at first slowly and then more urgently as though he were trapping something under my skin. Finding his quarry, he squeezed his hands together directly on my stomach and grunted in satisfaction. He rubbed his hands and then showed me my disease. It looked like an inert brown worm. I wanted to touch it but was strongly advised not to, as it was dangerous.

Then, as I watched, he took another puff of smoke and blew it onto the brown thing in his hands. It disappeared. Through the translator he remarked that it was a disease related to a fish spirit.

This seemed highly unlikely, as I had contracted the disease in Africa and I was fairly certain that it hadn't come from fish. Also, I had to wonder whether Brazilian spirits and African spirits were one and the same. And, of course, the rainforests were entirely different, too.

My skepticism notwithstanding, the treatment did work. I felt better almost immediately, and the disease really did vanish. Here again was a case in which something worked in practice (or at least produced the sought-for result), though I certainly knew of no credible theory to support it. Least credible of all was Sydney's explanation of what he had done. But it worked.

Robert Thompson, the noted authority on Congo influences on African American culture, later told me that black healers in the tidewater regions of Georgia and South Carolina would similarly trap and "concretize" a disease, producing a tiny lizard after they successfully captured the ailment. Thompson thought such displays were clearly feats of prestidigitation intended to impress future clients. I suppose that could be precisely what Sydney Sapaim had done, and I suppose that my immediate recovery could have been the result of the placebo effect (making me one of the more suggestible people on the planet). It's also possible that what Sydney referred to as spirits were energy fields ignored by or as yet inexplicable in the Western medical paradigm, and perhaps Zev Kolman was tapping into something similar.

———

Regardless of the source of these men's powers, shamans are fast disappearing. Of the 10,000 to 15,000 cultures on the planet, only a handful of groups still live outside the market economy. Most are deep in the Amazon rainforest, hidden in New Guinea, the Far North, or clustered in other remote areas that are too difficult to penetrate. A few tribes—people inevitably cite the Masai of Kenya—do seem to be able to preserve some aspects of traditional life even in proximity to modernity and its inducements.

Preserving some aspects of a culture, however, is not the same as perpetuating the curative rituals, knowledge and beliefs that comprise a complete worldview. Consider what Sydney Sapaim had to go through to become a shaman. Would he have endured this ordeal if he had had any doubts about the existence of the forest spirits and their life-and-death powers? Many tribal people continue to value their extended family and clan, but in the long run the mystique of a shaman cannot really hope to compete with the technological magic of the consumer society. And so the shaman begins to seem a relic of the past, the spirits retreat along with the forest, and the best and brightest children go off to schools to learn the ways of the West rather than the secrets of the ancestors.

CHAPTER 18

Esotéricas

One of the predictable ironies of the ragged edge of the world is that both ecosystems and cultures finally begin to receive the appreciation they deserve just before they disappear. Wolves were demonized and exterminated from the West, and in their absence mule deer proliferated wildly. Now that they've been reintroduced to rebalance the ecosystem, tourists by the thousands flock to see the very animals that had been disparaged as vermin just a few decades earlier. For much of our history, a primary responsibility of the Army Corps of Engineers had been to drain wetlands, which were viewed as pestilential incubators of insects and disease. Today the national mantra is wetland restoration, as these areas have come to be recognized as nurseries of fish, shrimp and migratory birds.

So it is in the realm of culture. When I began my career traditional cultures were widely viewed as impediments to development. In my book *The Alms Race,* I quoted a development official who stated this principle succinctly: "The village way of life is the root cause of poverty." Now that development and modernity have driven traditional cultures to the brink of eradication, more and more people from developed countries have come to recognize that not only do traditional cultures provide safety nets and meaning for tribes around the world, they are stores of knowledge and often-wondrous expertise. And, since we're the type of people who never let something that can be overdone remain underdone, the enthusiasm with which visitors from the developed world have embraced the wisdom of tribal ancients sometimes surpasses that of members of the tribes themselves. Ground zero for such enthusiasm is Machu Picchu in Peru.

In 1998 I returned to Machu Picchu after several years' absence. I had come to Peru with my wife, Mary, on an itinerary that included Machu Pic-chu, as well as a trip into one of the most vibrant parts of the Amazon. We'd flown overnight from New York to Cusco and then taken a bus down to Machu Picchu, arriving in the late afternoon. The vibrancy we encountered there was of a different sort than what I had experienced in the rainforest.

My first thought as we wandered around the ruins was that the stunning archaeological site had been taken over by a new species of cold-blooded human. Arrayed on various rocks were tourists of various nationalities, seemingly gathering warmth to kick-start their reptilian metabolism. As I was to discover, however, it was not the sun's energy these pilgrims were after, but rather the vibrations from the interior of the mountain itself. It appears that sometime during the past few decades word had gotten out that Machu Picchu sits atop a giant crystal.

I learned as much back at the Machu Picchu Ruinas Hotel (the three-star hotel with four-star prices and five-star views that stands next to the entrance of the archaeological site) when I overheard a woman with a rich Texas drawl casually telling a younger friend, "That's the rock where you gather your wizard energy." Indeed, the fragments of conversation I over-heard in the lobby and dining room were littered with comments about astral bodies, reincarnation and other New Age touchstones. When I asked one man why his group had come to Machu Picchu, he cheerfully explained, "We all lived here hundreds of years ago, and so this is a reunion of sorts."

For decades the staggering physical beauty of Machu Picchu, and the mysteries surrounding its purpose and abrupt decline, eclipsed other aspects of the region that might enthrall visitors. Now that is changing as pilgrims come to explore new dimensions of the area. Clearly, one of these new dimensions is the fifth dimension. A hotel manager told me that what was once a mere trickle of grungy hippies, scorned by the locals for their lack of cash, had become a flood of well-heeled New Age types who arrived in package tours as large as sixty people. Known locally as "esotéricas," these seekers are assiduously courted by the local hotels and merchants.

As I walked into the temples I could hear the sounding of conch shell trumpets as New Age imams summoned the faithful to devotions. I came upon one such group at the "Hitching Post of the Sun," an altar that Inca priests used to mark key points in the passage of the seasons. As I watched, a tall Peruvian man guided a clutch of Italian esotéricas toward the energies of the sun, the water and the mountains.

The fifteen acolytes lined up at the edge of the terrace, facing west toward the setting sun. Standing in front of each initiate by turn, the priest-leader held a pouch under his or her chin. I stared, mesmerized—not so much by the prospect of the initiation as by the potential for imminent calamity. If any of the initiates flinched or stepped backward, he would find himself plummeting a long way down in this temple complex (whose Peruvian administrators seem to have taken a caveat emptor approach to warnings about cliffs and other dangers). The Peruvian priest murmured some words and then bowed by turn to the sun and then other quadrants of the compass.

While this was taking place, another priest was in the middle of his own ceremony at the Hitching Post itself. He had reverently spread out an assortment of objects—including a conch shell, a crystal and a cocoa leaf—on the altar. When another group arrived one of its members approached the priest who had been leading the Italians and asked, "Why does the 'Temple of Three Windows' have five windows?" Perhaps irritated by the interruption, the priest brusquely replied, "I don't know."

Later I caught up with this priest, who turned out to be Juan Nunez Del Prado, a charming former anthropologist. We sat on one of the myriad walls of the temple complex, and Nunez told me a bit about his own conversion from academic to spiritual guide, and about the special energies of Machu Picchu that drew so many visitors.

Despite the conventional wisdom that the old religion had died out not long after the Spanish conquest, studies of Inca traditions that Nunez undertook in the 1960s convinced him that the traditional gods continued to endure in remote villages. He hypothesized that if people were continuing to perform Inca rituals, there had to be some priesthood or other support system involved. With funding from the Ford Foundation he gradually uncovered a network of acolytes, who in parallel with their work as Catholic priests kept alive the old Inca traditions. One of the most senior of this secret clergy was a revered priest named Don Benito Corihuaman.

It was during a meeting with Don Benito that Nunez had an epiphany that caused him to abandon academia. The old priest began speaking to the young scholar in a strange language. "Although I did not understand a word," says Nunez, "I received images in my mind." Stunned by the experience, Nunez spent the next ten years as a student of Don Benito, eventually being given what Nunez called "Hatun Karpay," the initiation ritual of the sacred kings.

Nunez described the Inca beliefs as a powerful system of personal growth, in some ways analogous to Tibetan Buddhism. Their focus is on enhancing powers of perception so that initiates can receive the living energies of the world around them. The physical setting of Machu Picchu abounds in such energies, he explained. The temple complex—which in its entirety has the shape of the sacred bird of the Incas, the condor—functions as a repository of the collective spirit of the Andes. To help tap these energies, Nunez uses the little pouch, or *mesa,* that I saw him holding under the chin of the Italian visitors. Nunez unfurled the pouch and showed me what it held—a shell symbolizing water, a cross symbolizing the male spirit and entrance to the "upper world," the seal of Don Benito, a coin given by a Buddhist priest, and other *khuyas,* or ritual gifts, that Nunez believes are charged with the powers of the elements and offer a connection to the spirit of the giver. Nunez believes that the *mesa* helps connect initiates to the energies of the hills and to the spirits of the builders of the temple complex and other holy people.

It's easy to make light of such ideas, but the spirit of the quest that draws these seekers is benign if not laudable. Moreover, there is no question that Machu Picchu has a dramatic effect on even the most jaded visitor. For me, the sheer physical beauty of the area is sufficient explanation for its effect.

Awakening at dawn in the Ruinas Hotel, I spent a couple of hours watching a spellbinding moisture-and-light show performed by a cast that included an equatorial sun, the Andes and the Pacific Ocean, with the script written by the laws of physics. At first the view was almost one-dimensional as the pale lumens of dawn light imparted a phosphorescent glow to the canopy of the surrounding cloud forest. Then fog completely sealed the area, to be replaced by a drenching rainfall, which lifted by 7:15. Walking around a little later, I caught the first glimpses of the impossibly high snow peaks that crowd the vast site from the west and east so closely that the view has a two-dimensional flavor. Only on those intermittent occasions when the sky is completely clear can one appreciate the staggering grandeur of the valley Machu Picchu occupies, perched below the high peaks and vertiginously above the rushing Vilcanota River below. The great vault defined by the surrounding mountains forms an inverted cathedral of air. I had no need of rituals or arcana to experience the profound thrall of this magical place.

———

Those who come to Peru solely to capture the energy of Machu Picchu miss out on another vibration of the region: the pulsing tropical life force of the

Amazon rainforest, just a short trip away. While I was intrigued and a little amused by the West's newfound passion for traditional lore, my first inclination has always been to get to the wildlands, and Peru has some of the richest and most intact portions of the vast Amazonian rainforest. After a couple of days in Machu Picchu it was time to travel into the jungle.

Our guide to the rainforest was Charlie Munn, an ornithologist who has worked in the surrounding forests for nearly two decades. We met up with him halfway between Cusco and Machu Picchu, and retracing our route, spent the night in the Monasterio, a converted monastery that aspired to be a five-star hotel. The rooms were ordinary, but the lobby, bar, courtyard and restaurants took full advantage of the stonework and architectural detail of the ancient structure. After dinner we took a leisurely walk (at 11,300 feet, a walk can only be leisurely) through the narrow cobblestone streets in the colonial heart of the city. Worried about muggers in a particularly dark area, Charlie stopped a local and asked in Spanish, "If we go down that street will robbers jump out of the shadows and choke us?" The man laughed and replied, "No, that's gone out of style."

The next morning Mary and I headed to the airport for the thirty-five-minute flight to a jungle strip on the Madre de Dios River in the heart of the Manu, one of the most pristine regions of the Peruvian Amazon. It's territory in which Charlie Munn has invested a good deal of time and money. He has studied its flora and fauna, tirelessly lobbied various Peruvian governments for its protection, and dipped into his inheritance to provide loans to local Indians who wanted to start ecotourist ventures. So far, Charlie has helped launch twenty-five such ventures, including a nonprofit travel agency called InkaNatura that brings groups to Machu Picchu and the Manu, and that returns its profits to conservation.

From the Boca Manu airstrip we traveled by motorized longboat up the Madre de Dios to the Manu Wildlife Center, a small ecotourist lodge that Charlie helped launch. In contrast to the crisp air of Machu Picchu, the Manu is all about heat. One either fries in the sun out on the river or is slowly poached in the sweltering, close air of the rainforest.

During the ninety-minute river trip to the Manu Wildlife Center, Charlie pointed out macaws, horned screamers, bat falcons, roseate spoonbills and other birds flying over or picking their way along the banks, and he also described the various stratagems they employed to survive. Most amusing was his description of the zone-tailed hawk, which imitates a vulture by flying with its wings cocked up and rocking back and forth to approach prey. "It flies along saying, 'I'm a vulture, I'm a vulture,'" explained Charlie. Once it gets within striking distance of a macaw the hawk folds its wings and swoops down on its unsuspecting victim. The rainforest is full of such trickery. One small songbird imitates the alarm call that other species make when a hawk is in the area, and, when the spooked birds take flight, it steals their food.

The Manu Wildlife Center is a collection of thatch-roofed huts strung along walkways beside the river. There is no electricity save for that generated to refrigerate food, and the facilities are spartan, but Walter, a Piro Indian and former guide who runs the lodge, chose the site for its proximity to the nearby clay and mineral licks that attract some of the most elusive animals in the rainforest. Just downstream, for instance, hundreds of macaws regularly gather to eat clay—the minerals it contains help counteract the acids that build up in the birds' stomachs from eating rubber tree seeds and other hard-to-digest foods—from the exposed banks of the river.

As with any wildlife viewing, getting a look at the local fauna required that one adjust to the rhythms of the forest. We set off at 6:00 one morning so that we could get settled into a floating blind on the river before the birds arrived. We waited four and a half hours before the first birds began gathering in the trees along the banks. They were very skittish, well aware that predators also knew their schedule. They descended lower and lower in the trees, and then finally, at 12:30, the first brave soul found a perch on the vertical bank and began chomping away at the clay. Within minutes the bank was covered with red-and-green macaws as well as their scarlet cousins.

Later that evening, lured by the promise of what Charlie called "the best tapir viewing in South America," we visited another lick, which lay in the forest a few kilometers from the camp. This lick was a *colpa,* a muddy pool where the giant mammals came to settle their stomachs. On stilts overlooking the lick Walter and his staff have constructed another covered blind. In our *colpa* cabana we curled up in blankets on mattresses, slumber-party style, and awaited the 550-pound tapirs. Just after sunset the first arrived. I have to say that only those aware of the extreme elusiveness of the big animals were likely to have appreciated the drama of the moment.

For most visitors three or four days in the Manu are more than sufficient to get a taste of the rainforest. And, I might add, for the rainforest to get a taste of them. A short swim in the Madre de Dios left me covered with an archipelago of bites as insects vectored in on me during the brief moments my skin was exposed while getting out of the water. I didn't mind. I had gathered energy in Machu Picchu and I left a little bit of myself behind in the digestive tracts of bugs living on the "mother of god" river. This synergistic exchange of the mystical and the corporeal seemed entirely in keeping with the new dimensions of the Machu Picchu region.

Final Thoughts

Many questions cloud the future of Midway, the Manu, the Ndoki, and indeed the future of every sanctuary and refuge on the planet. In recent years I've watched as hard-fought conservation victories have been mooted by global change or simply steamrolled by the juggernaut of the consumer society and its attendant greed and corruption. For a few moments in the 1990s, for instance, I had some hope that enough of Sumatra's main park, Gunung Leuser, could be preserved to maintain a place where orangutans and tigers might persist in the wild. That looks increasingly unlikely, as Indonesian businessmen bribe officials to look the other way as they log forests or illegally convert parklands to a palm-oil plantation.

This list goes on. The Galápagos are under increasing stress, even though they lie over 1,000 miles from the mainland. Ecuador has a hard time managing the Galápagos's population of migrant farmers and fishermen, even though tourists coming to see the islands' flora and fauna are one of the biggest sources of foreign currency reserves that the nation has. The same is true for Kenya and Tanzania, where nature tourism represents a huge cash cow, but poaching and encroachment by farmers continue.

The countdown continues not just for places, but for specific species. The number of animals whose populations have been reduced by more than 90 percent is staggering, as are the consequences. One of the unpleasant surprises in recent years has been an explosion of jellyfish in the oceans around the world. Much has been written about this phenomenon, but far less attention has been paid to the connection between this indication of oceanic distress and the disappearance of jellyfish predators. The giant leatherback turtle, which has patrolled the oceans since dinosaurs roamed the planet, consumes jellyfish as its primary source of sustenance. Having survived asteroid hits and other extinction-level events, however, the turtle is now being driven to the edge by fishing nets, egg collectors and even something so seemingly innocuous as lights near beaches, which fatally divert baby turtles away from the water after they hatch.

In the mid-1990s I wrote a cover story for *Time* on the fate of the tiger in the wild. We did a lot of thinking about the title, and eventually settled on "Doomed." The usual hedge in journalism would have been to put a question mark after that word, but John Stacks, the editor, and I wanted to make the point that habitat was disappearing at a rate that would crowd the wild tiger out of existence, even if poaching for the traditional medicine market in Asia was completely stopped. The article caused quite a stir, and I attended more than one conference where the title was brought up, snidely dismissed as needlessly pessimistic by conservationists.

Here was a case where I would dearly love to have been proven wrong. Since that article was published in 1995, however, the tiger has almost completely disappeared from Indonesia, China, Vietnam, Thailand and Burma. It hangs on in India, though its numbers are dwindling in almost all the reserves, including the swampy Sunderbans, which until recently had hosted the healthiest populations. In the Russian Far East, the Siberian tiger has a chance because its range is in a thinly populated habitat, and there is some slim hope the tiger can persist in Cambodia, which recently has taken action to slow deforestation.

But confining an animal that once was the keystone predator in a 5,000-mile swath of Asia to zoos and a few tightly guarded small reserves is not saving the species. Still, as with Yellowstone and the wolf, so long as the tiger lives in the wild somewhere there is the hope that someday it might recolonize its once vast territory and restore the balance of the many different ecosystems in which it was king.

The cultural entropy I wrote about in "Lost Tribes, Lost Knowledge" is all but complete, leaving behind thousands of deracinated tribes. Those who have decided that the modern market economy is not nearly as fulfilling as their former life discover they can no longer return, for either the forest and animals that supported them are gone, or the knowledge and rituals that bound them to the wildlands have disappeared. Huge amounts of knowledge are vanishing simply because the young are no longer learning the languages of their elders.

Andrew Vayda, an anthropologist I spoke with during my research in Indonesia, was somewhat sanguine about the loss of knowledge, observing that knowledge is continually lost, just as it is continually gained. Such cultural holocausts have occurred in the past, after all. A trove of wonderful insights and skills certainly vanished when the Neanderthal died out, or when the Library of Alexandria burned, and we have learned to live without that lost expertise and knowledge. We will likely one day miss this knowledge, however, because at a point where we urgently need a better understanding of the ecosystems of the world, the hard-learned lessons of thousands of tribes will no longer be available.

Forty years ago, when I first began exploring the ragged edge of the world, the frontiers it demarcated were larger than they are now, if only because the world's ancient forests were so much larger then. Although the ragged edge itself may be smaller now, the rate at which the cultural and literal fires of this boundary are consuming what remains is actually accelerating, because so many of the world's wildlands have been cut or degraded. What's especially disheartening is to see the warnings of my early adulthood proven right by the daily developments of my middle age.

I was in my early twenties when I first read the dire predictions of Dillon Ripley and Tom Lovejoy, who warned of the consequences of habitat destruction, particularly in the world's wet tropical forests. Despite countless conferences, initiatives and declarations, laws, and even treaties, destruction of the rainforests continues unabated. Some nations and consumers have gotten religion about the destruction wrought by cutting these forests, but for every Japan that reforms its bad old ways, there is a China waiting in the wings.

In 1979 a blue-ribbon panel that included George Woodwell, founder of the Woods Hole Research Center, and climate scientist Roger Revelle presented a paper to President Jimmy Carter that warned that if nations did not take action to stem greenhouse gas emissions, we would see changes in climate by the end of the twentieth century. No action was taken on GHG emissions, and the world indeed saw changes, ranging from the rapid disappearance of Arctic sea ice to increasingly intense droughts and weather extremes predicted two generations earlier.

In 1972 the Club of Rome published *Limits to Growth*, based on an approach to modeling called Systems Dynamics, which had been developed at MIT by Jay Forrester, one of the fathers of the computer. Using sophisticated feedback loops, the book projected possible outcomes for the world economy based on various usage rates of nonrenewable resources. The typical outcome was overshoot and collapse. For years afterward the book was widely ridiculed by libertarians and technological optimists. As of 2008, however, the trajectories it modeled were closer to what had actually taken place than any scenarios offered by so-called cornucopians.

One bomb that didn't go off, at least on the projected schedule, was the "Population Bomb," a catastrophe that, in 1968, the ecologist Paul Ehrlich predicted would occur by the late 1970s. Ehrlich underestimated the impact of green revolution agricultural technologies on food production in places like India and China, but while he may have been wrong on his time-table, unfortunately he is now being vindicated on his premise. During the worldwide economic boom following the collapse of communism, concerns about population growth dropped from the headlines, but now they're back with a vengeance, as persistently high commodity prices and alarmingly tight stocks of grain remind people that population and material aspirations cannot continue to rise indefinitely in a world of finite resources.

So here we are in the beginning of the twenty-first century, pretty much where a chorus of voices in the twentieth century warned that we would be. (Those who are interested in where I think we are going are invited to read my books *The Future in Plain Sight* and *Winds of Change*.) Virtually every large predator, both on the land and in the sea, is on death row, and the only creatures that thrive are pests of all stripes and animals that can live off our copious garbage. We've so overtaxed the planet that we can't throw anything away without its landing on someone's or something's head. Atmospheric toxins get dumped on the formerly pristine north courtesy of the Arctic Front, while plastics from the entire North Pacific region are collected by the great gyres of the ocean. It's as though nature were saying, "Here is what I see when I gaze upon humanity's works."

We live in an incongruous situation in which industry and individuals talk a greener line than ever before, while the world is more tattered than ever. Despite the environment's much-heralded ascendance as an American value, U.S. voters are willing to cast their ballots against environmental protections, such as the U.S. bans on offshore drilling on the outer shelf and in the Arctic National Wildlife Reserve, just because gasoline prices hit $4 a gallon. Imagine what will happen when, as is likely, we face a real resource shortage.

During the past fifty years conservationists and champions of indigenous peoples have won many battles, but on every front the war is being lost. I can't blame the cornucopians like the late Julian Simon. They provided a handy justification for ignoring the environment, but greed would have found another intellectual and moral justification if free market ideology hadn't been around.

One of my heroes is a decent man named James Gustave Speth, universally known as Gus, who in some sense is the last Boy Scout. He has devoted his life to working within the system. After Yale Law School he helped found the now-giant Natural Resources Defense Council, reasoning that experienced lobbyists and litigators could be crucial advocates in environmental battles. Later he worked in the White House, advising Jimmy Carter on environmental issues. Then he helped found the World Resources Institute to try to get corporations to work with governments and nonprofits on environmental issues. He tried to prod the international community to action when he headed the United Nations Development Program. He headed up Yale's celebrated School of Forestry and Environment, one of the institutions that will produce the next generation of environmental leaders. He has also written books, networked at the highest level, and lectured tirelessly around the country. Any one of these achievements would be extraordinary; to have all of them in the span of one career puts him in the company of America's greatest conservationists.

His long tenure at the forefront of America's environmental movement has given him a unique perch from which to assess how far we've come since the great environmental pulse began in the late 1960s. One might also think, given his front-row seat at many of these battles, that he would single out accomplishments like the Endangered Species Act, the Clean Air and Clean Water Bills, and the National Environmental Policy Act, among many other environmental victories. One might think that, but one would be wrong. Taking a dry-eyed look back at his career, what Gus Speth sees is failure.

In 2008 I participated in a Yale panel with Gus in which we discussed climate change, oil and the future of the world economy. Usually I'm the darkest voice at such gatherings, particularly if I'm sharing the stage with pillars of the establishment like Gus. This time, however, armed with a devastating series of charts, he made the case that while his and others' efforts had won many individual victories over the decades, overall they had failed to halt decline by virtually any metric one could produce.

Basically, Gus says that if you examine the charts of extinction rates, loss of wildlands, and the wholesale transformation of ecosystems during the tenure of the modern environmental movement, you might rationally conclude that an asteroid had hit the planet. There *has* been a Great Collision, says Gus, but the asteroid in question is the global economy. Looking back over a lifetime of working within the system, Gus has come to the conclusion that the system is the problem. (He spells out his argument in his book *Between Two Worlds*.)

I believe he's right. For forty years I've been working out my own view of the nature of the consumer, and modern politics and the modern free market system have developed a perfect immune response for neutering any attempts to represent the long-term interests of either an economy or an ecosystem. Our only hope is that the present system gives way to one that does reintroduce our long-term requirements into present-day decision making.

During the past decades, when I traveled to remote places, I never imagined that my visits to the ragged edge of the world were a farewell tour. Perhaps, more accurately, I hoped they wouldn't prove to be a farewell tour. And there is just the tiniest ray of hope that they weren't. It won't be pretty, but there is a chance that we will awaken to the obvious.

When something goes on inexorably despite decades of warnings from the best minds and most prominent people in a society, we have to stop and think about why. This is not just a matter of the destruction of wildlands and loss of species. The scientific consensus on the threat of climate change is overwhelming and has been so for over fifteen years (and the threat has been discussed at the international level for thirty years), yet the world has done virtually nothing to contain greenhouse emissions.

Looking around, we see this pattern everywhere. Consider a couple of recent examples. The Deepwater Horizon oil spill: The recent Gulf oil spill, the most catastrophic environmental event in American history, directly followed from the neutering of regulations, safety mechanisms and procedures put in place after earlier spills such as the Ixtoc spill of 1979 and the *Exxon Valdez* spill in Alaska in 1989. Does anyone seriously believe that new regulations that arise from this disaster won't also be neutered? We need oil, and the easy-to-find oil is gone, so we need to drill in the most inaccessible, politically hostile and/or environmentally vulnerable places on the planet.

This raises some obvious questions: If oil is getting harder to find and our dependence on the fuel leaves us exposed to catastrophic risks, wouldn't an intelligent society focus on developing alternatives? Yes. And, since all these costs and looming scarcities have been discussed for decades, wouldn't an intelligent society have started developing alternatives long ago? Again yes. Has the United States done so? No; we had the lead on alternatives through the 1980s, but we handed it to the Europeans and Asians.

Or consider the financial crisis that began in 2008 and continues as of the writing of this book. As was the case with the Deepwater Horizon oil spill, the crisis followed ignored warnings and years of deregulation that stripped away protections instituted after past financial crises dating back to before the Great Depression. Despite this financial near-death experience Congress has not even reinstituted past protections that governed financial institutions, such as the Glass-Steagall Act. And even if politicians summon the political courage to do so, does anyone think that such regulations would remain in place long enough to prevent some new financial crisis?

Time and again our best and brightest have alerted society to looming problems, but our persistent pattern has been to ignore the warnings and suffer the consequences. The pathetic refrain of recent years—"Nobody saw this coming"—is always a self-serving lie. Something is making us stupid. My candidate is capitalism, specifically the skewed incentives of capitalism as practiced in the United States that give us hyperfocus on short-term gains, while leaving us effectively blind to long-term threats. Like Gus Speth, I believe the system is the threat. In each case cited above, actions to head off a threat were perceived to impinge on present profits, and, as a society, we have consistently made the decision that we'd rather head off a cliff in the future than limit the gains of those with access to the levers of power. What we have seen everywhere is that economic interests ultimately control the lawmakers. We've created a system that leaves us constantly surprised by the inevitable.

Can this be fixed? Sure, and by no means am I suggesting that we replace free market capitalism with socialism or communism (a system that inflicted grievous environmental harm in Russia, China and Eastern Europe). Free market capitalism does efficiently match resources with demand and it does foster innovation, but, as recent crises have shown, it desperately requires real regulation. Moreover (and perhaps this is a naïve hope), free market decisions need to be tempered by values or beliefs that recognize the health of the systems that support us, both economic and natural. While we may aspire to a society that is governed by reasoned debate and enlightened policies, a look at history suggests that environmental protection that derives from religious fear—think about the role of *maselai* in New Guinea as discussed earlier in the book—has a far better track record than any system of regulations. Regulations can be gamed; God or the ancestors cannot.

Will any of this happen? Apparently, not without shock therapy far worse than what we have recently endured, and that's exactly what we are likely to get.

———

Ironically, it is the ongoing economic crisis that gives me hope that we might divert ourselves from our express ride off a cliff. While politicians are able to blithely ignore the ecological calamity that has followed from free market ideology run amok, voters won't let them ignore the economic calamity now being visited upon households around the world. If the global economy merely picks up where we left off before the bubble burst in 2008, then we can expect that our human-produced Great Extinction will resume as well. My guess, though, is that the current economic crisis will get bad enough to profoundly reshape both values and thinking, and in that there is hope.

There is also hope in the fact that the Ndoki persists intact, and that Cuba may not go the way of every other Caribbean island, that Yellowstone is now actually a more complete ecosystem since I was last there, and that, if they can survive climate change and plastics, the Northwestern Hawaiian Islands have a shot. So do many other places I've visited but not described in this book, such as the forests of the Guyana Shield and the extraordinary landscape of Kamchatka.

There are scores, hundreds, perhaps even thousands more places that have also remained relatively intact. Even today biologists are finding new lost worlds, such as a haven bursting with lowland gorillas just to the east of the Ndoki, or a healthy population of more than 100,000 gibbons (one of the most endangered of the great apes) in a reserve in Cambodia. Even if we're losing the war, we can't give up. And so, in closing this book, I'll offer a proposal.

I'll offer this proposal even though this is not a how-to-fix-it book. I'll offer an idea because it's critical that we try to preserve what are in essence the vital organs of the planet, for our sake as well as out of obligation to those countless life forms we are crowding out, hunting or poisoning. My thoughts about how we can tackle conservation at the scale of the problem follow. They are just one possible solution; there may be many others.

Continental-Scale Conservation

Upon leaving the Ndoki in 1992, I attended the Rio Earth Summit in Brazil. I was traveling lighter, since I'd lost about 15 pounds in the forest, and flew to Rio via Cape Town. I wrote a story from Rio as part of *Time*'s coverage of the overhyped event, and then a few weeks later *Time* ran my cover story on the Ndoki. I'd hoped to raise the profile of the area so that loggers could not move in by stealth, and in that respect the article was a success. It received a good deal of attention, and the World Bank subsequently helped broker a deal that kept the region inviolate, while opening other parts of the Congo for logging.

Now, nineteen years later, the Ndoki still remains largely untouched. Following my article, *National Geographic* did its own major feature on the region, again focusing on Mike Fay. These and other articles have firmly lodged the Ndoki in the minds of conservationists as an extraordinary place, and it remains protected despite on-and-off civil war, many changes of government, and the encroachment of loggers from all sides. The question remains, however, is the Ndoki large enough to endure if the forests surrounding it are cut? It was a key question when I visited the region, and it is even more relevant today, when logging has stripped the forest right up to the preserve's edge.

Therein lies the conundrum of conservation: Dedicated people can save a forest and yet still lose it if the surrounding land that supports it no longer has the ability to deliver water and moderate climate. I pondered this problem for many years after I went to the Ndoki. Having written about many of the grand failures of conservation, I didn't want to contribute to that huge and growing literature by offering a plan that required a huge infrastructure, detailed studies, approvals from various bureaucracies, or any of the other factors that I had watched subvert many well-intentioned proposals. Instead I wanted a plan that would be large enough to save the systems that support gems like the Ndoki, one that could be deployed quickly, one that was largely self-policing, one that was cheap, and one that required very little infrastructure and expertise.

One day the answer hit me. The next time Mike Fay came through New

York, we had lunch, and I laid out my idea. He immediately fastened on the necessity of what he called "wall-to-wall" coverage of the rainforest. Emboldened, I then developed the concept further.

The first opportunity to test reactions to my idea came on the tenth anniversary of the Rio Earth Summit, when I was invited to come back to Rio and participate in the "handover" of the summit to Johannesburg. There I had the chance to present my thoughts on continental-scale conservation at the plenary to the assembled heads of state and other dignitaries, and got an enthusiastic reception. But, as it was with Rio, and as it is with many conferences, my proposals were forgotten by the time delegates picked up their first cocktail at the receptions following the sessions.

Then in 2003, Tom Lovejoy, the celebrated conservationist and tropical biologist, hosted a dinner that brought together the heads of some of the biggest conservation groups in the country for an informal discussion of my idea. Once again, there seemed to be some interest, but I left the dinner with the conviction that ultimately it was not going to get out of the gate unless I took the lead.

And so I decided to write an article for *Foreign Affairs,* inviting Tom Lovejoy and Dan Phillips, who had played a key role in getting protection for the Ndoki when he was ambassador to the Democratic Republic of the Congo, to join me as coauthors. The piece was published in the July-August issue in 2004. What I present here is a longer explication of my thoughts that uses the structure I first presented in Rio:

Consider the Ndoki rainforest: Nestled in the northeast corner of the Democratic Republic of the Congo and bordered on three sides by vast swamps, the Ndoki was so inaccessible ten years ago that its animals were naïve of humans. Not even neighboring Ba'Aka Pygmies knew its elephant trails. Since then this forest has received protection (the 4,000-square-mile Nuabale-Ndoki National Park was created in 1993), and the Ndoki has survived political upheaval and civil war. Given the tumultuous politics and endemic corruption of the Congo basin, the protection of the Ndoki ranks as a conservation triumph.

There's just one problem: The forest seems to be drying out. While rainfall records are spotty, changes in flora and the more frequent appearance of desert dust from the Harmattan winds are worrisome developments in one of the drier wet tropical forests in Africa. As logging consortiums cut other unprotected forests throughout the Congo basin, reducing the system's capacity to store and recycle moisture, regional rainfall, now ranging between 1,273 mm and 1,650 mm, may stay below the threshold needed to sustain a wet tropical forest. If that happens, the present denizens of this enchanted forest may find themselves with nothing to eat and nowhere to go. The message from the Ndoki is that saving the parts is necessary, but it is not always sufficient. Conservationists must find ways to preserve the vitality of the systems that support a particular forest, lest other factors such as regional climate change trump even the most effective legal protection. Moreover, the pace of deforestation is such that, in many cases, conservationists will have to act without perfect knowledge of the vulnerabilities of the systems they are trying to preserve.

Since this dilemma first surfaced in the early 1990s, two pertinent issues have shifted from the realm of the debatable to the obvious:

1. The Problem of Scale: The mismatch between efforts to preserve the life support systems of the planet and the scale of the threat has risen into bold relief. Presently, roughly 5 percent of earth's tropical forests have effective protection. At the same time, the rate of moist tropical forest deforestation and degradation—8.1 million hectares from 1990 to 1997—has actually accelerated, in part because the fall of the Suharto regime in May 1998 loosed a fury of illegal logging in Indonesia.

2. Anemic International Action: Even as this mismatch between the scale of efforts and the scale of the problem has become apparent, it has also become clear that official action from the international community will offer too little, too late to close the gap. The United Nations Conference on Environment and Development, the so-called Earth Summit in Rio in 1992, brought together heads of state from around the world to address environmental problems. Commitments made there were largely forgotten by the time the fleet of presidential jets left the runway. For instance, ten years after G-7 nations promised $1.2 billion to preserve the Amazon in the PPG-7 agreement (the Pilot Programme for the Protection of Tropical Forests of Brazil), only $350 million has been committed and $120 million disbursed. As Gus Speth argues in *Red Sky at Morning,* virtually the only international agreement

ratified during the past thirty years that has had any major positive effect has been the Montreal Protocol on Substances That Deplete the Ozone. Partly as a result of the failure of international treaties, history is ratifying some of the nightmare scenarios of the past. In the past fifteen years, 60 percent of Indonesia's protected areas have been logged, and, at present rates of logging, Sumatra is now largely devoid of undisturbed forest and Borneo is not far behind, with dire consequences for the orangutan, Sumatra's pygmy elephant and countless other life forms.

Even as we rush toward these deadlines, new discoveries underscore the interdependencies of earth's ecosystems. Deforestation in Sumatra and Kalimantan in Indonesia has contributed to regional droughts and wildfires, and residents of Brazil's Mato Grosso assert that the rainy season has diminished in the past decade, though most do not make the connection to the retreat of the Amazon forest northward.

Despite this, all is not lost. For some time conservationists have recognized the problem of scale. Indeed, the big conservation groups (the Wildlife Conservation Society through Living Landscapes, the World Wildlife Fund through ecoregional planning, and Conservation International in its Tropical Wilderness initiative) have focused on working on larger scales. George Woodwell of the Woods Hole Research Center has called for action to protect the "functional integrity of landscapes" and points out the obvious but ignored truth that human economic activity benefits from ecosystems that sustain themselves and provide services indefinitely, while embedding natural systems into a human matrix works to the benefit of neither humans nor nature.

Moreover, in recent years there have been a number of ambitious initiatives aimed at protecting larger stretches of forest and preserving biologically functional units. For instance, the Ecological Corridor Project links a thousand reserves between Bahia and Paraná in Brazil's Atlantic Forest. The Cordillera del Cóndor Peace Park in Ecuador and Peru shows that even nations with long histories of conflict can find common ground in "peace parks."

━━ ━

Even more ambitious initiatives are in the works. One such undertaking is the Amazon Region Protected Area program. Once added to existing reserves for indigenous people and other set-asides, roughly 40 percent of the Brazilian Amazon would have some form of protection—at least on paper. Achieving this would depend on a huge number of ifs (not the least of which is the political will of Brazil's future presidents).

———

In Africa, the Congo Basin Initiative has new life. The region's seven nations have officially endorsed it, and the U.S. government has committed its prestige and $36 million of new money over three years to implementing the Plan de Convergence to bring this initiative to life. If the current plan achieves its goals, roughly 23 percent of the Congo basin forest would have some form of protection.

These initiatives represent unprecedented steps toward protecting moist tropical forests at the system level. They also provide strong evidence that governments and nongovernmental organizations (NGOs) can still launch ambitious conservation efforts absent strong international agreements. The question remains whether these efforts, even if perfectly executed, will provide sufficient forest protection to safeguard the integrity of these two crucial forest systems.

At present no one knows how much of a giant system such as the Amazon or Congo basin must remain intact to avert a self-reinforcing cycle of drying out. Much depends on how and where the forest is logged or clear-cut, plus what happens to the land afterward. Absent any certainty about the tipping points for the world's great forest systems, prudence suggests preserving as much of the system as possible. This in turn forces environmentalists to look beyond parks and indigenous zones, beyond biosphere reserves and wildlife refuges, to find ways to preserve forest cover in areas of lower biological diversity, in areas of lesser ecological interest, in privately held lands and lands currently being converted to other uses. While there is widespread recognition of the urgency of landscape-scale initiatives, there remains a need for a continental-scale plan that would extend to areas that are not a priority with donors and conservation organizations; a plan that could be rolled out rapidly and without endless negotiations, and something that would excite the interest of both donors and the host countries.

It will be years before anyone knows whether the Congo Basin Initiative, still in its formative stages, provides a model for harnessing and efficiently deploying resources. The most ambitious prior effort to address tropical deforestation—the Tropical Forest Action Plan (TFAP), sponsored by the

UN's Food and Agricultural Organization (FAO) and the World Bank in the late 1980s—became mired in bureaucratic haggling and actually intensified deforestation in Cameroon and some other tropical nations. The idea of tying forest preservation to efforts to avert climate change by giving credit to polluters for preserving "carbon sinks" first arose in the late 1980s in the preliminary talks leading to the Kyoto Treaty (though significant effects could come from national schemes and trading outside the treaty). Even if such sinks are eventually included in the treaty, the concept might not have any material effect on forests for at least another ten years—twenty-five years from first efforts in that direction. The lessons of the TFAP and Kyoto are that the more players there are, and the more there is to negotiate, the more the players will negotiate. Noble intentions very quickly devolve into a game in which players seek to gain access to resources while preserving their own competitive position.

There are alternatives. One possibility would be to use a simple market-like system that minimizes opportunities for negotiation, and that funnels champions and resources into every part of a forest system. Here's how such an approach might work:

Imagine two continents. Let's call them Pangea and Gondwanaland. Each has vast wet tropical forests that extend over seven nations. On Pangea, the largest country is called Hectaria; on Gondwanaland, the largest nation is Forestia.

Pangea and Gondwanaland have similar problems. Forests are being cut for timber exports, cleared for agricultural land, and pushed back by urbanization. Both continents have problems with illegal tree cutting, land invasions, out-of-control burning seasons, and all the other factors that remorselessly reduce the size and resilience of the rainforest.

Hectaria established a system of parks and reserves, but, as deforestation continued outside the parks and outside the nation's borders, Hectaria lost one of its two rainy seasons. Fires and pests destroyed areas that had escaped the chain saw. Downstream areas became vulnerable to floods.

Over on Gondwanaland, Forestians watched these events unfold. They decided to learn from Hectaria's tragedy. One lesson was that nations could not go it alone; all seven forested nations had to be involved in a continental-scale effort to save the system.

But how? These were poor countries. They needed outside funding. First off, the Forestians realized that to attract foreign donors the plan would have to be grand. They also realized that to allay the suspicions of neighboring countries and minimize the potential for negotiation, endless studies and bureaucratic haggling, the plan would also have to be both simple and transparent.

With these design features in mind, the president asked a former chief justice of Forestia's Supreme Court to design a plan. He chose the man because he had never been heard to use a word of more than three syllables. Here's what he came up with:

For purposes of conservation, cartographers created a map that divided the entire Gondwanaland rainforest of 600,000 square miles into 100 contiguous blocks, each 77 miles on a side. These blocks might cross national borders or ethnic territories; no matter. Forestia's conservation biologists started to object, saying that the grid ignored biogeographic realities. The justice held up his hand, pointing out that biogeography was a six-syllable word, and noting that the grid's uniformity was its virtue because it eliminated any opportunity for negotiation.

The next part of the plan impaneled a committee to seek credible bidders to take responsibility for preserving forest cover in each and every tile in that grid. The seven nations selected a few trusted members of the international environmental community to solicit bids from NGOs, corporations, international organizations and other credible parties, to take responsibility for forest cover and forest viability in each of those blocks. In essence they created a market for shares in the Gondwanan Forest, only in this market the successful bidder was obligated to put in resources, not take them out. The committee served as overseers of the market, certifying the bona fides of those bidding for blocks, acting as a clearinghouse where approaches could be compared and special problems addressed, and monitoring performance. Bidders had no supervisory authority over their blocks; they had to win over local people, governments and NGOs through offers of assistance and resources.

Those who ended up with a block could pursue any path they liked in order to preserve the forest in their area. The only criterion for success would be a periodic review of forest cover and forest viability a few years down the road (something that could be accomplished through remote sensing). Successful bidders could pour additional funds into existing projects, beef up enforcement, spur ecotourism, develop markets for environmental services or carbon credits, pursue urban development projects, whatever. The key to the plan was to have a group take responsibility for each and every block of the Gondwanaland rainforest—wall-to-wall coverage. Since many groups would want to bid for the most prized parts of the forest, a successful bid for one of the gems came with the obligation to take responsibility for one of the orphans.

The approach began showing results immediately. First the Gondwanaland Refugium Project (as it was called) seeded the area with champions, and that alone improved reporting on what was going on in the forest. Different groups found they could compete to show that their approach was better. Groups also found that they could cooperate and borrow expertise, and even subcontract to others when necessary. With many different groups competing and adapting, the project was like an ecosystem itself.

Environmental groups already working in Gondwanaland welcomed the initiative because it brought new sources of funding and publicity. Surprising new donors, attracted by the scale and high profile of the initiative, began showing an interest in the refugium because the project offered opportunities for green branding, market differentiation, and in some specific cases, the possibility of environmental credits and offsets that might later be applied to satisfy legal obligations. The Scallop Oil Company, which had suffered a black eye for some of its previous environmental practices, adopted several blocks and then promptly subcontracted its commitment to various NGOs already working in the area.

There were other surprises. Preserving the "orphan" forest areas of low biological diversity turned out to be surprisingly easy, as donors helped certify carbon credits and water credits that provided host governments with more income than they had been getting from forest concessions. For instance, Everglades Light and Power pledged to spend $5 million a year over twenty years on an "avoided deforestation" credit in an orphan block to meet a voluntary commitment to reduce its CO_2 emissions by 2 million tons a year. Government officials realized that the $150-per-hectare fee they would receive for the pro rata portion of carbon sequestered exceeded the logging concession bids for the remote area. They also got credit for conservation spending in the communities, giving them a stake in the success of the enterprise.

Forest nations on other continents looked at this initiative with enormous interest. The dozens of different approaches offered a test bed for conservation and development ideas. If something wasn't working in one block, there was nothing to stop the group from switching gears and trying something that was working in another block. Three years down the road, the committee pored over satellite maps to check on the progress of various groups. Forest cover continued to deteriorate in some blocks, but it improved in others. Overall, deforestation slowed.

Could such an approach work in the real world? The risks are low, and it is hard to argue that anything else is working at the scale of the problem. The structure is loose enough to allow bidding, or the lots might be allocated through blind lottery. There are various incentives for different classes of donors, ranging from financial incentives for credible corporations looking for credit for carbon offsets to the purely philanthropic. For host nations, the plan offers the possibility of new resources, new relationships with powerful institutions and corporations, development funds, and international credibility on a high-profile environmental issue. The plan requires no studies or surveys, only effective marketing to host governments and sponsors. It promises the delivery of resources and real action without the endless haggling that has seen perhaps a third of the world's moist tropical forests disappear since alarms first sounded in the 1970s. The only way to find out if such an approach will work is to try.

That's my idea. What's yours?

Acknowledgments

The raw material for this book comes from my travels going back forty years. Over those decades I had the help of many people who facilitated my trips, helped me understand these far-flung places, and, in some cases, saved me from getting killed or imprisoned. Many of these people are mentioned in the book, but many more are not. I don't remember the name of the driver who got Nick Nichols and me out of a market in Kinshasa just as an angry mob was forming, for instance, but I'm grateful for his timing and urban driving skills.

While I mention a number of scientists and conservationists from different organizations in the pages of this book, I benefited enormously from the practical advice and hospitality of the staff of scores of scientific institutions, conservation groups, and other organizations, ranging from the big groups such as the Wildlife Conservation Society, the World Wildlife Fund, and Conservation International to smaller groups such as RARE, Ecotrust, WAHLI in Indonesia, Global Witness in Asia, and the Southeast Alaska Conservation Council, among many others.

Quite a few of the groups that helped me along the way had nothing to do with conservation, but reacted with openness and generosity out of simple hospitality. I mention the Mill Hill missions in the book, but in other parts of the world I benefited from the insights and advice of people from Doctors Without Borders. In Central Africa, I received wonderful cooperation from the U.S. embassies in the Republic of the Congo, the Central African Republic, and what was then called Zaire.

Then there are the people with a passion for nature whose observations and local knowledge gave me an enormous head start in understanding different peoples and landscapes. Steve Galster, a courageous and resourceful conservationist, proved very helpful in my research into the plight of the tiger in India, and then again in my reporting on conservation issues in Siberia. At different times I traveled with Spencer Beebe from the Queen Charlotte Islands to Costa Rica in North and Central America. Tundi Agardy is wonderfully eloquent on the condition of the oceans, and she also taught me to scuba dive. Dan Nepstad helped immeasurably in my understanding of the workings and vulnerabilities of the Amazon rainforest. In many cases, I turned to accompanying photographers—an intrepid group that includes Frans Lanting, Nick Nichols, Tony Suau, and Bill Campbell—for perspective, and they never disappointed.

One group of people not mentioned elsewhere deserves special mention here because it was their assignments that got me to the ragged edges of the planet. The late Norman Cousins of the now defunct *Saturday Review* started me off on my travels by giving me an assignment to investigate fragging in Vietnam. Mary Griswold Smith—whose title at *National Geographic,* senior assistant editor for research grant projects, did not begin to do justice to her role in many of the magazine's groundbreaking articles and expeditions—championed my dream assignment on apes and humans. John Stacks brought me to *Time* magazine, and more than once responded to my pitching a story in some ridiculously remote place by saying, "Why are you still standing here?" (an answer I took to mean "Get going on the story," although it is entirely possible that he was saying "Get out of my office"). I tried for years to get an assignment to write an article on Cuban conservation, and I'm grateful to Carey Winfrey and Terry Monmaney of *Smithsonian* for sending me to Cuba. Allison Humes of *Condé Nast Traveler* enabled me to return to Polynesia after a hiatus of many years. There are many others, and I thank them all.

The impetus for several trips came from entirely outside journalism. Tim Wirth, the head of the United Nations Foundation, encouraged me to visit Antarctica and pointed me toward the National Science Foundation program that enabled me to travel freely on the continent. Bill Chameides, dean of the Nicholas School of the Environment at Duke University, invited me to be a guest lecturer on a school-sponsored trip to Midway Atoll.

In the early days, I financed some of my trips from book advances (something upon which I look back in wonder, as those advances were not large). In such cases, which included my first journey to Africa in 1974, I faced huge logistical obstacles as well as a skeptical reception from those I wanted to interview, as a contract from a publishing house presented by a disheveled guy who looked about fourteen years old was not the kind of press credential local officials (or expatriates) were used to seeing. In many places, I got past the door only because I had a letter of introduction from someone who had the credentials that I then lacked. I'm enormously grateful to the many academics, officials and journalists who provided these letters (some of whom are mentioned in the book).

Once I began writing, I was able to go off and focus on the book thanks to the generosity of friends who offered places where I could disappear and work. Jerry and Ani Moss provided the solitude to start writing the book, and Stephen and Valerie Evans-Freke provided a refuge when I did my final revisions. In between, another refuge—the Mesa Refuge—offered a place where I could write several chapters. The Mesa Refuge offers peace and quiet, but it is set amid one of the most stunning landscapes on the Pacific coast, and that poses a true test of an author's willpower. I hope to return and be tested again in the future. And many thanks to my wife, Mary, for understanding my need to go off to these places to write.

I'm grateful to Clare Ferraro, the president of Viking Penguin, for her patience in allowing me the time to finish this book, and to Rick Kot for his wonderfully deft edit. Thanks to Paige West for confirming Bruce Beehler's translation of pidgin. As always, Esther Newberg provided me with peerless representation.

Finally, I'm deeply grateful to Jim Bennett, an adventurer in his own right in the world of finance and an exemplar of loyalty and friendship, who has been both creative and flexible in structuring my role at Bennett Management so that I can continue to pursue my writing. In fact, neither this book nor any of my other writing since 1976 would have taken place had not Jim extended a foot for me to grab after I began sliding off a cliff when we were hiking outside Tucson. Thanks for that, too, Jim!

Index